24 HOURS TO CREDIT POWER

Additional copies of this book may be purchased directly from the publisher. To order, please enclose $25.95 plus $3 postage and handling. Send to:

24 HOURS TO CREDIT POWER
Post Office Box 15196
Montclair, CA 91763-9945

Printed in the United States of America

0 9 8 7 6 5 4 3 2 1

TABLE OF CONTENTS

CHAPTER 1. What credit is- Where it comes from? 1

What is credit? 1

Where does credit come from?................................2

Why everyone wants to give us credit 3

How to apply for credit 4

How to get credit when you have nothing to offer..............6

Who are the credit grantors? 7

What are credit bureaus, or who do they call to
    check up on your credit?................................8

Does a good job equal good credit? 9

6 easy ways to establish credit.............................11

Should you deal with credit repair companies? 12

Filing out a credit application form 13

How much should your credit cost? 14

3 of the cheapest sources of credit?.....................15

How you can get a copy of your credit record 16

How to read your credit record 18

**CHAPTER 2. How to use credit and stay out
    trouble** 20

Paying off your balance each month 20

Limiting credit to buying cars and homes 21

How much of your income should go for payments? 22

Is a line of credit on your home a good idea?.............24

Should you use credit for vacations? 24

10 good emergency uses for credit 26

Using credit to pay for college 28

10 bad emergency uses for credit 28

CHAPTER 3. How we get our credit in trouble **33**

Can you be plunged into a credit mess? 34

Do you have too many credit cards? 35

Did you lose your job? 38

Divorce problems 39

Can you buy too much house or car on credit? 41

What are the ten warning signs of credit problems?.....43

CHAPTER 4. Credit problems? What to expect...............**47**

What to do about nasty letters in the mail.....................47

Can creditors get you fired from your job? 48

Can creditors take part of your income?.......................49

How will creditors let you know you're in trouble? 49

CHAPTER 5. Paths to fixing credit problems **52**

Credit repair companies -- you can do as
    well or better without them?.....................................53

If you still feel you must use a credit repair company.. 55

Start by contacting your creditors 57

Get your credit record 58

Improving credit histories 58

A 5 step plan to resolving mistakes in
    your credit record..58

Cleaning up credit problems you have caused 66

Retail store credit 67

Mortgage lenders and banks 70

Credit cards 71

Auto loans...73

Student loans 75

Medical bills 77

Debt collection agencies...78

Does bad credit ever die? How to tell,
    and what to do about it 81

Cleaning up your public record 82

Is bankruptcy the right path for you? 85

A 12 step plan for filing for bankruptcy 87

     1. Preparation 87

     2. Finding a bankruptcy court 89

     3. What forms you will need 89

     4. Filling the forms..92

     5. The court schedules a meeting of your
        creditors 93

     6. The creditors meeting 94

     7. Working with exempt and non-exempt
        property to get the best deal 94

     8. The discharge hearing 95

     9. Filing an amendment 96

     10. After bankruptcy problems 96

     11. Re-opening your bankruptcy case 97

     12. Can they revoke your discharge? 98

How to work out payment plans 99

Can you get creditors to cancel part of your debt?..............100

Should you pay everyone off? 101

Tear up my credit cards? Are you mad?...............................103

How long should it take to fix credit? 104

Should you use credit to fix credit?......................................105

When all else fails, play the lottery 107

CHAPTER 6. The benefits of bankruptcy 108

The proceedings 109

How to figure out your Chapter 13 budget 109

An example of a Chapter 13 budget 110

What happens after you file 111

What the court will do 111

Limits and laws governing Chapter 13 111

Which debts cannot be paid off with Chapter 13 113

Can my creditors veto my repayment plan? 113

Will a Chapter 13 filing show up on my credit report? 113

Do I need to hire a lawyer to file a Chapter 13? 114

What would a lawyer cost? 114

How can I find a lawyer who will do a good job? 114

CHAPTER 7. Staying out of trouble 116

Watch the balance of income and credit payments 116

Saving up for big purchases 118

Limiting your credit loses 119

Stay away from the loan sharks 120

Don't get suckered in by easy credit...................................121

Become a cash buyer of most everything............................123

CHAPTER 8. Surviving credit boondoggles 126

What to do when you can't fix it 127

Surviving bankruptcy 128

Buying with bad credit...129

Looking for private sources of credit...................................130

Should you just change your name and run away 130

CHAPTER 9. Credit advice for women only 132

The special problems women face in getting credit 132

Do creditors give women a hard time? 133

Why you should have credit in your own name 134

How you should manage your money for a good credit
report 135

Tips on building your own credit history 138

What to do if you already have good credit and getting
married 140

How your husband's bankruptcy affects your credit 141

How does divorce affect your credit 142

How you can plan for a divorce 143

What happens to your credit when you become a widow......145

CHAPTER 10. How to slash your interest rate 149

Slash your payment in half 150

**CHAPTER 11. How to buy a home with no
money down**...152

The government 152

Don't forget the VA 154

**CHAPTER 12. Ways to create, make and raise your
own credit**..157

1. Form your own corporation 158

2. Seek personal loans 158

3. Borrow from Uncle Sam..159

4. Seek venture capital 160

Startup funding..160

First round funding 161

Second round funding 161

Later stage funding 161

Equity loan 161

Mezzanine funding..............................161

Merger and acquisition........................161

What's the best approach 161

5. Money from your house 163

The best investment— yourself 163

Real estate 164

Investing in discounted mortgages 164

Beat the DOW with this investment strategy 165

Franchising 165

Making money with credit cards 166

CHAPTER 13. Mortgage interest reducing 170

Trim a little, trim a lot 170

CHAPTER 14. Non-bank sources of credit 172

1. The government..172

The Small Business Administration 173

Farmers Home Administration 173

The Minority Business Development Agency 174

The Overseas Private Investment Corporation 174

Export-Import Bank of the United States 174

The Small Business Investment Company 175

2. Venture capital...175

3. Start your own investment club 176

4. A silent partner..176

5. Borrow from professional people 177

CHAPTER 15. Getting bankers to beg for your business 178

They need you 179

What about banker losses? 180

The application form 180

The three Cs: Capacity-character-collateral 181

The score 182

Get creative 185

What if you are self employed? 185

What if you lie? 186

More credit application form tips.....................................187

A final warning 188

CHAPTER 16. 17 businesses to start without money or credit 189

Bill auditing service 192

Business broker 195

Grant writing 197

How do you write a grant? 198

How much should you charge? 200

Publish your own newsletter 201

Printing broker 204

Resume writer..206

Business plan writer 207

Credit card marketing to college students 210

Loan marketing to health care professionals 211

Indoor environmental tester 212

Information broker...214

Medical billing service...217

Medical claims processing service 218

Medical transcript service 220

Professional organizer 222

Professional practice consultant 224

New luxury car free 225

You can have it all 226

Different states, different laws 227

Naming your corporation 228

Contact the car dealer 228

Get a client list 228

How do you buy the cars? 230

**CHAPTER 17. Five sources of private credit --
and five you avoid** **231**

1. Unclaimed property 231

Commerce Department announces over $5
   million in unclaimed property 232

2. People who give money away 233

3. Computers can sniff out credit for you 238

4. Another great source of funds 238

5. Seek out joint government-private sources 239

6. Check your own non-liquid assets—how $100
   can get you $10,000 239

Five credit sources you must avoid 241

   1. Illegal sources of money 241

   2. High interest credit cards 242

   3. Rent-to-own 242

   4. Pawn shops 242

   5. Mail order credit companies 243

CHAPTER 18. How to get a lower interest rate **244**

Shop around 244

   1. Truth in lending 245

2. Consumer leasing 245

Cost of open end credit...246

Getting interest to work for you 248

File variation 249

Glossary of credit and other financial terms 251

Special Bonus Sections

Bonus #1 - The Credit Game 266

Bonus #2 - How To Buy A Car For The
              Lowest Possible Price 278

Bonus #3 - Businesses You Can Start With $500 or Less-
              And Make Money 306

Bonus #4 - How To Get A Part Of Billions Of Dollars
              That The Government Is Holding 339

1 WHAT CREDIT IS-
WHERE IT COMES FROM?

Since you can't discuss anything until you define it I thought that I would start off this book with some information about credit. You know, what is it and what can we do with it. Once you know where it comes from it will be much easier to see how to get it, and what you should do with it when you have it.

WHAT IS CREDIT?

Have you ever gone out to buy something you want when you have no money in your pocket?---That's credit. How about buying a house? Do you have a couple of hundred thousand dollars in the bank so that you can buy your dream home? No, and I don't either, but the bank does and it will give me the money I want as credit.

Credit can't be handled, but it can let you buy anything that you can handle. You can't even carry it around in your pocket or your car, but you can carry a little piece of plastic that will give you the buying power of $10,000. Credit, properly used, can be a wonderful thing. It can make up for all of our financial shortcomings. And it is so handy that nearly everyone in America depends on it on almost a daily basis.

Credit is used to purchase both goods and services without immediately paying for them. What makes the idea of credit work is the trust that whatever is bought with credit will eventually be paid for with real money. Of course money is the coins and bills that we have in circulation, and that we seem to have so little success at keeping in our pockets.

There is nothing mysterious about credit, after all it's just buying now and paying later, and we do that all of the time.

WHERE DOES CREDIT COME FROM?

Credit can come from anyone who has anything to sell. The only thing that banks have to sell is money so they issue credit cards which allow you to spend money. Furniture stores can issue credit on the purchase of their furniture, and then take the furniture back if you don't make your payments. Stores that sell many different things issue credit cards that look like bank cards, but they can only be used to purchase things they sell in their stores.

While the most common places that comes from are banks and savings and loans, it can just as well come from private persons, oil companies, and department stores. Even our Federal government gives out credit, except that it calls the payments taxes. You might look at credit as the way we spread around money and goods to make more money. No matter who you are, if you are giving out credit you expect to get it all back plus a little extra for your trouble and risk.

Credit comes out of the desire to put idle money and goods to work in order to make a profit. Banks put their money to work by giving out credit and charging for everything that they do for the public. They don't risk any of their own money any way since it's all money that they have taken from somebody else. Now you could look at it as giving a loan to the bank when you deposit your money in a bank account since the bank pays you interest on most of your money that it has.

In turn the bank loans out the same money to someone else who needs it even more and charges that person more money than they are paying you. The only money a bank will have available is what they need to satisfy the law, and what they need to pay out on any particular day. After all, the money they have sitting around isn't earning its way by making a profit. It's only the money that has been given out in the form of credit that is making a profit.

Granting credit is just another way of putting money to work, except that you let the money work directly instead of through tools you might buy to make something else.

WHY EVERYONE WANTS TO GIVE US CREDIT

This is only an impression I get when I look through the daily newspaper, or take a walk in a mall. Stores in the mall scream out at you to take use store credit. You know how it is, just apply for instant store credit and you can have anything and take 10% off. The mails are even worse with credit card applications coming every week, and phone calls from lenders every time you sit down. Now this last is true only if your credit record is fairly clean, but they do come after you. It is not worthwhile being concerned over a lack of credit so long as there are few black marks against you.

In fact you should have all of the confidence in the world so far as finding credit. There are more people with spare money around to give credit . If you are unlucky enough to need money rather than have extra money to loan, and most of us are, then they should be coming to you every day and asking you to accept credit. Just look at some of the many piles of money that we have surrounding us that someone needs to turn into working credit.

Banks take in money from everyone with an account. Obviously not everyone with a bank account is able to deposit money regularly, but they must have some money in the bank in order to have any kind of an account. Also businesses use banks to put in their monthly receipts, and many people put their money in each month so they can write checks to pay their bills. Banks have a lot of money coming in over a month, and they have to constantly look for ways to put it to work. They do this by granting credit in the form of credit cards, home loans, and car loans. Many banks have problems doing this efficiently and are always looking for someone to loan their money too as credit. For proof just look at how many bank credit card offers you get in your mail every month. An average would be between 2 and 5, and this goes on year after year.

People selling real estate are another prime source of credit givers, and they are made up of individual people who want to sell land. This is a group that you have to go look for, but they are out there. The trick is that the only form of credit they are offering is the purchase of their land, but it is possible to buy land with that kind of credit, improve it in some way, and sell it off yourself for a profit.

Since so much wealth is concentrated in so few hands, the only way many of these money collectors can get more money is to loan it out as credit. Just look in your Sunday paper's business section, there are organizations trying to loan money everywhere. We get pre-approved credit cards in the mail nearly every week. If you own property there are probably people on the phone every few weeks offering you re-financing or lines of credit. Every time you go into a department store these days there are ads offering you discounts if you will accept one of their credit cards. Now oil companies and air lines are sending you credit cards with rebates in their products if you will use them. While most of the money in our country is in the hands of very few people, if they can't get you to accept some of it back as credit it isn't of much good to anybody. The trouble with credit is when you go shopping for it because you need it, and then the ones with the credit to give can make you do anything that they want.

HOW TO APPLY FOR CREDIT

If you have money to loan you wouldn't just go out and give it to the first person you saw. You would look at all of the people who might want to borrow your money and loan it to the one who looked most likely to pay it back with interest. Of course if you didn't know these people very well you would have to ask them some questions. You might want to know how much they made, and whether they paid their bills on time, and especially whether or not they simply forgot to pay them back at all. Now I don't know about you, but I wouldn't loan money to anyone who I thought would not pay me back. If someone were just slow in payments once in awhile I might loan them money, but if they paid back all of their debts on time with interest, they would be first on my list of people to loan my money to.

Creditors do almost exactly this same thing when they decide whether or not to grant credit to an applicant. Of course there is nothing to prevent you from trying to look as much like the perfect applicant as possible. But to do that you should know as much about the rules the creditors go by in making their decisions. We will look at these rules in as much detail as possible for a few minutes with the idea that the more you know about what a lender or creditor is trying to do, the better your chance of getting it to come out in your favor.

The first of the major decision makers for lenders is what they call capacity, or the ability to pay back what you borrow or use in credit. In determining capacity creditors want to know how much income you have, and how much debt you have. If you have too much debt you will have trouble paying them back, and the same holds true if you have too little income. Some of the things they include of either debts or income, depending on whether you are paying or receiving, are alimony, child payments, and how many dependents you have. Debt to income ration is calculated by taking your total income and dividing it by the average amount per month that you have to pay out. In your debts are included any loans and finance charges you are paying, but also rent and mortgage payments, alimony, car payments, and insurance. All of these are added together and divided by 12. If the total amount of monthly debt that you have is greater than 1/2 of your monthly clear income you will probably be turned down for new credit. While the 50% rule is only a rule of thumb, it is pretty difficult to get creditors to give credit when the debt ratio is higher than that. If you figure out your debt to income ratio and you are over 50% you should check with the creditor before you make your application. This may save you some time and trouble.

Capacity questions: How much is your income? If you work on commission how much do you average a month? Do you have checking and savings accounts? What debts you owe now?

The second thing that the creditors are going to look at is your character. Character, in terms of credit, is whether or not you have a habit of paying your obligations, and whether you consistently pay on time. They will find this information through the credit reports they get from the credit bureaus. Other factors they consider important are how long you have worked at your job, and how long you have lived at your address. Are you a good solid citizen who sticks to what he starts and finishes it out successfully? If you are the type of person who always finishes out what he starts you will probably also pay off any credit that you are granted.

Character questions: How long have you worked in your present profession, and how long have you worked for your present employer? If you are self employed how long have you had your current occupation? Have you established a credit history? Have you kept your credit accounts up to date?

Creditors also look at your collateral. These are assets, or things worth money other than income, which you own. Your home, savings, investments, and even your car and home furnishings would all be included as collateral. Collateral shows what you are worth, in terms of money, and how likely you might be to pick up and disappear. If all of your collateral is in the form of bank accounts you could take all of your money and be gone tomorrow. But if it is all in the form of land you might be around for years before you could dispose of it all. Actually they like to see a balance of the two, assets you get use to pay off your credit if need be, and assets which would be hard to move so that you would stay put until you did pay off the creditors.

Collateral questions: Do you own or rent your home? Do you have retirement accounts, stock, bonds, or investment property?

Once you have assembled all of the relevant information and approach a creditor, you must turn in a full and complete application. Even though the creditor will check your credit record from the credit bureau, they will ask you to list much of the same information on your credit application form. If a creditor finds out that you have simply left off negative information rather than trying to explain problems you will be rejected. However, if they grant you credit and then later on find that you have lied on your application they may prosecute you or sue you. In either case you will be much worse off simply forgetting information than by reporting truthfully and trying to work around it.

HOW TO GET CREDIT WHEN YOU HAVE NOTHING TO OFFER

If you think that you need to have property or an income in order to get credit, you are generally wrong. Often you may need collateral, but many times what the credit is granted for will take care of that. Of course you do need people to believe in you, and that you will pay back the credit that you are given.

The easiest offer that I have ever seen for credit, when you had nothing to offer, was at the colleges. At virtually every college in the country representatives from the Bank of America, or some other credit card offering bank, show up each spring and fall offering students credit cards. The credit cards usually have a very low maximum of around $1,000, but the banks are so anxious to give them out to students that they often offer to give out 2 liter bottles of soda along with the credit cards. Where else in America can you get free food along with a credit.

Pre-approved credit cards have to rank high in credit offered when you have no means to repay. Of course the banks want to know where you work and where you have money in the bank, but I would wager that most of them will send you a card anyway even if you didn't fill that portion out. Besides, even most people without savings have a job that would satisfy the banks.

Department stores should not be forgotten. Since they are selling their own merchandise, and if you have one of their credit cards they think you will buy more of it, they will give you a credit card just so long as your credit doesn't look too bad on the credit reporting agency. Of course they will run a background check on you, as will the banks, and if you have a lot of delinquencies against you they will take back their credit offer. But if you are fairly clean, you can be pretty sure they will happily give you the credit you want.

Now I'm back to the real estate salespersons. In selling real estate, when times are tough, sellers will often carry back loans on the property to help sell. When they do this they are giving you credit. Your job is to find property in which the seller will carry back a loan, and which has a potential to either sell at a higher price, or which can serve as a regular loan at a bank, with the property serving as collateral. Of course if you just want a house but have little amount of money, having the seller carry part of the loan may be the best way to go to get into it if you can't qualify for a regular loan from a bank. Sellers will often do this to give themselves an income or get the property sold, and if you fail to pay back the loan they figure they will get the property back anyway, and be able to re-sell it. However, you can do well to if you pick the right properties, and you can't get credit anywhere else.

WHO ARE THE CREDIT GRANTORS?

At this point, if you are looking for credit for the first time, or if you have no other troubles, you need to know who you should contact to get credit. That is what people and institutions you should write to or call to get a credit card or loan. But let's assume that you are at least ready to apply for a credit card, either because you need it or because there is something that you want and you need to use credit to buy it, who do you call to get the process started? As a suggestion, you can begin with the nationwide banks and savings and loans, each of which can issue credit cards anywhere in the country:

First USA Bank	1-800-955-9900
Citibank	1-800-843-0777
Household Credit Services	1-800-477-6000
Chase Manhattan	1-800-441-7683
Chemical Bank	1-800-648-3355
Wachovia Bank	1-800-842-3262
Bank of New York	1-800-942-1977
MBNA	1-800-847-7378

WHAT ARE CREDIT BUREAUS, OR WHO DO THEY CALL TO CHECK UP ON YOUR CREDIT?

Credit bureaus are also known as credit reporting agencies, and they are the organizations in the United States which have made a business out of collecting credit information on every person in the country, and selling it to businesses who are thinking about giving you credit. Of course there are some minor credit bureaus around the country, but the big three that everyone has to deal with sooner or later, and who you will no doubt have many dealings with, are TRW Credit Information Service, Trans Union Credit Information, and CBI/EQUIFAX.

Even if the stores in your area check with a credit bureau other than these three, 500 of the 800 total in the country use the same credit base anyway.   You can't escape the big three.

There is one more question that remains that is important to getting and keeping credit, where do the credit bureaus get their information? If you know the source of the information they use, then you have the chance to influence it. There are three major sources of information: the businesses that subscribe to their services, public records, and information you supply to credit organizations. The business subscribers are the stores and businesses where you have credit accounts. When you go to charge a purchase and the store calls to check on your credit, these are the companies that are called. And when you are late with a payment, this is where it gets recorded. Of course mistakes can be made as well, and you might even fix any payment problems that you have with a store and still have it on your credit record. When that happens you have developed a bad credit report and you can be denied loans or credit cards as a result.

Public records consist of information that goes through the legal system. This includes bankruptcies, tax liens against you or your property, and judgements against you such as garnishments on your salary or even lawsuits. This would also include mechanics liens on property you own by contractors who were not paid. It may not always be fair, but they are public records and they are entered into your credit reports.

The information you supply yourself is perhaps the most frustrating, particularly if you want to keep some things private. Take a look at the next credit application that you fill out. Included are your name, current address, previous addresses, possibly your age although that is often illegal these days, and your social security number even though the law that originally established social security forbids using the social security number as a means of identification. Of course savings accounts, banks, and employers are also asked for. If you refuse to answer these questions, many of which really have nothing to do with your ability to pay back credit, you will not be granted the credit in the first place.

In any case, since these are the sources of information that go into your credit report, by knowing your own credit history you can see what negative information may be in circulation, and what you can do about it.

DOES A GOOD JOB EQUAL GOOD CREDIT?

A good job is a job that pays a living wage, in which there is security, and in which you have spent a few years. A living wage these days is usually over $30,000 a year, although the amount has to be higher the more credit you are interested in getting. Security in a job means that your employer is unlikely to lay you off, fire you, or go out of business himself. Time on the job is also crucial, since the longer you have worked for a company the more likely you are to be around for a few more years. Of course this works quite well for people who have worked 10 or 20 years in a field, but once you get much above that you start approaching retirement and a loss of income. Therefore, 30 or 40 years on a job, even at a high income level, will usually work against you because of age and health problems.

Now, saying you fall into all of these prime categories, does that mean that you will have good credit, or have an easy time getting credit when you need it. The answer is that it depends upon your own credit history. If you have never had credit or any kind of credit problem, then having a good job will usually work very well in your favor in getting credit when you need it. The key to getting credit when you need it though is your credit history. If you have gone along for many years without credit and suddenly want to buy a house or a car you may very well be discriminated against because you have no credit history. In that case you might have to establish your credit by getting a credit card or a charge account at a department store for a year or two before a bank will give you a car or home loan at favorable rates.

The other problem, and it is major, is if you have a good job but you have a tarnished credit history. If you are chronically late in making credit card payments, house payments, or car payments. Or worse yet, if you have actually ended up with a bankruptcy on your record in the last 7 years, you might find it impossible to get credit when you need it no matter how good your job looks.

We won't go into the steps to take to fix credit problems right now, look at the chapter on dealing with bad credit and how to fix it, but there is still one step you should keep in mind in all of these cases, tell the credit grantor about your credit problems when you fill out the application. Nothing will kill your credit chances faster than if a creditor thinks that you are trying to hide negative information. When they discover something that you might have hidden they naturally assume that you have probably hidden a lot worse things, and they will not want to have anything to do with you and your credit needs.

6 EASY WAYS TO ESTABLISH YOUR CREDIT

This is just a little guide for those of you with no credit, or who want to get some good credit references so they can obtain more credit later, say to buy a car. Incidentally, don't try going to a car dealer first if you want to establish credit. If your credit is bad, they will soak you, and they check with the same credit bureaus as everyone else before they will give you credit. Here is an easy guide to get started:

1. Accept one of the pre-approved credit cards that comes in the mail. At this point it doesn't matter what the interest rate is, or whether the limit is low or high.

2. If you are a college student, get one of the cards offered at the colleges. They usually have a $1,000 limit to start, but they don't require any credit history.

3. Go through a local department store. Many of them virtually beg for you to take one of their cards, and they will probably be more lenient with you if you don't have a credit history, or even if you have a few bad marks against you. When you take one of their cards use it for only small purchases, and pay each one off each month for at least 6 months before applying for any more credit. This will give you a positive credit record.

4. Join a credit union. If you are working for any of the many public organizations you are eligible for credit union memberships, and since your job guarantees that you will make your payments they approve all reasonable applications for credit by their members.

5. Put some money in a timed savings account and then borrow against it. This is a way of guaranteeing yourself while establishing your credit. Then if you are short of money for a payment any month you just take it out of your account, at a penalty of course, and keep current.

6. If you have life insurance, borrow against it. Since the money in life insurance any way, insurance companies will always loan against it. If you don't pay as you should they just deduct what you owe from your policy. There is risk to you but not to the insurance company, and it can't give you a bad credit record.

SHOULD YOU DEAL WITH CREDIT REPAIR COMPANIES?

I would like to say no, absolutely not, but I can't do that unless I first explain what credit repair companies do. But once you know what they do you still need to know if you can do the same thing yourself and save their fees.

Basically these are companies that come into the picture after you have developed credit problems. What they offer to do is to clean up your credit record. Some even claim that they can make a record of a bankruptcy disappear, which is false since a bankruptcy becomes part of the public record. What they all have in common is that they all have up-front fees, and you are never offered a money back guarantee of success for their claims. If they fail they still keep your money. Fees are also not cheap, they are gauged to what the credit repair companies think they can get out of you. For this reason they can range from $50 to more than $2,000.

In addition to the problems of dealing with legitimate companies of this type there is the problem of dealing with direct fraudulent companies that come into an area, open a credit repair business, and then leave after a month or two keeping all of your fees.

Legal or not, should you deal with them? In most cases you don't have to, and along the way in this book you will find out how to fix your own credit because they cannot do anything that you can't do yourself.

You still need to avoid getting trapped by one of these companies however, since they will come after you if you get in trouble. They go through credit materials all of the time, and every time that someone gets in trouble one or more of these companies will be calling and sending literature. The literature and calls will make one or more of three claims: The first is wild claims about wiping out bankruptcies, and cleaning up your credit report no matter what your credit history. Your credit history is your credit history, and you can legally take steps to correct or improve it as well as anyone else. There will also be statements to the effect that little known loopholes will be used to get rid of negative credit information. The only reason the loopholes are little known is that you just haven't heard of them yet, they aren't really little known to those who deal with credit problems. The third lie that they claim is that they can get you a major bankcard no matter what your credit history. For one thing many minor bankcards are just as good as major ones, and for another major banks are often more conservative than other banks and are less likely to give you credit than a lot of other sources. It just sounds better in the advertising to say that they can get you a major credit bank credit card. To be wise, ignore all of these claims, none of them mean any thing. Pay attention to everything you are going to learn by reading and you can do it all yourself.

FILLING OUT A CREDIT APPLICATION FORM

While there is some variation in the information required to fill out credit application forms, most things stay the same from one to another. If you can prepare your information in advance it will make it much less stressful for you when you actually get a form, and much easier if you have to fill out more than one form. You can also find out where you have weaknesses and work to strengthen them. While this may sound a little difficult, having all of it organized means that you will only have to worry about a very few problem areas rather than an entire form when you go for your credit application.

1. Your full name

2. Social Security number

3. Full address

4. Previous address if less than 10 years at current

   address

5. Business and home phone numbers

6. Employer's name and address

7. If married, spouse's:

   a. Name

   b. Social Security number

   c. Address, if different from yours.

   d. Business and home phone numbers

   e. Employer's name and address

8. Bank and saving's account institutions and account

   numbers

9. Other assets: property, and saving's accounts, and how much

10. Creditors

    a. Credit cards

    b. Bank loans

    c. Home and car loans

    d. Personal loans

11. Credit problems that you know you have.

You may not be asked all of these, after all some of it is public information, and if its just a credit card or a department store charge account they don't need that much information. But if you are borrowing for a house or an investment the lender will want all of the information on you they can get. If you have all of this with you when you go to apply for credit you will never have to plead a lack of information, which could make you look bad even before you make an application for a loan.

HOW MUCH SHOULD YOUR CREDIT COST?

Credit can cost you in two or three different ways. It often costs to apply for credit, if it means an appraisal on property that you own, and many credit cards charge an annual fee just for having them. The most familiar cost though is the interest that you pay on the credit that you use. Let's take a look at each of these costs and see how much you are going to have to spend in order to get credit.

Up front fees are generally linked to getting credit on property. This is where some people go wrong with credit agencies that charge you a fee and say that they will get you charge cards at banks. There should be no up front fee for that type of credit. But, getting back to credit on property. This credit will probably take one of two forms, either a straight loan, such as on a Trust Deed, or a line of credit. Both will require appraisals as well as loan origination fees, which are really fees for doing the paperwork on the loan in the bank. To save on out of pocket money have these fees added into your payment schedule. They are only deductible over the life of the loan anyway, so there is no advantage for you to put out $2,000 or $3,000 when you are getting your loan.

Credit card fees vary greatly. A few are free, but these aren't from the biggest banks and you may have trouble qualifying for one of these if you have had credit problems. Most commonly you will be charged from $50 to $70 a year, and the only way you will know is if you read the information the bank sends you with your statement each month. If you keep the card after you get the notice the fee will be added onto your account balance.

Monthly rates also vary hugely. The lowest ones are around 6.9%, and are generally tied to a variable interest rate or an introductory rate. Many others are in the area of 8.9% to 12.9%, and they will keep that rate indefinitely. The biggest ones go in the area of 15.9% to 21%. The most common that I have run across are 18.9%, and they still charge a $50 per year fee for their cards. I think it is all a rip-off, but it is very hard to avoid most of these fees if you want a credit card.

While these are the big three costs everyone will face, the credit card companies keep an ace in the hole just to gouge you a little more if you are so sloppy as to really need your credit. Almost every credit card has a limit, but, just to keep you from being embarrassed, the companies will let you run up charges to 10% over your limit. Now while they are doing their good deed for you they are also looking out for themselves. For every month that you have a balance over the limit they charge you an over-your-limit penalty. They won't just cut off credit purchases at the limit, not even if you tell them to. This little added fee is usually $15 a month, although a few credit card companies only charge $10 or $12 a month.

Credit costs re-cap:

Appraisal and loan origination fees	$350
Annual credit card fees	50
Interest rates on unpaid balance	19%
Over-the limit credit card fees	15

3 OF THE CHEAPEST SOURCES OF CREDIT?

Seeing that credit comes in all shapes and sizes, you might

as well use the cheapest sources available when you get the chance. Here are the 5 cheapest sources of credit you are likely to find.

1. Low introductory rate credit cards with adjustable rates. These go for as little as 6.9% on the unpaid balance, and often have no first year fees. Over-the-limit charges are the same as for other cards, but limits are also the same. To get full advantage of these you may have to find a new company every year or two and transfer your balances.

2. Line of credit accounts on your home. Oftentimes these are offered without appraisal fees, and rates can be as low as 3.9% annually. The danger in them is that you are putting your home on the line for a few thousand dollars in credit. The advantages, other than the low rates, is that they are easy to get, your income and credit history is less important, and you can find them at most banks and credit brokers. You pay them off in the same way that you pay any credit card, but the limits can easily go to $10,000 or $20,000 since they are tied to the equity in your home.

3. Borrow against savings. This will usually cost you no more than about 2% above the rate you are receiving on the savings, but is limited by the amount of money you have saved. The advantage of this type of credit is that you can still list the savings amount as an asset, to qualify for more credit, while you only have to count the payment amounts as against your earnings. One of the hardest processes to trying to accumulate liquid money, and it is often better to borrow against what you have saved than to take the money out of your savings and spend it directly. The source of the savings can be a bank savings account, an insurance account, or even a retirement account that you can't spend legally without a penalty.

HOW YOU CAN GET A COPY OF YOUR CREDIT RECORD

As discussed earlier, there are three major companies that keep track of your credit history in the United States. The problem with these records, for many people, is that they never take notice of their credit record until they are denied credit by someone. It is often too late to fix the credit satisfactorily if you wait until this happens, making it important that you inspect your own credit record at least once each year. Then, if anything bad has shown up, whether deserved or not, you will have a chance to get it removed or add your own explanation as a means of keeping your future credit applications successful.

As it so happens, by law, you are permitted to request one free copy of your credit record from any credit reporting companies, if you do it within 30 days of the denial of credit. Otherwise the credit companies will charge around $7 to $8 a copy, except that TRW will give you one copy a year free. All that you need is the proper method to go about making the request, and that is what is offered here.

You can use the three addresses and phone numbers below to check on your credit. It is best to give a call before you send money for a report since rates may change at any time.

Equifax Information Service

Customer Correspondence

P.O. Box 740193

Atlanta, GA 30374-0193

1-800-685-1111

TRW

12606 Greenville Avenue

P.O. Box 749-029

Dallas, TX 75374

1-800-392-1122

TransUnion

P.O. Box 8070

North Olmsted, OH 44070-8070

1-800-922-5490

When you call a credit reporting company, before requesting your credit report, ask them exactly what they require in terms of verification of your identity before they will send you the information. Do this once a year, or whenever you are denied credit, and it will go a long way toward keeping you out of credit trouble.

HOW TO READ YOUR CREDIT RECORD

Credit records vary somewhat according to which organization you receive yours from. However, they all supply the same basic information, and they can all be interpreted rather easily if you follow the guide given here.

1. The heading: contained is your identifying information and the date the report is issued. When you get your record make certain that it is really your record and not someone elses. This is important because you do not want anyone elses credit mixed up with yours, and the worst way it could be mixed up is by getting the people reported on confused. With 275 million people in the United States, there are going to be other people with your name, and they may even match other vital information with you.

2. The information heading: The first listing is the inscriber name, that is the name of the business that has supplied credit information. The name may be followed by the account number and subscriber number, you can ignore these. Next will be billing dates, which will be followed by amounts past due. Past due entries are negative information and must be answered or erased to clear your credit. The last entry will be a current status report. Even if you haven't used an account in a year or two the store may be listed along with all of this information

3. Your credit history: This consists of the individual entries under the headings just given. You should look at these entries to confirm that each account listed is yours, and does not belong to someone else. Check the entries of account status for the same information. If you have returned merchandise its charge amount should not be listed on your record. Be very careful about records of late payments and current account status.

An inquiry into your credit history will look for the number of accounts that you have, your total credit amounts in relation to your income, whether you have any problems in making payments on time, and how much credit use you have made lately. Being overextended on credit can be just as much of a problem as being slow to make payments since it may indicate that you won't be able to pay on time for the new account. This is especially true in large purchases like homes and cars.

Bankruptcies will also show up on this report, and if the bankruptcy is within the last 3 or 4 years you may have a very difficult time qualifying for credit now. Many creditors will tell you that if you have everhad a bankruptcy they will not give you an account, or a loan. If this problem has arisen for you, it is best to take great pains to clear up the record as soon as you can.

2 HOW TO USE CREDIT AND STAY OUT OF TROUBLE

We should use our credit so that we don't lose it. What is worse about having credit than using it incorrectly, so that it creates more problems than it solves. Credit is not meant to make life harder for us to live but to make it easier and more enjoyable. If we are using credit to relieve our feelings of frustration with life, we will end up in trouble. The same goes if we use credit in any of the incorrect ways that are open to us. Credit itself does not care what we do with it. Credit does not think, it is only there. You make the decision as to what you really want to use credit for, actually decide what you really need to use credit for. Always keep an eye on the fact that you are going to have to pay for the credit you use. And, yes, you can file for bankruptcy and wipe out your debts, but that also means wiping out your credit at the same time for many years to come. The entries in this chapter are meant to help you keep on the straight and narrow, not to dictate how you should live your life. If a compelling need for credit arises in life that does not match one of the topic herein discussed, you must make the final decision as to whether you should use your credit to handle it. It should not make your decision wrong, to fail to find it listed here, but it should make you thoughtful. You can rarely get in trouble for failing to use credit, but using it poorly always results in more problems in life than we need to face to be comfortable.

PAYING OFF YOUR BALANCE EACH MONTH

This is certainly the safest way to avoid credit problems. The only real concern with this strategy is that it defeats much of the proper use of credit, and leaves you in the same situation you would be in if you didn't use any credit. Other than staying out of trouble, a major effect of paying off your balance each month is to establish a good credit record. If you have a few credit accounts, and all of the balances have been paid off within one month, you will have the best and cleanest credit record you can get. This won't always get you a home loan or another credit card, but no lender can argue that you have more credit than you can pay.

The negatives to paying off credit monthly are few, but they must be mentioned. Creditors will know what you are doing when they see your credit record and will discount it for exactly what it is, a cheap way to establish a good credit record. Furthermore, businesses grant credit because they want you to have a balance. A larger profit is made from the balance you take a year or two, or more, to pay off than is built into the original sales of merchandise. If you have a $5,000 balance you are paying faithfully on each month, you will gladly be offered a $7,000 limit if you ask for it. Creditors may even offer it if you don't ask. But if you are charging and paying off $200 each month, a business will have a lot of processing costs and very little profit. They will conclude, and correctly, that you don't really need or want their credit.

Keeping zero balances is still useful for you though, in most cases. If you have a record like this, and get into a situation where you must have credit it is difficult to see why any company would deny it to you. This is the safest and most secure route to a good credit history.

One caution that is worth giving you, paying off your credit each month is not guarantee that you won't become a credit junky in the future. Just becoming dependent upon credit gives you the feeling of how it is used, of how easy it is to use to get out of trouble and buy a gift or a new wardrobe. Credit is a powerful drug, and using it for good can end up creating just as many problems as misusing it.

LIMITING CREDIT TO BUYING CARS AND HOMES

Once upon a time the only reason that anyone had credit was to purchase very expensive things that they could never buy for cash. In those days buying cars and homes, making investments in your basic needs, was the only reason strong enough for people to borrow. With this type of very conservative buying on credit you were never overextended so long as you didn't lose your job.

Of course these were the days before the invention of the credit report. Lenders had to depend on what you told them about your income and credit history. This worked pretty well most of the time, and it would work just as well today, even with the credit records and income histories you have to supply now. If you can limit your use of credit to buying cars and homes it is unlikely that you will ever have any problem with your credit.

There is no real downside to limiting your credit use severely. If you ask around to all of your friends and family you may actually find someone who has taken this route to credit management. However, unless they are very well off financially you will also find that they are doing without many of the little things that many of us think are necessary for a good life. If you like to buy new clothes when you feel like it, go out to dinner regularly, take nice trips each year, and treat everyone to a party even when money is tight. you probably won't be able to limit your credit use to the big ticket items.

On the other hand, if you can commit yourself to this credit plan you can avoid all of the pitfalls of overextended credit. There will be only a couple of credit payments each month, and you will know exactly what they are. If you do have an emergency and really need the credit you will be able to get it on short notice. You should actually be better off in the future instead of just deeper in debt to pay off a credit card that you charged a trip on 10 years before. If you have credit cards now with a few thousand dollars balance, can you remember what you bought that ran up all of that debt?

HOW MUCH OF YOUR INCOME SHOULD GO FOR PAYMENTS?

Those who make loans and give credit cards know that you have to eat, keep your car running, and do many other things in your life. For these reasons they will not give you credit if it means that too much of your income is already committed to paying for credit that you have. The numbers they use to determine the maximum amount of credit you should have come from the Federal Government.

To make this a little more real let us look at an income of $2,000 a month, and see how much credit you can expect to get, and in what form. If you are interested in buying a house a bank will loan you up to 3 times your annual income, if you do not already have too much credit. At $2,000 a month you would have an annual income of $24,000, and a bank would lend you up to $72,000, or 3 times $24,000, to buy a home. In many parts of the country this isn't very much money to buy a home, although there are parts of our land where you can get a nice home for $72,000.

Before they will lend you the money to buy this home, the bank will want to look at your whole credit record. While they will be interested in evidence that you don't pay your bills, aside from that they will also look at your total credit obligations. The rule of thumb in judging your credit worthiness is that you have less than 25% of your monthly income going out to short term credit payments, that's less than $500 a month.

At this point you say fine, I only have $250 a month going out to pay for my credit cards. But banks don't look just at credit cards, they also look at personal loans, bank loans, payments for furniture, and payments for cars, none of which you might think of initially. Since car loans can easily be $200 a month, it is easy to get your credit payments over $500 a month.

What all of this means is that you should take the monthly income of your family, all those who will be responsible for the loan, and all of the credit debts of that same group of people, and see if the monthly payments for those debts is more than one-forth, or 25%, of the total income you have each month. If your payments are higher than that you are going to have a very difficult time getting any additional credit. Even worse, if you have allowed your credit payments to get up into the 30% or 40% range, or even more, you are in serious danger of going bankrupt since you do not have enough income to pay your debts comfortably and live. If you are overextended in this manner any sickness or layoff, or even a change of job, is likely to put you into credit difficulties that will take you years to get out of.

To stay out of credit trouble keep your credit obligations at less than 25% of your total monthly, household income.

IS A LINE OF CREDIT ON YOUR HOME A GOOD IDEA?

A line of credit can have a very important place in your credit picture, but it must be used with caution. Do not get a line of credit so that you will have a credit card with a $50,000 limit, this will only result in your financial ruin. Do get a line of credit, at 8% interest, or thereabouts, to consolidate all of your 19% credit cards. And then tear up all of the other credit cards.

Getting a line of credit is a lot cheaper and easier than taking out additional conventional loans on your home, or even of getting new credit cards. The interest you use is secured by the equity you have in your home, and your home is put at risk every time that you use this form of credit.

Getting a line of credit is so easy every bank offers it to every home owner. They make it so easy that appraisals are free, or not even required, and rates are low. I have gotten at least one call a month from a bank offering me a line of credit, but if I tell them I would rather re-finance my home they hang up. Banks would rather give you a line of credit than a re-finance because they are offering you much less money, at variable rates that can go up or down with the prosperity of the country, and if you can't pay they will take your home. While a line of credit might be attractive for you, it is a chance for the banks to get back all of the property they sold over many years, and not at fair market value either.

But is the line of credit any good for you? I've already mentioned a couple of places where the line of credit can be a good idea, and one or two where it would be a bad idea, and this is what I would like to leave you with. Do not get a line of credit on your home unless you can payoff all of your other debts and lower your monthly cash flow. Then throw away and cancel all of your other credit sources. If you can't bring yourself to do the last thing, don't get a line of credit, it's too dangerous and what you stand to lose if you can't make the payments is worth too much. Don't make yourself homeless over charging a few clothes so that you feel good for a day.

SHOULD YOU USE CREDIT FOR VACATIONS?

As a general rule you should not use credit for vacations if you want to keep good credit. It is not that using credit for vacations, all by itself, is going to end up ruining your credit, but it is bad practice nevertheless. On vacations you naturally feel more relaxed and happier than you do at home. You also feel less responsible to your creditors, and all of those other ones that you pay each month through the long cold winter. As a result the idea of spending extra money to make the vacation more memorable seems to be a very good idea, and well worth the money. Of course it would be well worth the money if you never had to go home and pay off your credit card bills. Unfortunately, as is the nature of vacations, they come to an end and you have to come back to the real world of bills and house payments.

You do not want to be paying for your vacation, no matter how memorable, 2 or 3 years after you have gotten home. The concern with making monthly payments for months or years after any vacation will long outweigh any benefit you will have gotten by your indulgence.

If you must have an extravagant vacation, open a vacation savings account the year before you want to go. It may not seem as spontaneous, but once the vacation is over it will also be paid for. Alternatively plan to go on a cheaper vacation package. Instead of going to Hawaii, go to Mexico and save half of the costs. To have memorable vacations often means planning, and delaying, but it can be done responsibly, it is always preferable to using credit to pay for it.

There are exceptions to this general rule, however. It may be necessary to take a vacation on short notice for your health, and in that case use any money or credit you can get to do it. What kind of medical emergency do I mean? It could be a mental breakdown, a nasty divorce, a serious or fatal illness, or one of those needs in a close friend or family member. You are going to have to make up your own decision on what qualifies as a real emergency and what is just a great need that you have to get away from your daily life.

We all need vacations, but few of us are able to judge accurately the level of vacation that we need for renewal. It is too easy to be impressed by travel brochures and stories and feel that we have to do the same thing or we can't live. Generally we are wrong in this, and taking a day or two at a bed and breakfast will do us about the same amount of good. Be real about vacations and be realistic about what you can afford before you commit to doing something you can't afford except with credit. As you may have found out by now I tend to be very conservative in the use of credit. It should be used, but it should never be squandered.

10 GOOD EMERGENCY USES FOR CREDIT

Why have I included this section when emergency and appropriate uses of credit are mentioned all through this book? These 10 have been gathered to give you a guideline of when to resort to credit in special situations. Of course we all want to use credit for our own convenience, but we also need to use it for those situations in which nothing else is as easily available. Read over these 10 to get an idea of what to look cut for, and why you should keep a credit reserve just for these emergencies.

1. Auto breakdowns away from home. Anyone can suffer a breakdown out on the highway far from home. In many such cases you may have to depend entirely upon yourself to get your car fixed and get moving again.

2. Death or illness in the family. How many of us have family members in poor health scattered around the country, and even around the world. When death or serious illness strikes it is always unexpected, and the only solution for many of us is to go to join the family at whatever the cost.

3. Emergency repairs to the home. We can live in our homes for many years with nothing unexpected ever happening. But one day, we know not when, we can be hit with an emergency which has to be corrected as rapidly as possible. How would you like a roof with a big hole in it on a dark and stormy night? No one would, but when it happens we can't wait around for the insurance people to show up in a day or two and help us take care of it, the hole needs to be fixed now, and we will worry about insurance later.

4. The big interview. This may not look like an emergency requiring credit to many of you, but if you have been out of work for a while and then suddenly have a real chance for a job, it qualifies. When going to a job interview we need to look as sharp as possible. After all, the more you look like you need a job the less likely you are to get it. At least that is the way the world seems to work. If you get

one of these interviews take out your credit cards and buy the best interview outfit you can find, it may just pay off.

5. Whenever you can pay off the balance at the end of the month. You may be asking what kind of an emergency use this is referring to? Well, it isn't exactly an emergency use, but any time that you can pay off your balance at the end of a month you are not abusing your credit, and you won't get into any problems through its use.

6. For a necessary gift. When is a gift a necessary gift, such that it qualifies as an emergency? Have you ever forgotten a birthday present or anniversary present to an important person in your life? If you don't think that this qualifies as an emergency that requires the use of credit, just try it once. To keep peace in your home and family it is sometimes necessary that we purchase a gift when we have not planned to do so, and when we don't have any other method of doing so.

7. For an investment. Normally I would not suggest that you use credit to make an investment. However, sometimes you can come across an investment which is so good that it must be taken advantage of now, and credit is the only way. Excluded from this category would be gambling in any form, and anything sold over the phone on a "you must buy now to take advantage of this wonderful offer," type. If you are a regular investor, and know a lot about what you are investing in, then occasional use of credit to make an investment is entirely appropriate.

8. To avoid bankruptcy. Admittedly this is taking a chance, but if you are in a bind where you can lose your house, or on the verge of going totally broke, using credit as a last resort to avoid this dire outcome is entirely justified. This does not mean that you should just shift your credit payments around from one source to another. That would result in certain bankruptcy, but actually taking care of a credit crunch in order to give yourself some breathing room is a worthwhile intent that can justify using credit.

9. Medical care for your pets. This falls into the same area as using credit when family members become sick. For many of us our pets are the only ones close to us. In addition, no one has health insurance for pets, and pet care can easily run into the hundreds of dollars. If you come to the point of allowing your pet to be untreated or using credit, then use your credit. Whatever the outcome you will

sleep better for the choice.

10. Because you are filing for bankruptcy. This bit of advice seems to counter what was said in number 8. However, if you are filing for bankruptcy this may be your last chance to use credit for the next 7 years. Using it to prepare for the next 7 years may not be a decision of high moral value, but it can help to make your life tolerable, as well as help you to get over one of the roughest periods of time you may have to face. This is something that creditors hate, and that you should not warn them you are doing, but you can be sure that they have all faced the problem of bankrupt debtor and have survived.

USING CREDIT TO PAY FOR COLLEGE

College is meant to include any training or educational program that is going to give you employment and survival skills. There is nothing better for you to invest in then yourself, and the best way to invest in yourself is to continue to learn throughout your life.

For college I would resort to any source of money that I could. While you might make a mistake by giving your money to a program that doesn't teach you the skills that you need, you are still safer putting your money in your own education than you will if you put it into any other investment.

But what do you need? The basic educational cost, for a Bachelor's degree at a public college, is around $10,000. Other programs that are shorter in time cost less, such as getting a license as a Practical Nurse. But back to the appropriate uses of credit. Look at the $10,000 over 4 years as you would the cost of buying a car. To buy a car for this same amount of money you know that you are not going to get a Cadillac, and the same goes for public education. Nevertheless, at the end of 4 years you will either have a worn out car or an education that can double your income. Which do you want?

10 BAD EMERGENCY USES FOR CREDIT

Not all emergencies should be solved with credit. Just as I listed 10 good emergency uses of credit, it is necessary to provide a list of bad uses so that you can avoid them. Credit does not care where it is used, that is your choice. Only you can make the final decision as to whether your credit expenditures are good or bad, and this little discussion may assist you in making good decisions rather than bad ones.

1. To make you feel good. Why do most Americans overeat, to make us feel good when we feel bad. Why do we go on binges of any kind, to make us feel good when we feel bad. If we took the trouble to express ourselves in a more constructive manner there would be no drunks, or drug addicts, or speeders on our highways. There wouldn't even be very many people who have misused their credit to the point that they now have no money, but that they did not even have the money they needed to pay their credit bills. I don't know how people in other countries handle day to day stresses, but Americans tend to go and do something that is bad for us in order to feel good. The next time that you feel bad and depressed, do not go and buy things on credit. Take a long walk instead, or rent a movie you love. Talk to a friend. Anything except go on a binge, especially a credit binge that can leave you feeling sorry for yourself several years from now.

2. To reward yourself. Flipping the coin over and going on a credit binge because you deserve it to reward yourself is just as bad as doing it to make you feel good. Hopefully all of us do things on occasion for which we should be rewarded. Of course in our society we never reward everyone who deserves it, and many people feel compelled to reward themselves. If you lose a pound reward yourself. If you get a raise reward yourself. If you have a good date reward yourself. The list of reasons to reward ourselves is endless, but the ways of doing it constructively requires thought. Don't give yourself a reward by using credit for something that you can't afford. A reward could be to take a day with a friend, or to go to a movie that you would like to see. Just do something that you can afford. If you are accomplishing tasks for which you deserve rewards, then there should be many types of rewards that you could give yourself, and very few should require you to go out and max out your credit cards.

3. To avoid depriving yourself for a month. Over the course of any given year we come up a little short of money once in a while. Now if you have some savings, and can cut back and eat beans for a couple of days, you can get through to the next month without too much discomfort. But if you are totally committed to maintaining your life style every day of every year you might consider cutting back to

be a great hardship. If this causes you to go out and use your credit accounts to keep from never having a bad day you are on your way to ruin. In life there will always be an occasional bad day, but if you are basically doing all right the few bad days will usually give way to many good days. The next time you have a bad day or a bad month don't turn to your credit cards to make it all right, cut back on life for a few days and you will come out way ahead in the future.

4. For groceries. I have only thrown this in because of the recent growth of pay point cards at supermarkets and gas stations. As you can guess I buy with cash whenever possible. Others, who like the plastic, carry very little cash and resort to the charge card at every opportunity. This includes going to the grocery store for the family food, or to pick up all the goodies for that Friday night party. Using credit like this is putting it out of your control. You never know how much you have in the bank, and you never know how much you have on your credit accounts. For those of you who are already addicted to this form of purchase I would advise to be very careful. To those of you haven't gotten into pay point as yet, steer clear of it if you can. It's a trap that can suck you in like quicksand. Never use a credit source unless you can keep track of how much you are spending. If you can buy groceries with credit and keep track of, you can probably handle it.

5. To pay off other credit cards. Paying off credit card bills with other credit cards is a sure trial to financial ruin. If you have gotten to the point of being unable to make your credit card payments each month, but you haven't yet gotten behind, contact each of your creditors and work out lower payment plans. This will keep your credit in good shape and will prevent you from getting deeper in debt each month as you try to keep up with payments you can't afford. If credit cards are used wisely and not overused to the extent that we owe more than we have, there should never be the need to consider using credit to pay credit. This goes for bill consolidation loans as well. Use these only when you are willing to tear up all of your old credit cards and live cheaply long enough to pay down your balance. Don't get overextended in the first place and you will never have to make this choice.

6. For a vacation. Do not use credit to pay for your vacations. There are exceptions, but most vacations can be planned in advance, and should be. The most common reason given for borrowing for a vacation is that everyone wants to have something

really special to remember. The problem with that attitude is that what you will remember the longest are all of the payments you are making afterwards. If you want a vacation to always remember then start saving and planning for it 2 or 3 years in advance. Find the best vacation package or travel fares that you can. With this type of planning you can often save half or more of the money you would spend on a spur of the moment super vacation that you paid for with credit.

7. For spur of the moment purchases. If you like to go window shopping leave your credit cards at home. In general, spur of the moment purchases are bad for your home budget, but they are especially bad for your credit and your future survival. You might even say that if you live by impulse buying, you will also go broke by impulse buying. Simply the nature of this type of purchase means that you have made it without much reflection on whether you want what you are buying, or whether you can afford it. But, and here is a way out, if you must buy those things that you see when you see them, only buy on cash. Cash buying will never ruin your credit, and you can decide in advance how much you can spend. This simple control may save your credit status.

8. Because it's there. This is a slight modification of the impulse buyer. The typical buyer who simply buys things because they are there is the one who never misses a sale. If you are not sure if you fit into this category you can easily find out by looking around your house. If it is cluttered with a million purchases that you have never made use of and never think about, you qualify. Now if you can shop these sales and specials and pay with cash you may still have a cluttered house, but you won't have more credit than you can pay for. If you are addicted to buying at garage sales and the like you still qualify as an impulse buyer, but you are safe from the credit monster.

9. To gamble. This is a very bad area to get into the use of credit. I thought that it should be mentioned because there has been so much growth in instant cash machines that it is now possible to spend both your bank account and your credit limit at one of our gambling capitals around the country. Unfortunately the United States also seems to have more than its share of gambling addicts. When you have money to spend gambling is glamorous. It is done in palaces and important people pay attention to you. You can even rub elbows with millionaires. But once you have gone broke, and you

will if you keep it up long enough, no one will even give you the time of day. No matter what anyone says, every addiction is just as bad as every other addiction, and all will ruin you in the end.

10. To buy something offered over the phone. Never buy anything that is offered to you over the phone that has to be purchased now or you lose the chance to buy. You will be cheated and you will be robbed. In addition never give a credit card number to anyone over the phone either. Telephone sales are a growing and insidious menace to the credit of the people of the United States. If you are ever called and offered anything over the phone have the information sent to you and make your final decision in your own home in private. Until you do this do not set up appointments with these people to come to your home to sell you anything.

While I intend this book to have a lot of good advice on credit that anyone can use, I am mostly concerned with the problems that credit can cause us. It is not that credit has to be a problem in our lives, it's just that we can get into credit trouble so easily. Having too much credit is a problem that can creep up on us over a period of years, like arthritis or heart disease. Initially we feel fine, using just a little credit now and then, and paying off the balance each month. Then we have a good Christmas and a car repair emergency and we are carrying a balance that is going to take a year of paying each month in order to pay off. Although we don't seem to be using our credit very much, each year finds our balances a little larger. Eventually our credit payments are eating up a fourth of our income, and we are beginning to have trouble making all of the payments each month. At this point we begin getting the reminders in the mail from our creditors, and getting refused on a credit application here and there. Even if we haven't recognized it yet ourselves, we are in credit trouble and the next few months will leave us going toward bankruptcy. With this chapter I will be pointing out some of the ways that this condition can come about in the hope that you can avoid them.

3 HOW WE GET OUR CREDIT IN TROUBLE?

A few pages ago you were given some general guidelines as to how much of your income should go for credit card payments. The rule of thumb is 25%, or one fourth, of your take-home income. The problem with using this figure is that it only takes part of your credit picture into account. You probably have many forms of credit than just credit cards, and they can all get you into trouble. It is not only necessary to keep your credit card payment as low as possible, it is also required that you keep all of your credit obligations under control. When your credit goes out of control your creditors are going to end up taking control of your life.

Another way of asking this question is to take a look as how much of your income you need to have available in cash, and how much credit you can afford with the remainder. If you are not a person who likes to carry much cash you can probably get along best by putting most of your cash into a Versatel type of account that will give you a little cash money any time that you ask for it, but doesn't require you to actually carry any. For the sake of argument let's say you only need about 25% of your income in cash. Out of each $1,000 you get a month you would then have $250 available. After all, everyone needs petty cash nearly every day.

Of the rest of your money you are going to have to put aside some for bills that you don't pay every month, but that you can expect. These are things like taxes or a vacation trip. Not true emergencies in the sense that you don't know how much they will cost, or have any idea of when they will happen. Just stuff that comes up all the time and has to be paid for when it does.

Let's now say that you have half of your money left for credit. Since credit rates vary so much half of your money might be enough for a $100,000 home loan, or a $40,000 car loan, or $15,000 in credit card bills. At least this is what $500 a month can get you. But then no one can really live on $1,000 a month any more, so this is not a real case. If you are living in our land on anything less than $2,000 a month for one person, or quite a bit more than that for more than one, you are in trouble.

For an income of $1,000 a month I would not advise you to have any credit cards, and to drive the cheapest cars, and use the cheapest housing, you can get. But if you are in the $2,000 area and are alone you have a chance to enjoy some of the good things in life and use credit to smooth the way.

But how does this all come out? The original question was when are your credit payments taking too much of your income. The answer I have been getting around to is one half. If your credit payments take more than 50% of your take home income you are paying too much toward credit, and you could very well end up in financial trouble. Money may go through your fingers like water but credit has a memory. If you use credit you can't pay for; your creditors will be there month after month no matter what else may have happened to you in the meantime

If your credit is such that it will take you at least 5 years to pay it off, because you owe too much, can you guarantee that you will be able to continue making payments for the next 5 years? Can you guarantee that over this time you will not be laid off or fired from a job, or that you will not become too sick to work for a month or two? Can you even guarantee that you won't need to draw on your credit for a real emergency at any time in the next 5 years? To all of these questions I will bet you that you can't give any guarantees. Keeping your credit payments, and obligations, at a level that matches your income is an absolute necessity if you are to keep your credit from driving you to bankruptcy.

CAN YOU BE PLUNGED INTO A CREDIT MESS BY CATASTROPHE

It is not always our fault when we get into trouble with credit. Personal catastrophes can occur at any time. These include the death of a spouse, divorce, loss of a job, natural disasters such as tornadoes and floods, and investment disasters such as a radioactive disposal site going in next to some land we invested in. The point is that they can happen to anyone at any time, and chances are very good that every one will have several of these disasters over their lifetime.

Because they are disasters and can never be predicted it is impossible to prepare for all of them. However, it is possible to protect yourself from the most common disasters that you are likely to face. You can take out life insurance and health insurance to protect you from death and serious illness. You can insure your home against floods and fires, and even against robbery and accidents on your property. In other words, with planning you can almost eliminate the chance that one of these disasters is going to destroy you financially.

DO YOU HAVE TOO MANY CREDIT CARDS?

Credit card numbers can sneak up on you. While I would like to say that you only need one credit card, I can't go that far. Different credit cards function for different purposes. If you have too many of the same kind, then you have too many. Also, if you have credit cards of types you don't need, you have too many no matter how many you have at the time. To make an accurate judgement as to whether you have the right numbers and types of credit cards we will take a look at some of the different kinds you can get, or that you may have been offered already.

Visa and MasterCard are two cards that are often issued by the same banking institutions. It is not only simple to get one of each of these, say from Bank of America, but they will continue to offer you new cards from the same banks long after you have gotten them. They are also granted from saving's and loans, and it doesn't seem to matter where you get them from since I have never found anyone discriminate against a credit card because it was offered through a minor bank or saving's and loan. But how many of these do you need, and do you need both? I would say that one of either one is plenty. In spite of seeing these cards around for years I have never been able to discover any difference between them. Having more than one will probably end up confusing you as well as leading you to overcharge. After all, if you max out your account on one Visa or

MasterCard you will probably end up maxing out on three or four, or even more. The rule of thumb is that the more credit cards you have the more credit you will use. Have multiple cards of the same type just confuses the issue even more by keeping you from knowing how much   you owe on any one of them.

Oil company cards are less well known, and their interest rates are about the same as Visa and Mastercard. The hook with the oil company cards is that they give rebates on their purchases. The usual rebate is around 2%, but the amount is limited. Thus, if you spend $1,000 on the card you would get a $20 rebate in oil company products such as gasoline. But if you spend $10,000 on the card they do not give you $200 in products. The limit per year is around $50, and you get nothing back for charging above that amount. The last such card that I saw was from Richfield, and the interest rate it offered was 16.9%, or a savings of 2-3% from the bank cards. The main danger we face in using these cards is thinking that we are getting something for nothing because of the rebates, and overusing the cards. If you use this particular companies products anyway then you might as well use one of their credit cards, otherwise leave them alone. You certainly don't need an extra card of this type for anything other than a temptation.

Airline cards are in the same category as oil company cards, but they are sexier. After all, flying is more interesting then buying gas for your car. The danger is the same as with other cards, but the reasons for overusing your credit may seem much better. Who could argue with making purchases on an airline credit card so that you could take a vacation that you could never save up for on your own. If you use a lot of credit, and you want to travel this is a good card to have. There is a caution though, since the airlines now have so many people out taking free flights they have started increasing the number of credit miles you must have to get a free ticket. By the way, normally they will give you 1,000 miles or so credit when you take the card, and credit of one mile for every dollar you charge after that. Depending on their rules they may even give you the same credit for credit transferred onto your new cards. So you can see that these cards have merit, but you have to beware the trap of just adding them to what you already have. If you take one of these cards then get rid of one of your other ones.

Department store cards can be another source of trouble. Because they are issued by department stores and not by banks it is not difficult to consider them somehow different. If you do not consider this credit source as of the same category as every other bank and savings and loan card you are mistaken. The only major difference in department store cards and other credit cards is that they cannot be used to purchase anything not sold by that one store. Of course since they are so limited you might think that they would have something to really attract you, like very low interest rates. Think again, the interest rates are the same as are the conditions for payment. What they do often offer you is a discount when you sign up for them, and credit at the store. The department store chains that use these kinds of cards usually do not accept any other credit cards. While this may seem to limit them a great deal, it also keeps all of the profit in the organization itself and keeps everyone else out. I do not recommend this form of credit card for anyone unless there is a store you shop at regularly, and credit would be of real use to you. Otherwise one of these credit cards is simply going to be another temptation to use credit buying things you don't need simply because someone convinced you that you needed them.

Gold cards are kind of a fancy version of the usual Visas and MasterCards. The main advantages they have to offer are higher limits. Both interest rates and payment schedules are the same as for the other cards. One more thing, they cost more than the other cards, as much as $20-30 more each year. I have never seen anyone turned down for a credit purchase because they didn't have a gold card and it is my opinion that they are just an excuse by the credit agencies to charge you more money for the same services. I can't see how this card would get you into any more credit problems than any other one, but it is just an added expense that no one needs.

American Express, Diner's Club, and Carte Blanche cards come under the category of travel and entertainment cards. American express is advertised as the go anywhere card, and Diner's Club and Carte Blanche are used for meals and purchases in many areas of the world. These cards are different from the Visa type in that balances are required to be paid off each month. If charges are not paid off you will then be charged interest and eventually be turned over to a collection agency. While you normally pay no interest with these cards, since they are paid off monthly, there is an annual fee for the cards themselves. These cards cost much more than bank cards, and merchants are charged higher rates when you use them. Because the balances have to be paid off each month it is harder to qualify to get the card in the first place. These cards are also easier to get in trouble with. If you do not have a reasonable and bonafied reason for a travel and entertainment card do not get one. If you are at all shaky in your credit you can end up in default very quickly. Even if you have, and need, one make it one of the priority cards that you pay off before you make your other payments. The consequences may not be as bad as not making your housing payments, but you can ruin your credit just as quickly.

Maximum rate Vs. minimum rate cards are really no different when it comes to services. Of course it is easier to find high interest credit cards than low interest ones. Low interest cards are generally offered in such states as New Jersey, but they are national cards and anyone who qualifies should be able to get one. Naturally most of the credit card offers you get in the mail will be for high rate cards. I believe that everyone should have credit cards from local banks, but even if you do you may be getting billed from Texas. Based on the way credit is granted you might as well get the lowest cost credit card you can get. In fact unless you are just getting your first credit card, and have to get it from whoever will give one to someone with no credit record, go out and find a low rate card. The difference in interest that you would pay on a $7,000 balance is about $1,000 a year in interest. A 19% credit card will cost about $1,600 a year, and a 6.9% card will cost about $600 a year. That extra $1,000 could be used to pay down the balance on the credit card, or you could use it to buy more credit if you wanted to. In any case you might as well keep the money yourself instead of giving it to your local friendly bank.

DID YOU LOSE YOUR JOB? WHAT IT MEANS TO YOUR CREDIT

Losing your job does not necessarily mean the end of your credit. Of course it is going to impact your credit, and you may not be able to get new credit. But as long as you keep up your credit payments all of the accounts that you have current will stay available.

What should you do if you lose your job? Keep your credit payments up as long as you can, and if you can't then contact the creditors and explain your situation to them. Creditors do not want you to go bankrupt since it means the end of your accounts and a loss to them. On the other hand creditors do not want to simply have you stop making payments altogether. I guess that they are afraid you will forget to make the payments later on when your finances improve. They will give you a reduced payment plan. Perhaps interest only, or even less. If you are paying less than the interest on your credit the leftover interest will be added to the account and interest will be charged on that too.

It may even be permissible for you to borrow from one credit source to pay another, but this is also a sure fire method of going broke. For every month that you live on your credit in this manner your credit problems will double. The maximum amount of time you might get by this way is 6 to 12 months, but you may never get credit again. Remember that even those who lose their jobs have futures. You will probably be able to get unemployment for 9 to 12 months, and hopefully you will have a little money in the bank. Even without a job most families can get by for a year before things start to get desperate. But within that year you have to go out and find yourself another source of money.

But this is not a book of job hunting tips, but of what to do to get, keep, and maintain credit. So if you lose your job keep paying your bills. Stop everything else except paying your bills and job hunting, but pay your bills. When that gets too difficult, in maybe a year, contact all of your creditors and negotiate a decreased payment schedule. These steps will maintain your credit. Do not live on your credit, ever, as this is a sure road to ruin.

If it comes to bankruptcy, and it might, read the sections included here to find the best paths to follow, and pay special attention to those that have the best opportunity to keep your credit in tact.

DIVORCE PROBLEMS

The problems of credit and divorce have much to do with the way families work these days. In most families both the husband and the wife work. However, if only one works it is almost as common for it to be the woman as the man. This is important in divorce because one of the marriage partners may have been the primary source of income qualifying the couple for credit. In divorce the person with the lowest income is going to lose much of their credit.

To guard yourself against divorce, and any other unforeseen event such as death or loss of income of your spouse you need to qualify your own credit. This is one of the best insurance policies you can take out, and all that you have to do to take advantage of it is to plan ahead and look after your own affairs.

If you are anticipating a divorce in the near future there are some steps you need to take in advance to protect your credit. To begin an in depth plan for your approaching divorce follow this 5 step plan:

1.   Talk to financial professionals for tips as to managing your own credit. You don't have to tell them that you are anticipating a divorce, just that you feel that you should have your own credit established to protect yourself financially. If you talk to a lawyer you will probably have to pay, but if your bank offers a financial adviser service they should talk to you for free. When you go in to talk be prepared with information regarding your current credit status and income. Financial advisers are used to acting in confidence so there should be no problem with keeping your consultation to yourself. Do not use the same adviser that you and your husband have been using together however, or your inquiry might get back to your spouse before you are ready to communicate your plans.

2.   Build your own personal credit, independent of your spouse if you want to have credit after the divorce. This is best done well in advance of a divorce, and will require that you get a bank account in your own name. The amount of credit you establish is not important initially, simply that it is in your own name. It is often more simple to get department store cards in one spouse's name since joint accounts are much less common, and men and women tend to shop in separate stores as well. If you are a member of a credit union credit is commonly granted in the members name rather than the families, and your salary is accepted as insurance for payment.

3.   Get a copy of your credit record now that you have talked to a financial adviser and gotten credit in your own name. You need to see if your credit has any problems. To be certain that you know everything you can about your current credit status get reports from each of the three main credit agencies.

4.   Clean up any negatives in your joint credit record since these can come back to plague you later, even if your own credit record is clean. Begin by getting copies of your joint credit records

from each of the big three, in the same manner that you did for yourself. For every negative statement you see in the joint record prepare a written explanation, and try to get the negatives removed if that seems possible. When you go to apply for additional credit disclose the problems and your answers to them on the applications. Credit agencies that are surprised by negative are much more likely to turn you down in your credit needs.

5. Use your joint funds to pay off joint obligations in order to protect yourself later on. You can never tell for sure how a court will divide credit payments and income. You could very well end up with most of the bills and the least of the income after a divorce, when you are in the most need of clean credit. If there is money in your bank account use it to pay off creditors who have both of your names. You want to come out of a divorce with as clean a credit record and as few outstanding obligations as possible.

If you have gotten a divorce, or have gotten one already, and you still have joint accounts with your ex-spouse, cancel them. Joint credit accounts go on the credit record of both partners, and are the responsibility of both to pay. If your ex-spouse is irresponsible and you have a joint account they could refuse to make a timely payment, or charge amounts greatly beyond their ability to pay. Will spiteful spouses resort to such antics to get even for the divorce? Of course they will, in fact that type of activity should be looked on as expected. Shed all joint accounts as early as possible to protect yourself in cases of divorce.

Just to summarize the advice given here. Get credit in your own name, if you only have joint accounts and they are closed you will have no credit. When you apply for credit be sure to list non-job income as well as job related income, if you need to. Collect proof of your new income status to prove your credit worthiness to the credit agencies. Put explanations of credit record problems in the credit record. If you are a woman, and you are taking back a previous family name, let your creditors know. Especially do this if you are applying for credit with banks or other agencies who don't know who you are. In considering credit problems, disclose the problems and your answers before they show up on your credit record and ruin your chances of getting the credit you need.

CAN YOU BUY TOO MUCH HOUSE OR CAR ON CREDIT?

Houses and cars seem to be appropriate areas to examine to see if someone will give you too much credit. Too much credit is credit which you can't pay back because you don't have enough money. Buying a house, any house, or a new car always means going to the bank and applying for financing. A complete credit check is done, and you are required to list your sources of income and all of your other debtors. The loan is made only if the lending institution believes that you can afford to pay it back with interest.

So, theoretically at least, if you can get it financed, you can never buy too big a house, or too nice of a car. Of course this is only by theory, and in the real world theory is not always the truth. Of course there is abundant truth that lenders make mistakes. There is always a default rate of 2-3%, and if the economy gets so bad that a lot of people are losing their jobs as much as 10-15% may eventually be unable to pay off their loans.

What is the result of such failure? It is just as you see now, banks have repossessed more homes, and more cars are taken away from people through their inability to keep up payments. This brings up the next logical question, whose fault is it that these people have gotten too much credit, and can't pay it back?

With the checks that the banks do it would seem to be their fault if you get into credit trouble over a house or a car. But things are never that simple. Some of our debts do not show upon credit reports. For example, why would a personal loan be on such a report, and even credit union loans are not usually reported. But the main reason that the buyers of cars and homes end up defaulting on their loans is that they have lost income somewhere along the way. Lost jobs are the usual problem. Of course any addiction that uses a lot of money, or any other such mental illness, will cause the same problem. Many people do not even know that they have an addiction to gambling until they decide to gamble their rent and food money and then are threatened with being thrown into the street and can't feed their wives or children.

But aside from all of this, what is the problem? Conditions change over time. Not usually over short periods of time like 6 months or a year, but over 5, or 10, or 30 years everyone's financial situation changes. While most of the time you will earn more money over time, this has become less true recently. The trend in jobs has been for less benefits and less income. In fact it has been for fewer jobs for everyone. This does not happen to everyone, but it is happening to more and more people every day. Your best bet is to buy less in a car or home than you would like to. Compromise to the point that you can still live with your purchases, but that you have a wide margin of safety.

Because Americans get so much of their identity from the homes they live in and the cars they drive, most of us are not good judges of what we really need in a home or car. We want to buy the very best available. The home and the car that makes our blood run fast, and that gives us a feeling of accomplishment. In terms of credit, and as a tribute to the salesmen, we always want to buy more than we can afford at the time. It is the job of the lending institutions to prevent us from doing that. But since they are also out to make money, and because they believe when we say that we will pay back every cent we borrow plus interest, they will often loan us more money then they should.

You cannot trust the lending agencies to prevent you from buying a larger house or more expensive car than you can afford. You have to depend upon yourself. To depend upon yourself you look at your needs first. If you have a large family you need a large car or a van. If there is only you, and possibly one or two others, then any car will probably satisfy your needs. And if it is only you, then get the smallest car, and simplest home, you can be comfortable in. These are all common sense decisions, but they are ones you are going to have to make before you try to buy that house or that car. Good credit management, even in the case of homes and cars, is up to the consumer, not the lender.

WHAT ARE THE 10 WARNING SIGNS OF CREDIT PROBLEMS?

There are clues for you to watch out for. When any more than three of these warning signs appear in your life, you are in danger of credit problems, and if more than six appear at any one time, you are already in trouble. If all of them appear, then leave the country and change your name.

1. You can't keep track of your monthly charges. If you are going along through the month thinking that you are charging $200 to $300, and then find at the end of the month that you have charged

$500, and you tend to do this frequently, you are in trouble. Take a look at your monthly payments for the past several months. If the minimum payments have been going up each month then you are running up credit charges faster than you are paying them off. Sooner or later you are going to have minimums so high that you can't even meet those, much less pay anything extra toward your principal. Because the main balance of a credit card decreases so slowly with minimum payments, financial advisers always recommend that you make double or triple payments on at least one card to keep your credit levels under control. If you can't do this you are probably carrying too much credit, and you need to get rid of, or cut down on, some of your credit sources.

2. You sometimes skip a credit payment so that you can pay more important bills. As your credit payments become too heavy you are going to be faced with months in which you don't have enough money to pay for everything. Credit cards, or even a house or car payment, can conveniently be skipped for a month now and then. Of course if you make a habit of skipping payments your credit record will list late payments, and you will have more trouble in the future in getting additional credit.

3. You have cancelled a credit card because it is out of control. Although credit cards are only supposed to be used by the person they are issued to, no one checks very often, whose name is on a credit card when a charge is made. Of course you might do this to yourself, but it is more likely that other family members are using the same card. If you have gotten into such a situation and have been unable to get things under control through talking or threatening, the only choice you may have had left was to cancel the card. This is a sure sign that some of your credit is out of control. Just think what could happen to you if you had a line of credit on your home and someone went crazy with charging things, you could be broke and on the street in 6 months.

4. A bank or savings and loan has turned down one of your credit applications. While there is nothing deadly in being turned down for credit occasionally, this should still be taken as a signal that you have something negative in your credit record. If you get turned down for credit get a credit report and find out what is wrong. If there is something negative in your credit record you can be sure that everyone else you apply to for credit is going to see it too.

5. You sometimes go from cash to credit for monthly living expenses. Monthly living expenses are mainly food, gas, entertainment, and the incidentals that we use everyday. Most of the time we budget enough cash money to take care of these costs, and on occasion we may use checks. Since these expenses come up every single month they are one of the easiest costs to budget for. Because they are so predictable there should never be a reason to use credit to pay for them, but if you do you have a credit problem. Now it could just be that you are using credit where you should be using cash, and it means nothing. It is more likely, however, that you are having so much trouble managing your budget that it is impossible for you to keep enough cash to even make it from one month to another without resorting to credit. If this is a problem you have to cut down on your credit load so that you will have the cash you need each month.

6. You have gone to a home loan company for quick credit. Now home loan companies can provide a great service. Since they will take virtually anything for collateral, they will loan to anyone who has a car, furniture, or a job. In emergency situations this can be a great help. On the other hand if you have gone to a home loan company because no one else will give you credit, you have a problem. It is a problem even if you have done this because it is easier for you to borrow on everything you own rather than finding a regular lender. The use of home loan companies is always a sign of poor financial management.

7. You have used a cash withdrawal from one credit card to pay another. This has been mentioned before as one of the ways in which we get into trouble with our credit. While that is true, it must also be included as one of the signs of approaching credit problems. Borrowing from one credit card to make payments on another ends up increasing the amount owed while giving us no benefits. Well, that is a little harsh. Paying credit cards with other credit cards does buy time, but that is all that it buys. If you cannot keep up with your credit card payments contact your creditors and get them to take lower payments. This will make it longer to pay off your balances, but it won't increase the amount you owe. Borrowing to make credit payments will end up costing you all of your credit in the long run.

8. Your car has been seized for failure to make payments. What can be more traumatic to your feeling of self worth than to have your car taken away from you? Since cars are so important to

everyone in our society they are one of the last possessions we cease to pay for. If your car has been re-possessed you are not very many steps removed from losing all of your credit, or even from filing for bankruptcy.

9. Your home is being re-possessed. If your home is being taken by your lender you are already in bankruptcy, or you should be. Because house payments are so high it is not difficult to get behind when things go bad. If this is happening to you then your credit has been damaged almost as much as if you had a bankruptcy on your credit record.

10. You are in the process of, or have already, declared bankruptcy. Yes, this is the last and most definite sign that your credit is dead. Even though you cannot file for bankruptcy more often than every 7 years, no lender wants to touch anyone who has ever filed for bankruptcy. If you have been forced to resort to this solution to your financial problems immediately start taking the steps that will restore your credit. A list of steps you can take will be given a little later on.

4 CREDIT PROBLEMS? WHAT TO EXPECT

When you have problems with credit you cannot expect your creditors to leave you alone. They are going to contact you at home and at work. They will threaten you and tell you all of the evil things that will happen to you if you do not pay their bill. Each creditor cares only about their own account, and complaining about other accounts is unlikely to get you any sympathy. Creditors are not just out to get you in trouble with their credit. Credit is where they make most of their money, and if you get into trouble with your credit they are afraid that they won't get their money back. That is why they will listen to you and try to work out a payment plan at a reduced rate. But before you get to the point of negotiation you are probably going to go through some pain. This chapter presents some of the problems you may encounter, and how you might be able to deal with them.

WHAT TO DO ABOUT NASTY LETTERS IN THE MAIL

If you skip a payment to your creditors all that you can expect is that the old payment amount will be added to your new payment, and a penalty may be added. It is not that creditors like this kind of behavior by people who owe them money, but they realize that it can happen to anyone occasionally, and they don't want to lose the good will of their customers because of one missed payment. If all goes well for them and for you the back payment, with interest and penalty, will be made up the following month.

If you miss two payments, or you are getting behind by one payment frequently, you will probably get a reminder letter and maybe a phone call. Contact at this time won't be nasty, but it will be insistent. They will not let you alone from this point on unless you bring your payments up to date. The letters and phone calls will also say pretty much the same thing: We see that you have gotten behind in your payments to us, and we would like to know when you will be able to get your account current. If you cannot pay the delinquent payments at this time explain your problems to us and we will see what we can work out. If you can make payments, even partial payments, and you maintain contact with the creditors the level of communication will remain pretty much as shown here.

But if you get three, or more, months behind, or you stop replying to their phone calls and reminders, the creditors will begin to turn nasty. They will start to remind you of your good credit rating, and mention things like foreclosure and repossession if you have bought cars, homes, appliances, or furniture. Others may even go so far as to talk about law suits and garnishing your wages.

So how do you respond to these letters and phone calls before they begin to take legal action against your earnings and assets. Your need, if you are in financial trouble, is to gain time. You want to gain time whether or not you can ever pay off the money that you owe because it leaves you in control for as long as possible. If you have a chance of getting a new job, or of selling something to get money, you can probably work your way out of debt over time. But even if you are in the process of filing for bankruptcy you want to assure your creditors that everything is going to be fine and that you will send a little money each month until you get on your feet. Do not let your creditors on to your true situation until you have to. If you do they will take steps to seize your possessions first, and file against you before you can protect yourself. Never cut creditors off when you are in trouble. A lack of communication with creditors is the next worst thing to filing bankruptcy in their face.

CAN CREDITORS GET YOU FIRED FROM YOUR JOB?

It is against the law for creditors to harass you at your job in order to get the money you owe them. Now this doesn't stop some creditors from calling you at work occasionally, but if they do this to the point at which it threatens your job you can sue them.

This law was passed to protect employees when they were at work so that they could repay creditors, and because your relationship with your creditors should have nothing to do with your source of income. At least not until some sort of legal judgement has been brought against you. Employers do not want to interrupt their day and yours in order to give you messages from people you owe money to. While a creditor can't get you fired for owing them money, if a creditor calls an employer often enough you may find yourself out of work.

CAN CREDITORS TAKE PART OF YOUR INCOME?

Yes they can, by going through the courts they can get a judgement against you where your employer will pay them directly each payday instead of giving you all of your earnings. Virtually any creditor can do this, but the IRS is probably the most frequent user of this technique of bill collection. I once knew a man who had 80% of his salary garnished by the IRS. The judgement against him was the result of a business that had gone bad, and that had depended upon government contracts for most of its money. When the government failed to pay its bills, his business fell apart and the IRS suddenly wanted all of the money that was supposed to have been withheld from his employees. When it turned out that the money wasn't there, they came after him in the courts and ended up garnishing his wages for the next 5 years.

Any creditor can do this by going to court over a debt that you can't pay. You can beat it only by losing your job or by working out a payment plan directly with the creditor. If you are garnished, although an employer can't fire you for it, it looks very bad on your employment record and could show that you can't manage money efficiently. This is never something that a person should let happen to them. Keep your credit problems between you and your creditors, never let the courts get involved unless you bring them into it for some kind of a settlement to decrease your obligations.

HOW WILL CREDITORS LET YOU KNOW YOU'RE IN TROUBLE?

If you aren't paying attention to your finances, and many people don't, your creditors may figure out that you are in trouble before you do. If you get behind on payments regularly, or you have too many credit cards and charge accounts, or you have a tax bill that you have to pay over time you may be getting close to serious credit problems. But the real clue is how well do you keep track of your own monthly expenses. If you don't have at least a general idea of where you stand during each month as to paying your bills and having the cash you need on hand, you could be in trouble and not even know it. But your creditors will know it, and they will let you know in some very obvious ways.

A denial of credit is a pretty good sign that you have too much credit, or not enough income to cover your credit application. This is especially true if you start getting turned down by credit card companies. Most credit card issuers will give cards to anyone, and if you are getting turned down when you think you will be getting a card, you should do a budget and find out how your credit stands.

Reminders to make payments mean that you have been slow with your payments, and often more than once. These reminders should mean more to you than that you are just a little lax in taking care of your bills, it should be taken as a clear sign that you don't know what you have paid and what you haven't.

Denial of cash advances is a loss of a sacred rite to most Americans with credit cards. So long as your credit is current with a credit card company you have a right to cash advances. Many of us become dependent on these for the cash we need each month, and the loss of this source of income, or credit, can be a real hardship. However, you should never become dependent on cash advances, use a regular bank, or Versatel, account for cash. It costs you money every time that you use a credit card for cash. If you are denied credit card cash give the issuer a call immediately to find out the source of the problem, and fix it. If you already know why they won't give you the money, then you should also be making plans of how to fix your credit.

Negative statements on your credit record are probably the first thing that shows up when credit problems develop, but the last that you will be aware of. If any of the first three events happen to you, contact the credit records companies and get copies of your credit record. If you have negative statements which you did not expect than take steps to fix them. If your record is clean take it to the creditor and ask them why you were turned down for credit, or for a cash advance. If all that you have had so far is reminders for payment you may still have a clean credit record. If you do, be glad and keep it clean if you can.

These are just some of the ways creditors let us know that we can't quite be trusted with our credit. You may encounter others, but they should also show up in one of the forms just discussed.

5 PATHS TO FIXING CREDIT PROBLEMS

There are many paths to fixing credit problems, and it helps to have a road map if we want to find them. Fixing credit is a service offered by Credit Bureaus, but I am going to show you how to do it here. After all, why pay an agency $1,000 to help you out of credit problems every time that they crop up when you can find out how to do it yourself any time. Your best investment is always the one you make in yourself. Every hour you spend on learning how to do something for yourself will be an hour less that you have to pay someone else to do the same job for you. Read over the paths given here, and when you have problems use this as a guide. Some of this information will be rather detailed since it needs to be followed very closely. The more information and guidance you get the less need you will have for outside experts.

I may as well begin by giving you a rundown on credit repair companies. Personally I don't think that any of them are worth your money, but if you listen to their sales pitch they are likely to talk you into paying them to fix your credit problems for you. Of course they can't do anything more than you can. In fact there are so many people running around trying to sell services like credit repair that you can waste all of your money and never really know what anyone has done for you. Of course hiring someone else to handle your credit correspondence makes sense if you are so wealthy or so busy with responsibilities that you really don't have time to take care of your own problems, but for most people using a credit repair company is a convenience that you shouldn't take advantage of. Many of us are a little fearful of dealing with other people, and its easier to pay a nice person to go and be nasty for us than to do it ourselves. It is really a foolish way to go since we never know if the services we are paying for are worthwhile, or even if they are working up to the claims of their salespeople.

After trashing credit repair companies I am going to tell you how to go about repairing your own credit yourself. Credit repair is nothing more than making phone calls, writing letters, and paying bills. If the paying bills part is impossible for you at this time there are ways of at least cutting down the amount of money that you have to pay out. This is not an impossible task, its just one that is about as much fun as doing your income tax.

CREDIT REPAIR COMPANIES --

YOU CAN DO AS WELL OR BETTER WITHOUT THEM

Credit repair companies make all kinds of claims that they hope will scare you into buying their services. They say that they can wipe out bankruptcies (they can't), get rid of negative information in your credit record (they don't say that you can do the same thing), get you credit no matter how bad your record (they can't do this any better than you can), use loopholes to get you out of tough situations (we'll try to find some of those here), and get you a major bankcard that will be acceptable anywhere (of course that's the same as getting credit when you have some black marks on your credit record). In plain terms they are offering you nothing that you can't do for yourself.

Some of the things that the credit repair companies tell you are lies, and these need to be pointed out. FIrst, with a bankruptcy you won't be able to get credit for 10 years without their help. The only part of this that is true is that the bankruptcy stays on your credit record for 10 years, and that is not the same thing as whether or not you can qualify for credit. Creditors set their own standards for granting credit. The only thing that a creditor knows that you don't, at this time, is which creditors will be likely to give you credit with a bankruptcy on your record. If you can find out who these creditors are you can apply directly and save the credit agency fee. How do you go about talking to creditors in this case. Look at the reasons for your bankruptcy. If it was not the result of a mismanagement of credit all you may need is a good explanation of what drove you to bankruptcy. If you did have a problem in managing your credit you have to be able to show what you have done to turn things around. These would be accomplishments such as paying off some of the credit you had, decreasing the number of accounts, and having a stable job.

Credit repair companies sometimes try to show that they have some affiliation with the Federal Government. None of them have any such affiliation, and the Federal Government has nothing to do with whether or not an individual gets credit or has a clean credit record. The reason for trying to claim that the company is in some way a government agency is that they can try to force you into signing up with them. Just think: Official Agency for Credit Repair for the United States, or some such title. If you got a brown envelope from a company with this name you would be much more likely to hire them then if they were just called Joe's Credit Repair. Of course, since there is no official agency for credit repair you would be much more likely to get Joe as a representative than you would a government official.

Some credit repair companies advise you to use a technique called file segregation to clean up your credit. This is a technique in which you give false information on your credit applications, and simply leave off a few creditors so that it doesn't look like you have had many credit problems in the past. Now, past creditors and credit problems will probably show up on your credit record anyway when it is requested by the creditor, making it look like you are just trying to cover up past problems. File segregation actually goes beyond just not giving information about past problems, it is much closer to an effort to establish a false identity for yourself for the purpose of obtaining credit. The simplest way this might be done is to give basically honest information, but give a false Social Security number. Then when the creditor gets your credit record there will be nothing on it since they are coded by the Social Security number. In any case don't do this. Giving false information for the purpose of getting credit, file segregation, is a Federal crime. In certain states obtaining credit through file segregation may also make you libel for charges of civil fraud by the state. This is an illegal practice and you should not attempt it on your own, or on the advice of a credit repair company.

Resorting to a credit repair company for a loan, which many of them offer, will leave you with more debt than cash. They will hit you first with a large up front fee for processing your loan. This could run into hundreds of dollars even for a loan for as little as $2,000-3,000. In addition they will demand some sort of collateral, including your home and all of your possessions. The last insult they will make upon you is an interest rate much higher than you could get anywhere else for a property secured loan. It is more likely to be in the same area as the more expensive credit cards, and with low payments it might take you 15 years to pay them off at minimum payments.

I once took out one of these loans for the amount of $1,500. All of my furniture and cars were required for collateral, and payments were $45 per month. I made minimum payments for 3 years before my finances improved to the point that I could pay it off. At that time I still owed about $1,200. These are some of the worst loans you can ever take, and if you fail in your payments they will be after you in days. They are only friendly when they are giving you the loan, and never afterwards.

The bank credit card offers are not exactly lies, since that would violate the truth in advertising laws. What they do for you is give you an application for a secured bank credit card. These are a little different from the bank credit cards you have seen most of your life in that you have to give collateral to the bank in order to get the card. Of course you are not required to go through a credit repair company in order to get an application for one of these cards although not every bank does issue them. To get a list of the banks that issue secured bank credit cards you can send $4 to:

Bankcard Holders of America (BHA)

650 Herndon Pkwy., Ste. 120

Herndon, VA 22070

Or call 1-800-638-6407

IF YOU STILL FEEL YOU MUST USE A CREDIT REPAIR COMPANY

Most credit repair companies choose to operate from states where they are unregulated. If you have a problem with one of these companies you can still sue them, but you won't get the state to back you up and make sure that you aren't being cheated. If you want protection from state laws you are restricted to going to companies in just a few of the states. Here is a list of all of the states in which you get this protection:

Arkansas	California	Connecticut	Florida
Georgia	Louisiana	Maryland	
Massachusetts	Nevada	New York	Oklahoma
Texas	Utah	Virginia	Washington

These states require the credit repair companies--(1) to buy an insurance bond so that you can collect something should you win a law suit against them; (2) to inform you of your rights according to the Federal Credit Reporting Administration; (3) provide you with a written contract; and (4) to give you a time period in which you can cancel your contract should you change your mind.

There are 5 more steps you need to take to protect yourself when you look for a credit repair company to work with. Each step is very important to your protection, and none should be skipped because it doesn't seem important, or because a representative of the company is telling you not to bother with it:

1. Check with the state office of consumer affairs, in the state where the credit repair company is located, to see if complaints have been filed, or legal judgements have been made against the company.

2. For additional information of this same character check with the Better Business Bureau.

3. Now go to several credit repair companies with good records. Take your credit report and ask each of them what they can do for you and what their services will cost. If they won't given you a written statement forget about them. You want their claims in writing so that you can compare companies and costs, and to give you leverage later if a company fails to do as it has promised. Then you have some written grounds on which to sue. You need this protection because you may choose to work with a company whose claims are extravagant, and who never meant to carry them out, but only wished to get your name on a contract.

4.   This is also important.   Do not give a credit repair company money up front. Like any other incentive, the more of your money   one of these companies gets from you before it does anything the less likely they are to work hard for you. Their whole purpose of being in business is to obtain fees for their services. If they get all of their profits just by getting the contracts, and not by carrying out their services, they will be motivated to continue signing up people for services but never have any incentive to help anyone. They will probably go out of business after a few months with this attitude, but when they do they will take your money with you.

5.   Do not sign with companies that give money back guarantees. Have you ever known anyone who ever got money back from a service company with one of the guarantees? I doubt it, not without going to court. Such guarantees are just arguments they use to get up front money from you. After all, they will tell you, since we have a money back guarantee you can't lose anything if we aren't able to help you, you will always get your money back. Money back guarantee companies are more likely to have folded shop and left the state by the time you realize that they will do nothing for you, and you are getting ready to sue.

START BY CONTACTING YOUR CREDITORS

If you have read a few of the topics already presented you should have realized by now that you need to contact your creditors at the first sign of credit problems. When you write your creditors you are going to be asking for time to pay and for a lower cost payment plan. Although credit cards usually ask for a minimum payment of 2% of the unpaid balance, with about 80% of that payment going toward interest and only 20% toward your balance, there is no reason that they could not give you payments which are even below the interest amount and agree to keep your credit record clean. Of course you would have to make up the extra interest you will have built up if you are not paying the interest amount, but if you put yourself on a time table you should be able to do it given enough time.

Another strategy, should you be at the limit of your credit, is to request an increase in your credit, or even to request a new line of credit, if that is what you need.

Not contacting your creditors when you are behind in your payments will cause them to go to court to collect your debts, or turn your account over to a collection agency, or re-possess your purchases. As a result of these actions, for not talking to your creditors when you are in trouble, you can lose your credit as well as everything else you own, and part of your income.

GET YOUR CREDIT RECORD

This has already been mentioned several times so there is no need to go into it in detail at this point. There are 3 major credit agencies in the country. You are entitled to purchase a copy of your credit record from any of them at any time, and to a free copy from some of them if you are turned down for credit. As soon as you begin to suspect that you have a credit problem get copies of your credit records from each of the credit reporting agencies. This will give you the basic information you need to begin the process of fixing your credit.

IMPROVING CREDIT HISTORIES

Cleaning up your credit history is not extremely difficult to do, but it is very technical. It depends upon the source of your problems: whether they are due to simply a mistake you made in getting too much credit, or that they are the result of mistakes made by the credit bureau. You also have the right to correct statements removed from your record when they have been there a certain number of years. The technical part comes in with deciding which source is responsible for the problems, and in writing and calling the right people to resolve the negative statements.

A 5 STEP PLAN TO RESOLVING MISTAKES IN YOUR CREDIT RECORD

If, on looking over your credit record, you notice charges and problems that are clearly mistakes you will need to correct them up in order to clear up your credit record. It is best to do this through letters since any information that you give or receive over the phone can be easily misplaced or denied. If you supply information by registered letter you will have a record of who received the information and when. You can also compile a file and send the entire collection to the credit bureau at some later time if that were necessary. The process of clearing your credit record of mistake involves sending a series of letter to the credit bureau. Credit bureaus are reluctant to acknowledge mistakes in their records, since that would mean that their records were not accurate, and they will make you work for every mistake that they remove. The letters, or steps, given here may not produce the results you want. If they do not some more advanced means of dealing with these disputes will be discussed.

Mistakes in credit records come under Section 611 of the Fair Credit Reporting Act. According to this act, if you find a mistake in your credit record and bring it to the attention of the credit reporting bureaus they have a reasonable amount of time to reinvestigate your record and verify their information. If they find that their information is incorrect, or they are unable to verify the information that they have, they are required by law to remove the negative information from your record. Oftentimes a store or finance company has not retained their credit records for very long, and they are unable to verify the status of accounts more than a few months old. This is done because many of these organizations are only concerned with billings of the last few months. Generally it is only bills in this period which might be disputed, or where clients have not paid for merchandise or services. Items which cannot be verified after reinvestigation must be removed from your file with the same promptness and courtesy that they afford the credit users who pay for these services.

1. Send a letter recording that you have found a dispute, and define exactly what problem you have found. Ideally this one letter would result in a reinvestigation of the disputed credit record, and a correction or reaffirmation that the information they had was correct. However, things rarely work this well. Most of the time credit reporting bureaus are going to put you off and drag their feet, making it necessary for you to go to the second letter. When you go into the process of correcting errors in your credit record, only work on a maximum of three corrections at one time. If you tackle more than 3 problems at one time you run the risk of being ignored because the credit bureau will conclude that your entire credit record accurate, but that you are just trying to bluff your way out of your problems. They may not be entirely incorrect in this conclusion, but

you don't want them to know anything more about your motives than you want to tell them.

The first letter can have the following format:

> *your name*
>
> *address*
>
> *phone no.*
>
> *Soc. Sec. no.*
>
> *Today's date*

Customer Services

credit bureau name

and address

Dear Sirs,

Due to incorrect information in my credit record I have been placed in an embarrassing situation in regard to financing. Prompt correction of this information is necessary or I will suffer monetary damages pursuant to business and professional activities necessary to my livelihood.

I was informed that my account [put in your account names and numbers] are delinquent for [enter reasons, late payments, non-payment, or other]. This information is in error, all of my accounts are current, and I am meticulous in maintaining the payment schedules of my creditors.

I expect a prompt answer regarding this matter, in writing.

> Sincerely,

> *sign your name*
>
> *type your name*

Make a copy of this letter before you send it, and keep copies of all communications that you have with the credit bureaus and creditors. Also keep all of the letters and forms sent to you in the same file. If they have you fill out any standardized form of theirs, also keep a copy of it in your file.

2. The second letter is to be sent 30 days after the first, when they have failed to notify you of the outcome of the reinvestigation. This letter should spur the bureaus to hurry up and finish their reinvestigation. Of course they may also try to ignore you after the second letter, but according to the Fair Credit Reporting Act they must respond to your request for correction within a fair and reasonable time. They have been taken to court over just what this means, and the courts generally give them a period of 30 to 45 days. Since they will still be within this period when you send your second letter all that you are trying to do at this time is keep their attention on your problem.

The second letter should be sent by Certified Mail. This will give you a signed receipt proving that it was delivered. Also include a copy of your first dispute letter. Your receipt from the Certified letter will provide legal proof of your having sent the letter in case they do not act on it. It will also let the credit bureau know that you have information that you can go to court with if they fail to act, or fail to act properly on your request.

your name
address
phone no.

Soc. Sec.

Today's date

Customer Services

credit bureau name

and address

Dear Sirs,

This is my second request for correction of the errors in my credit report. It has been one month since I first notified you of these mistakes (see enclosed copy of first communication), and action is required immediately. By law you must respond to my query within a minimal amount of time. You have reached the time for resolution.

I would like to remined you that the errors on *[list creditors and account numbers]* are damaging to my credit record and must be corrected.

These accounts are not in a state of delinquency and must be cleared promptly. I expect your immediate reply, the resolution of this dispute.

Sincerely,

sign your name

type your name

At this point the credit bureau has been put on notice that you are not going to leave them alone if they simply do nothing. They will also know that you have copies of the materials you are sending them, and that you are aware of your rights under the law. Generally this will be sufficient to gain a partial or complete resolution of your dispute, but not always.

3. The third letter is a demand letter. You are demanding that they take action. It is to be sent 10 days after the second letter, but only if they haven't taken action on your first two letters. What is different about the third letter is that you also send a copy to the Federal Trade Commission. Along with the letter you send a copy of letter number 2 to both the credit company and the FTC.

This third letter has the same heading as the first two, but you are going to get a lot tougher in the main part of the letter. You want to let the credit bureau see that you know they have ignored two previous letters requesting corrections in your credit records, contrary to law , and that their actions are going to cost you money and make it difficult for you to live. You want to indicate the damage they are doing to you by their inaction because you will be able to cite these damages in a future law suit should that become necessary. Almost none of these disputes ever goes to the courts though, you just have to make the credit bureaus aware that you have enough documentation that continuing to ignore can end up costing them court costs and monetary damages. LIke any business the last thing that they want is a legal action that is going to affect their profits. Be as specific as you can about the damages you are suffering by their inaction. Could you lose the chance to buy a house, or could it affect your job or your ability to earn your living in some way. If you have specific damages, and it turns out that inaction are their part is partially the cause of your loss, you can sue them for the entire amount of the loss plus court costs.

On your complaints always list the full name of the creditor to whom you are applying, the account number, and the nature and amount of damages you are likely to suffer. Here is your third letter, but you must tailor it to your particular needs. Do not simply copy these letters. If you do the credit bureaus may see that you are using some sort of form letter and make it even more difficult than they usually do for you to make corrections. This is the letter to use when some of the corrections you requested have been made, not when they have ignored you completely.

your name
address
phone no.
Soc. Sec. no.

Today's date

Customer Services

credit bureau name

and address

Dear Sirs,

Upon receipt of my credit report I discovered that only a portion of the errors brought to your attention have been corrected. The information in my credit report is still in error, and immediate action is required.

According to your communication the items *[list those accounts not corrected]* have been verified. I protest that this information is in error and your verification has been derived from the same erroneous source as originally.

These accounts are in error:

[list the accounts and account numbers]

According to my records these accounts are current, and have been fully current for the duration of my association with these creditors. I am requesting the name of the customer service representative supplying this information to your organization.

According to FTC law, you are liable for errors on my account should you fail to correct them promptly. If there are additional delays in resolving this erroneous information I shall take stronger action.

Sincerely

sign your name

type your name

4. The structure of the fourth letter depends upon the response you have gotten from your letters up to this point. By now you should have heard from the credit company that your record has been totally or partially cleared. If it has been totally cleared then you are through and you need send no more letters. If it has been only partially cleared you need to go on with more contacts. If no items have been corrected send another demand letter, similar to the one used in 3, but detailing more of what you want done. The company will either have to go to a more extensive reinvestigation or make the corrections you are demanding. The chances that they will make the correction are good because they do not wish to spend their time and money investigating the records of non-paying people, even though they are required to do this by law. If some of the items have been corrected, but not all, go to the next step in the process.

You can use this letter to thank the credit bureau for the corrections they have made, but point out to them that they haven't yet cleared your record. If they have cleared all of the items you have questioned them on, you can now introduce new corrections that need to be made. If they have not cleared any of their mistakes you can go back to demand letter 1, that we talked about in number 3. But be very specific about difficulties and damages you are suffering because of their inaction.

your name
address
phone no.
Soc. Sec. no.

Today's date

Customer Services

credit bureau name

and address

Dear Sirs,

Sincerely

sign your name

type your name

5. At this point the credit bureau and your creditors have finished with you as far as reinvestigation of negative statements on your credit record. They are now convinced that your record has been corrected, and they will do nothing more for you as far as removing negative statements. You are next going to have to go to the creditors, as discussed in the next section, and deal with each individually in order to complete the clearing of your credit record.

CLEANING UP CREDIT PROBLEMS YOU HAVE CAUSED

Taking care of problems with creditors depends upon the type of creditor you are dealing with. Retail stores are different from mortgage lenders, both of these are different from banks and credit cards. In other words I am going to have to give you information on dealing with each of these credit sources individually for you to take care of credit problems. Of course when you put this information to use it is only necessary to deal with one type of creditor at a time, and to follow the steps given. With persistence you can clean up your own credit record, and learn enough about credit in the process to keep out of trouble in the future.

RETAIL STORE CREDIT

Retail stores are the source of many of the bad credit records that show up in reports. Because they are so competitive they tend to grant credit to many people who have shaky credit records, and who would be better off with a cheaper credit source. Retail stores do not give low rates on their credit accounts, and they are very particular about their customers being up to date. Thus, if you are more than a couple of months behind 2 or 3 times you will very likely find your account turned over to a collection agency, and marks made on your credit record for 30 and 60 day delinquencies. Retail stores use these devices, and the threat of them to ensure payment of their accounts. They are also much quicker to take accounts into court than banks or credit card issuers.

Now the good news, retail stores will also clear your credit much more rapidly than most other credit sources. They are also relatively easy to deal with. If you develop a credit problem with a retail store you go to the customer service department, tell them how sorry you are that this has happened, and how much you want to correct it. They will then negotiate with you and can clear your account in a day. This is the job of customer service, other than keeping track of which accounts are up to date and which are in delinquency. While you can get things started with a phone call, you can get much quicker service by going in and being pathetic and unhappy looking in person. In fact the sorry you are over the problem and the more anxious to fix the problem, the more sympathy and cooperation you will get from most retail stores.

However, there are exceptions. Much more hard nosed are Sears and JC Penny. While you can use the same tactics with them, it will be much more difficult to get them to clear your account before you have made substantial progress in making up any back payments you have.

But suppose you are not going to be able to clear your account promptly, what should you do? Approach them anyway. In most cases they will clear your account just because you have asked them to, and promised to come in and negotiate. If you do pay a visit to them shortly you will be in the same fix, and it will be much more difficult to clean it up the second time around. Basically, retail stores depend more upon the good will of their customers than most lending institutions, and their best bet to be paid is to make everyone happy as much as possible.

As you express your intent to clear your account, you might also tell them of the problems you are having as a result of their credit report. Also express your desire to remain a store customer, and that you consider this a simple lapse or misunderstanding, and it is not your practice to obtain charge accounts and fail to make payments. It is best to stay calm during your negotiations since any threat of violence is more likely to end up as a security problem than a credit resolution. If the desk clerk won't help you ask to see the supervisor, and go over their head as well if they can't help. No matter how they may resist your requests to clear your credit, keep at it. The more persistent you are the more likely they will be to succumb and let you off. LIke all organizations, retail stores are not set up to deal with people who won't go away. They will take care of your problem, if for no other reason, just to get rid of you.

Your strategy, on first approaching the retailer, depends on how your account stands at this time. If you are now paid up, you can just ask the retailer to clear your credit. This often works, although if they have taken you to court or given your account to a collection agency they probably will not feel very cooperative towards you. If you still owe money offer to pay it off, or if you can't do that immediately tell them you wish to work out a payment schedule. Conclude your opening conversations by asking that your credit be cleared at that time. If the credit is cleared and things worked out, you are free to go on to the next lender.

Hints to keep in mind on clearing retail store credit: offer to pay up your account if they will clear your credit. If the dispute is an error on their part, they didn't deliver the merchandise you ordered, they should clear your account without question, as well as all credit bureau records. If you have a single late payment against you plead a problem with the mails or in their processing section. If you have moved, and were then charged for a late payment, explain that it was not your fault because it took a few days for the mails to catch up to you. If you questioned a bill, and were listed as delinquent during this time, it should be cleared because you should not be charged with delinquencies on incorrect billings.

If you cannot get your credit cleared in spite of working with the customer service department, then simply submit a check in full, or to bring your account up to date if that is all that you can do, and enclose a letter that indicates that their acceptance of your check is an acknowledgment that they will remove negative information from your credit record. This is kind of a heavy handed way of getting a retailer's cooperation, but they are going to be reluctant to return a check on a delinquent account.

Customer Service

Creditor name,

address,

and phone

date

Dear Sirs,

You will find enclosed payment for account number ###########. Acceptance of this check acknowledges this account is current, and that you will delete notices of account delinquency from all credit record bureaus.

Thank you for your cooperation in this matter. It has been an unfortunate experience which I fully appreciate your assistance in resolving.

Sincerely,

Sign your name

Type Your name,

address,

phone number,

and account number

MORTGAGE LENDERS AND BANKS

Credit with banks and mortgage lenders is distinctly different from working with retailers, and has even changed in itself recently. A few years ago most bank loans were for auto or home purchases. Then came in credit cards, and, more recently, lines of credit on homes that work like secured credit cards, with your home standing as collateral for payments of the charge account.

Banking institutions are very different from retailers when it comes to credit, and clearing credit. First, they do not hand out credit as easily, and they are not as quick to clear it even when you pay up a delinquent account. While you can reach a central office of customer service, they will talk to you but they probably won't help you. In negotiations you are much better talking to the representatives at your local branch. These people may follow the same rules as the central bank, but they are also local businessmen, and want the good will of the public. Bank managers are judged on the success of their branch and not on the success of the central bank.

Because of the legalities involved mortgage lenders and banks are more restricted in what they can do. Of course if they have made a mistake in the delinquency they have put on your credit record, and you can prove it with cancelled checks or receipts, they should immediately remove all negative statements from your credit record. If the negative credit record is due to a single late payment, it may very well be a mistake, and you can ask them to remove it as a matter of courtesy in that you believe it to be in error. If you have a consistent, monthly, 30 day late delinquency against your account, it may be the result of a payment not being credited, or you may have actually missed a payment at some time. Bring this to their attention, and ask to have your record cleared when the misunderstanding is resolved. In all of these cases check your credit bureau records to assure yourself that the negative report has been removed. If it hasn't, get back in touch with the bank or mortgage lender and get them to act on it.

If, however, you have been delinquent as a result of over extensions of your credit, or loss of jobs, or poor planning on your part, have something to offer them before you knock on their door. They are not going to remove negative statements from your credit record unless you are correcting your past late and missed payments. If you can correct things, and they still won't clear your account, wait 6 months and approach them again. You can now come and tell them that your account is current or clear, and that you would be very appreciative if you could clear your credit record. Eventually they may cooperate with you if you keep in contact with them, but it may take time. Have patience.

CREDIT CARDS

Credit cards come in many forms, although the most common are MasterCard and Visa. The credit cards I am concerned with at this time are those which come under the signature loans, as opposed to the secured credit cards you get with a line of credit account on your home. Other popular forms of credit cards which you might have encountered are American Express, and Discover. Basically these all work on the same principles, and most merchants make no distinction in the type of credit card you are using. Some of these cards cost more and have higher credit limits, such as the gold cards, and some are required to be paid off each month. Credit limits may start as low as $1,000 for a card given to a college student, although the most common limits are $5,000 or $7,000.

All of the cards which offer revolving credit type plans, where you make monthly payments, operate on the same plan. Interest is charged on a monthly basis, and monthly payments, usually around 2% of the unpaid balance, are required . If your account has exceeded the limit you are charged a penalty each month the limit is exceeded, and your payments are doubled. This continues until the account balance is below the limit, at which time it reverts to the original payment plan.

If you make minimum payments it will take 5 or more years to pay off a balance, and it doesn't show how large or how small that balance is at the time. The intent of the card issuers is to have you keep a balance on your account so that you will pay them a great deal of interest and very little principal each year. With this kind of a plan, and it has been designed this way on purpose, it is not difficult to see that at some time over these many years you will be making payments on your credit cards that you may miss a payment, fail to have a payment credited to your account, or become overextended and begin missing payments. Credit cards are essentially an open ended commitment to send money to a credit card issuer for your entire lifetime. Problems with credit from this source are almost inevitable at some time in your life, and you need to know what to do to clear them up.

There are both pros and cons when dealing with credit card companies. The credit card industry is heavily regulated, and what they can and cannot do is generally determined by law. Because they must treat all customers equally, they are not likely to give you a special deal unless they can also offer it to the rest of their accounts. Because they depend upon unsecured credit they are very prompt about reporting late payments. Damaging your credit record is one of the few real weapons short of going to court or turning your account over to a collection agency that they can use. On the pro side is the fact that credit card companies also depend largely on the good will of their customers to keep a high level of profits. There are hundreds of companies issuing credit cards, and every one of them would like to get that $5,000 or $10,000 balance that you pay on each month. If a credit company makes you angry by ruining your credit, or refusing to work with you when you are trying to clean up your account, there is nothing to prevent you from cutting off your account with them and transferring to another account. You even have a chance, if you are truly in financial trouble, that they will settle for less than the entire balance on your account, and remove your bad credit records.

There are not very many good arguments if you are perpetually late in making your credit card payments, but there are certain instances in which it is not your fault, and by law nothing should go into your credit record. The law states that you must be billed accurately, and at your current address, as supplied by you to the company. You are protected from a report of late payments if the address is sent to the wrong address, and you will know that if the envelope is marked with re-routing information, or if there is a dispute concerning the amount of the bill. The first remedy naturally requires documentation involving the Post Office, and if you do not have that do not try to claim that your bill was sent to the wrong address. For the second, check your billing closely each month and if there are any discrepancies contact customer services for the credit company and request a correction. You will probably get a grace period of a week or two, if not a month, while they decide whether or not your billing is accurate.

If you already have a bad credit report, which is deserved, and you seriously wish to clear it, get to know one of the service representatives as well as possible. Whatever the rules, it is people who run organizations. Always be polite, and do not threaten legal action or violence. If you can convince them that you are just an average person who has made some mistakes with their credit, and that you are trying to correct everything and clear your record, they will be able to do it for you. If you never give up, chances are they will eventually. If you have no legal grounds to stand on in regard to getting your credit record cleared, it is still possible for individuals to bend the law if they think you are worthwhile, and do it anyway.

Thus, there are 4 basic approaches to clearing credit card problems: 1) If you know they are in error, and prove it to them and they clear your account, double check with the credit bureaus to make certain they are not listed; 2) If you have a single overdue, it could just as well be their fault as yours, and you should ask them to remove it since a single mistake should not ruin your credit. Check with the credit bureaus afterwards; 3) If a billing problem was caused by you moving to a new address, you are not liable for a late payment. Ask them to clear it and check with the credit bureau; 4) You have questioned a billing that you believed in error, and later found a late payment on your credit record. You cannot be charged for a late payment on a disputed billing. Ask to have it removed and check with the credit bureau.

AUTO LOANS

Auto loans are a unique class of credit debt. Autos are their own collateral for their purchase loan. When you buy a car, so long as you can be found, your car can be repossessed if you fail to keep your account up to date.

If you look through the auto section of your local paper you will see many car dealers offering to sell cars on credit, whether or not you have a clear credit record, or even a bankruptcy. A dealer can do this because his profit margins are high, and the auto business is very competitive. While getting a mortgage to buy a house can take 2 or 3 months, if you can get it at all, you can get a car loan in an hour, and almost without regard for your credit history.

Most dealers now use banks or finance companies as credit sources for cars. In fact when you go to buy a car, even if you say that you have your own financing, they will pressure you to fill out application forms and take possession of the car at that time. According to the car purchasing laws once you have taken delivery of the vehicle and driven it off the lot it is your responsibility and the dealer has earned his profit. This is the reason for the rush. If you leave a dealership without a car dealers know that only 1 in 100 will ever come back and buy a car. They don't want you to leave for anything, and if you can't qualify on the normal bank charges many dealers will give you the loan themselves.

For all of these reasons auto loans are very aggressively serviced. If you are late you will hear about it. It will also go on to your credit record, and they will soon be looking for you to get the car back. Out of all of the credit we use in this country, the majority of poor credit reports are the result of late and missed car payments. If you are buying a car, don't get behind and don't miss a car payment.

Negotiations in auto loans are very hard to carry out. If you are behind a payment, or have been charged with missing a payment, they will probably not negotiate with you but simply take action to repossess the car. To protect yourself you are going to have to makeup the missing payment, or supply records to show that you paid on time, and then wait for their decision.

Unless you have proof that the auto loan company is in error when they claim you have missed a payment or made a late payment, it is probably not worthwhile to try to negotiate with them. Working through the credit bureau will allow you to do much the same thing, but with people who are bound by law to have accurate credit records. If your car has been repossessed, which is the worst thing that can happen in an auto purchase, the repossession will go on your credit record and will probably stay there.

One other warning in dealing with auto loans, should your car have been stolen, destroyed in an accident, or spend its entire time in the shop for repairs, keep up with your payments. These people do not care why you have stopped making payments, if you are not current they will place it into your credit record.

As a final thought, in dealing with auto loans, they create more negative credit reports than any other source, and they are the most difficult creditor with which to negotiate. When you buy your next car go through your own credit union or bank, and give the dealership none of your personal information. If you are not financing through them they do not have to know where you work, how much you make, where you bank, or who you owe money to. Simply tell them that you have arranged your own financing, and then shut up and politely tell them that you do not wish to provide any further personal information.

STUDENT LOANS

Student loans are unique in that they are unsecured loans which are guaranteed by the government. They can be of any size, depending upon the educational program they have financed. That is they range in size from a few hundred dollars to $100,000. Student loans are made directly by the government however, they are made by banks or student loan agencies, according to which state they are obtained in. They are also an installment loan requiring monthly payments, but payments do not begin until after the end of the educational program. There are time limits though so that a part time student cannot stretch out this loan period indefinitely. Loan rates are also somewhat below the market for other loans.

Because the payment period for student loans does not begin until after you leave school, problems can develop when a lender does not know whether or not you are still a student. Suppose you had borrowed $5,000 in your senior year in college, and informed the lender of this at the time. If, at some time during the year you had decided to continue in your education in a graduate program, but failed to inform the lender they may have very well sent a notice to the credit bureaus that you had defaulted on your student loan. Now you may also have dropped out of school for some reason and can't afford to begin payments as yet since you aren't employed. You may also have graduated and don't have the funds to make payments. In any case the lender considers you to be in default and has now filed a notice of student loan default against you.

This is not the end of the problems though. While the lender has filed a loan default against you he has not given up on getting his money. In the next step he may well turn your account over to a collection agency. If the collection agency fails to find you or fails to collect the borrowed money from you they may file their own record of loan default. If the lender then goes to court and obtains a judgement against you, this public record is then entered into the credit record. Now you have three records of loan default against you which could all be based on a mistake in that you did not keep your lender informed of your status as a student. On the other hand, you could be in the same trouble because your income is too limited to make proper payments, and rather than embarrass yourself you have chosen to ignore your need to make payments until you have a higher income. The result, so far as your credit record is concerned, if the same.

Because of the manner in which a student loan default multiplies in the credit record it is extremely difficult to negotiate with. If you get the bank to clear your record the court and the collection agency may not. Do not forget that the Federal government originally guaranteed the loan and will have filed their own default statement to your record as well. Getting the attention of the Federal government even for information they ask for is extremely difficult. Getting their attention to clear up a credit record that was in default is next to impossible. If the credit record was damaged due to a misunderstanding with the lender, due to you not keeping them informed as to your student status, you at least have a reasonable argument for getting them to remove the default notice from your record.

According to current practices, should your loan go into default it will be placed in the hands of a federal or state student loan collection agency. If your loan has gone to one of these agencies, and you have now gotten the agreement of the lender that your loan is now current, you are still going to have a very difficult time getting the state agency to clear the account, or your credit record. They are terrible at this since they are always understaffed and overworked. The last thing they want to spend their time on is clearing credit records. They are rewarded by the state for making collections, not for clearing accounts of damaging information. If you deal with them get everything in writing, and always get the name of anyone you speak with. If they decide to go to court, they can do so, and get a judgement against you, without ever informing you of the action. This procedure is outlined in your student loan agreement, but no one reads that when they are applying for the loan since no one ever intends to default on these loans. Be cautious in all dealings with state collection agencies and get everything in writing, to protect yourself.

If you intend to clear a student loan default, or slow payment, begin by getting your payments current. So long as you have a stream of non-payments or late payments coming through the various organizations involved you will be unable to dispute the claim that you are in default. Once you are current, work through the credit bureaus. The section on credit bureau dealings provides you with a series of letters and arguments to present to the credit bureau that should get some action. This is a much more efficient approach than working with each of the student loan collection agencies because the credit bureau job of verifying student loan defaults is very complicated with the large number of organizations which must be worked with. Simply dispute the default to the credit bureau, and with luck, in a few months you may have a clear record.

MEDICAL BILLS

Medical bills have been included because they frequently involve a balance which is too great to be paid when it is incurred, and which becomes an installment debt. Also similar is the treatment of your bill if it becomes delinquent. In this unfortunate circumstance your medical bill is unceremoniously turned over to a collection agency. We will handle debt collection agencies in the next section, but you still need to know what to do with medical suppliers who bill you directly.

Now a plus for you is that medical bills do not show up on your credit report as a debt. Normally this should allow you to get more credit when you want it, say, to pay off your medical bills if that is what you wish to do. On the other side of the coin, however, is the case in which you allow your medical payments to become 60 days late. When that happen medical bills are sent to a collection agency where they will show up on your credit record as a strike against you. Medical billing services follow this rule even if you have a good excuse for getting behind on your payments. Don't try to use reasons such as you had debts from many medical services and they were not all submitted to your insurance or to you for payment, or that your payments were lost in the mail. When the bill is 60 days late, and you haven't paid it, it will be sent out for collection.

Bad debts resulting from from medical services usually end up creating 3 layers of debt problems: (1) doctor is the primary creditor and wants his money before anything will get moving; (2)

the collection agency has put in some time and effort and requires a strategy all of its own; and (3) it may very well have gone into some sort of court action and created a public record, which you will also have to clear. Except for dealing with the doctor, the others are dealt with in their own sections.

Doctors are very easy to deal with, but very hard to negotiate with. A doctor wants his money, and anything less than what is owed to him is a delinquent account and goes to the collection agencies. Of course doctors have very little interest in your credit records other than using them to get you to pay your bill. So if you can pay off the bill, or arrange a payment plan and begin making payments, he will generally be willing to clear your credit record. If this is how it goes don't ignore the collection agency or court records or they will result in even more problems in the future.

If you get the doctor to agree to clear your account get your credit report to make certain everything has been done. If the record is still there go back to contacting the credit bureau and dispute the delinquency. If you get the credit bureau to go back to the doctor for verification and he reports that your account is cleared it will be dropped from the record. If you get your credit record and the medical billing is already cleared, you are done with this phase of clearing your credit.

DEBT COLLECTION AGENCIES

Collection agencies are distinct among your creditors in that the only service they offer is the collection of money. If they fail to collect money on a debt they fail in the only task they have.

Because of their single mindedness, debt collection agencies are very likely to operate on the fringes of the law, so far as pursuing unpaid bills. For one thing they resort immediately to threats and intimidation, while for most debtors this is the last tactic they will use. The process of intimidation, through which they want to make you more concerned about them than about anything else, will frequently employ phone calls, letters, threats of various sorts, and contacts to your family, neighbors, and co-workers if the debt is large enough to warrant this level of effort.

In spite of all of these harassments, you should always attempt to negotiate with a collection agency to make your settlement as advantageous to you as possible. If you have the money to pay off your debt all at one time approach your original creditor and make your offer, in return for your credit being cleared. If for some reason you cannot get the creditor to cooperate with you, send the check to the collection agency, but with a letter stating that acceptance and cashing of the check is acknowledgement that your debt is paid and that they will clear your record. Enclose the statement:

" Your acceptance of my check signifies that the account for [list your account and account number] is clear of all delinquent payments, and that you will contact all credit bureaus to whom this account status has been reported with the instruction to remove all derogatory and collection account records."

If a credit collection agency does not accept your check under the conditions which you have given it to them, they will probably use one of two arguments. They may call and inform you that only the creditor who turned the account over to them can delete complaints on your credit report, or they may tell you that such statements cannot be deleted in any case. Do not accept these arguments. Just as statements can be added to your credit report because of delinquencies, they can be deleted when those delinquencies are repaired.

If they take this attitude raise the issue that you consider the original complaint against you as an error. You can state that notices were sent to the wrong address, or that you have paid but do not have the cancelled checks for some reason. In any such case offer to pay the account, in return for getting your record cleared, and you will seek further redress when you have found your records. You are trying to raise doubt in their minds that what has been done to you is entirely fair or legal, and then offer to fix it anyway. This should take them off the hook as far as clearing your credit, and seems to leave you with the responsibility cleaning up any further problems. They have done their job, satisfied the creditor, and gotten you out of their hair all at one time.

If they hesitate, and by now you will probably be talking to the manager of the agency, then demand that they return your billing to the original creditor and that you will work out your differences at that level. This is a threat to their operation since they are paid only if they collect money, not if you agree only to pay money to the creditor.

The next step in raising the heat is to call in a lawyer. This is a big threat to a collection agency since lawyers are expensive, and bringing one in can tie up an account for months or years. This will probably only be useful to you if the billing runs into the thousands of dollars. Of course all that may be required is a letter from a lawyer outlining the steps that will be taken if they refuse to negotiate a payback plan that allows you to clear your credit.

When they do agree to take your offer and clear your credit, get it in writing, and keep everything you get from them in a file. That way if they do not take care of your credit problems with this account you can go back and sue for damages. They know this, and it will spur them on to prompt action. Once you get the collection agency to agree to clear your credit, wait 30 days, and then check your credit records with the credit bureaus. If there is still a problem you can go back to the collection agency, although they may well have forgotten about you by now, or you can go to the credit bureau and dispute the negative record. If the credit agency has cleared you on their records they will not confirm the negative statement they put into your bureau records, and those should then be cleared without further action on your part.

As a check list here are the 4 general guidelines to follow when dealing with a credit collection agency: 1) They are in business to make money, and they do that by taking a portion of the money they collect. If you offer to pay them for something you want they will have a definite incentive to work with you on clearing your record; 2) The law controls the forms of contact they can use in prompting you to pay your bills. They can write you or call you at home, but they can't threaten you, harass you (say with calls in the middle of the night), or threaten your livelihood by calling you at work to the point that it disturbs your ability to earn a living. Credit agencies are limited by the laws of the "Fair Debt Collection Practices Act," which you can consult at a public library if you should have questions about what they say, or what they seem to be trying to do; 3) You can threaten them yourself by telling them you refuse to deal with them, and you will work only with the original creditor. Of course if you do this they will lose any commission they might have earned. This should prompt them to work with you, and if it doesn't you can carry through and go back to the original creditor to work out a payment that will clear your credit record; 4) Extra collection fees for the use of a collection agency cannot be charged against you unless your original financing agreement allowed them. To determine whether or not this applies to you it is necessary that you read all of the fine print in any credit papers you signed. If you see anything about the borrower or debtor being liable for debt collection charges, should they be used, then they have you. But if there is no language of this sort you ought to be free and clear, at least on that score.

DOES BAD CREDIT EVER DIE?

HOW TO TELL, AND WHAT TO DO ABOUT IT

Unlike many public records, bad credit does not live forever. Most negative entries on credit reports can only live a specific number of years, and then they are officially dead.   Dead credit information is supposed to be removed from your credit report by the credit bureaus, but things do not always happen as they should. You cannot count on the credit bureaus to remove records which have died a natural death. After all, they are not paid for removing out of date information from credit reports, they are paid for providing information on individuals to creditors who request it.

Because you, as an individual, are not paying the bill for your record, you must take the responsibility of cleaning up these records yourself, or at least of checking up on the credit bureaus to make sure that they are doing it. By law they are not supposed to be reporting out of date information to creditors, and if you catch them at it you can force them to remove it or sue them.

Your enemy in keeping your records current is that you do not know how long a negative statement should stay on your record. If you find something negative and you don't know it should be removed just because of age you might spend extra months trying to get it removed through all kinds of other communications which are unnecessary. It is always wise to use the simplest method available to clean up your credit. The more complicated the process you have to go through, the greater the chance that you or the credit bureau will make a mistake and your record will still be blemished.

Here is a list of the most common type of negative statements found on credit reports, and how long they should remain there. After getting copies of your credit report read over every negative statement carefully to check for dead records that should be buried out of sight and forgotten.

> no time limit -- unpaid tax liens
>
> > favorable or neutral information
> >
> > credit problems of $50,000 or more
> >
> > job information if the salary is $20,000
> >
> > or more
>
> 10 year items -- bankruptcies
>
> 7 year items --   unpaid bills and slow payment
>
> information from creditors
>
> Chapter 13 bankruptcies
>
> paid tax liens
>
> lawsuits
>
> civil judgements but varies by state
>
> bills collected through a collection agency
>
> criminal arrests and indictments if you were convicted

Never assume that just because records are supposed to have been removed that they have been. Go to the trouble of getting copies of your credit reports from the three main credit bureaus, and clean them yourself. Before you are done you should have a copy of your clean and up to date credit report in your hands. If you meet any opposition to taking this responsibility do not be afraid to threaten a lawsuit. Reports information contrary to law makes the credit bureaus liable for damages to your life.

CLEANING UP YOUR PUBLIC RECORD

Unlike your credit bureau files, your public record is open for anyone to see, and some information which can damage your chances of getting credit can stay on it forever, but in most cases it doesn't have to. In the last section you could see that unpaid tax liens don't begin to die until they are paid, and then they still have 7 years after that. The same thing goes for what are called Mechanic's liens on your home. Mechanic's liens are unpaid bills by people who have worked on your home or property. They may not always be your fault, such as when a contractor skips out without paying his painters or tile men for their work, but these people will usually file a Mechanic's lien against your property anyway in order to get their money. Sometimes the only way you can get one of these bills removed from your credit record is to pay twice for the work you have gotten, once to your general contractor and once more to the person who performed the work. So far as the law is concerned it is your problem and not the problem of the painter or other person, and you will have to pay them and then try to find the contractor and sue them to get your money back. It may not be fair but that is often how it works.

Bankruptcies, which may or may not be your own fault, at least have a set life. After 10 years they should be removed, and you have the right to demand they be taken off of your credit record. Of course a credit company may ask on your application if you have ever had a bankruptcy, but you are not legally obligated to give them this information if it happened over 10 years ago. According to law if you supply false information to get credit you are guilty of a crime and can be prosecuted, but in those areas where there is a time limit, you are not required to report out of date information even if a credit application asks for it.

Chapter 13 bankruptcies are also part of the public record, but they only stay around for 7 years, instead of the 10 years of a regular bankruptcy. Chapter 13 bankruptcies can be very useful in cleaning up credit problems, and will be discussed in much more detail later on so that you can find out how to put them to use if you get in a situation where you simply cannot make your payments, but you want to avoid getting a bankruptcy on your record. For now just keep in mind that a chapter 13 bankruptcy only remains on your credit record for 7 years.

Other than these obvious records that concern credit and money, your public records also includes information on criminal convictions, suits brought against you in court, and judgements against you for anything. The one exception to this rule is that if you can get your record sealed no one will be able to find out that you have a record even though there may be a newspaper report of the action in court. The most usual situation in which records are sealed is when you are a minor, and under 18 or 21 years of age. Of course you can request that your record be sealed as a condition of a plea bargain at any time, and control it at the source, but that may not work in most cases.

There are also credit problems with suits that are brought against you where you have been able to settle with someone out of court. Suppose, for instance, that you are charged with credit fraud, something that any credit bureau would be very interested in, and that you later get the case dismissed because you convince the group charging you that their interpretation was wrong, or the incorrect information you gave them was just an error on your part and not an attempt to qualify for credit fraudulently. Even though you have legitimately beaten the case, credit bureaus take the position that since you were charged with a credit problem in the public record they are justified in putting this information into your credit file. It may not be fair from your viewpoint, but it will hurt you anyway, and force you to explain what happened whenever you apply for credit in the future.

A lot of these kinds of problems are a result of the way that credit information is gathered. It is not always the major reporting agencies that are responsible for going out and getting it. Local companies, in your part of the country, keep track of such information sources as local records, and then go about selling it to anyone who is interested. These companies are not required by law to verify that everything they report is true since they do not supply this information directly to creditors, and if they find a court case filed against you it will probably go into their files. The credit bureaus are required to verify what they report, but they have very little incentive to do so unless you question them yourself. The problem of false public reporting of credit is a big one, and something that you are going to have to be on the lookout for. These companies are often very bad in this area.

Vacating the judgement. But supposing that you have been guilty of a credit problem, and a judgement has been made against you, what can you do? The creditor is not feeling kindly toward you and would like to see your credit ruined for as long as possible, but he is interested even more strongly in getting his money and costs for the trouble of suing you. This is where your opportunity comes in to remove the information from your record. While the negative report won't even go on the clock until you pay the debt, it doesn't have to stay there for 7 or 10 years either. Contact the creditor, or the collection attorney if they are using one. Offer to settle your bills without any further delays if they will vacate the judgement against you in exchange.

Vacating the judgement legally means that the suit is recognized as having been in some way recognized as defective. While a creditor may not believe this, especially when they have already gotten a judgement against you, they will often do it in order to get their money. When a lawsuit is vacated it is removed from the public record, and you can then have it removed from your credit report as well.

Should you decide to try to get a judgement vacated, you are still largely at the mercy of the creditor. The creditor has already gotten a judgement against you, and his only problem by this time is finding enough of your assets to seize to get his money. Once he has sold your assets and collected his money he has no need to deal with you, and no incentive to help you clean up your credit. But up to this point you still have something to begin with, and you should if you want to clear your credit.

Once you have gotten a judgement vacated, get your credit report cleared by going through the process of getting your credit reports, challenging the records, and asking for verification. This whole process has been covered in another section, and needn't be reviewed here.

IS BANKRUPTCY THE RIGHT PATH FOR YOU?

Bankruptcy is a very serious business when it comes as a way to fix your credit. Beware of anyone who says that bankruptcy is easy and safe, as a way to escape your debts, because what a bankruptcy can do is ruin your chances of getting credit for 10 years, or even more if creditors find out about it. A creditor looks at a bankruptcy on your record in the same way that you look at a person who welches on a bet. You borrowed money, or accepted credit, and then when things got tough you ran out on your debts.

Most creditors who have had their customers declare bankruptcy really believe that such people should be locked up for stealing, and most of those who are willing to grant credit will forever look at anyone like that as a person who will probably do it again and shouldn't be trusted.

Ok, those are some of the bad aspects of getting a bankruptcy, but there are good ones as well. There really are times when bankruptcy is your best course to save yourself financially. That is what we want to look at here: what are the circumstances when bankruptcy is the right path for you? If this is what you should do, after you weigh all of your options, then you should go ahead and do it without looking back. Its time to take the steps you must, look ahead, and forget about the past.

As a last resort there is nothing better than the bankruptcy laws. Bankruptcy should only be used when you have exhausted all of your other options, and the alternative is the loss of everything that you own. Creditors can seize your home, your car, all of your personal possessions except the tools that you use in your job or profession, For debt you can literally be thrown into the streets. Out of all of the street-people you can see around America, a lot of them ended up where they are because of debt.

But you can't look at bankruptcy just as a means of getting out of debt, you must also change the way you live afterwards. If the court leaves you with assets you may have to sell them off and move to another part of the country where living is cheaper, or where you can get a job. The problem with too many people is that they will file and bankruptcy and then just go back to doing the things that got them into trouble in the first place. These are not people who should use bankruptcy. You can only file a bankruptcy once every 7 years, and you will simply lose your home and property the second time around if you develop the same credit difficulties.

It should not be too difficult to find out if you are a candidate for bankruptcy no matter how much you may hate the idea. If you can't make your monthly payments, you are constantly being harassed by creditors of past due bills, you have lost your job or business, or are in danger of losing them, and creditors have turned you down for more credit even though you think that all you need is a few months to get things back on track. If this is how the world looks to you, you are in a position where bankruptcy may just save your life.

If you decide that you need to file a bankruptcy, read over the next section for instructions on how to go ahead. It is not impossible to save yourself some money in filing bankruptcy if you understand what you are trying to do, and you should always understand what you are trying to do when you are dealing with money and credit.

A 12 STEP PLAN FOR FILING FOR BANKRUPTCY

A bankruptcy is a legal procedure which is intended to relieve you of the responsibility of paying your debts. Filing a bankruptcy requires going through a set of steps to take you from a debtor to a debt free person, with a bankruptcy on your credit record. If you are going to file for bankruptcy you want to do it right so that you get all of the credit relief and personal protection to which you are entitled. The steps you should take to accomplish this are very important and very precise, and of course it involves going to court to see a bankruptcy judge. If you are well prepared before you go before the judge it will be much easier for you to get what you need, and to look like you know what you are doing. While the plan given here can't cover every type of bankruptcy case, it will give you the basics, and at least keep you from being unprepared when the time comes to file your papers.

1. Preparation; putting as much property into an exempt category as possible, and should you use a bankruptcy lawyer?

In the process of filing for bankruptcy there are two classes of property, exempt and non-exempt. Exempt property cannot be seized by creditors to satisfy debts. Non-exempt property can be disposed off to pay off your debts. The big question is just how do you decide what property is exempt and which is non-exempt. The more of your property that is exempt, the less you are going to lose in the bankruptcy.

Determining exempt property depends upon which state you are in at the time. Most states exempt personal property such as toiletries, your clothing, and the furniture in your home. Of course furniture can be worth a great deal of money, and there is often a dollar limit on the total amount of furniture that qualifies as well on the maximum value of each piece of furniture. The total value of exempt furniture is usually placed between $2,000 and $3,000 depending upon the state. Values of individual pieces are pretty low, and often cannot have a value of over $200. If your furniture values are higher than these they can be sold, and the exemption amounts returned to you by the court.

Cars also come under the exempt status, but only up to a value of around $3,000 depending upon the state. There is often an additional exemption of around $1,000 that you can attach to anything, even your car.

If you are married when you file for bankruptcy some states let you double your exemption so that you and your wife can each exempt personal property. If you aren't certain about this law, and there is any difficulty in finding out the information, go ahead and claim a double exemption. The worst that can happen is that you will be turned down, and you will then be in the same condition as if you had only taken a single exemption anyway.

Finding a list of property that can be exempt can be complicated. In California there are two lists called System 1 and System 2. You can only use one of these lists when you file your bankruptcy, and you have to choose between these two. You cannot mix exemptions from the two system lists.

An even more complicated decision comes up in 15 states, and Washington, D.C. In these states you have to choose between a state list and a federal list. Again you can only use one of the lists to make your selection. Here is a list of the states, just in case you aren't certain if this is something you have to consider: Arkansas, Connecticut, Washington, D.C., Hawaii, Massachusetts, Michigan, Minnesota, New Jersey, New Mexico, Pennsylvania, Rhode island, South Carolina, Texas, Vermont, Washington, and Wisconsin.

Normally all of your income is taken into consideration when a court computes how much you have to pay in a bankruptcy. In some cases pensions are exempt, and it doesn't matter how large they are. To be exempt a pension has to be covered by a federal law called ERISA, or the Employee Retirement Income Security Act. If you aren't sure ask your pension administrator if you come under this law. Now while ERISA pensions are always exempt, and needn't be listed as income sources, a non-ERISA pension can also be exempt, but to do so it has to satisfy two conditions: 1) You have to use your states exemption schedule; and 2) your pension must be listed in your state exemption list or the federal non-bankruptcy exemption list.

2. Finding a bankruptcy court.

Bankruptcies always involve courts, and finding the right bankruptcy court can make the difference between coming out with most of your property in tact, and coming out broke. Bankruptcies come under federal law, and the federal courts make the decisions. The federal court that you will file in is either the one where you have lived the last 180 days, or where your business has been located for the same period of time. If you live away from a city you will file in the nearest city in your state that has a federal district court. If you cannot decide which federal court to file in, or you don't know where to find the court in the first place you can call the National Bankruptcy Law Project at 800-542-0034, for information.

3. What forms you will need and some tips on filling them .

Filing a bankruptcy is largely a job of getting a hold of, and filling out forms, and there are 6 forms and types of forms that you need to be sure to include to get a complete package. As far as just getting the blank forms themselves, bankruptcy forms should be available in any local business supply store that carries legal forms, or you can call the National Bankruptcy Law Project at the number given above for information on how to get them at some other source. Just to keep it straight I have numbered the forms 1 through 6, although some of the forms contain several schedules for you to list things on, or to answer other types of questions.

1) The first form is called a **Chapter 7 Voluntary Petition**, and in it you are asking the bankruptcy court to discharge, or cancel, your debts.

2) The second form is actually a set of forms in which you must list your current assets, debts, income, real property such as land and cars, personal property like jewelry and clothes, your creditors, and of course your income and living expenses. These forms are called: **Schedule A** for real property; **Schedule B** for personal property'; **Schedule C** for your listing of exempt property; **Schedule D** for creditors with secured claims (that is claims against you where you have put up assets to guarantee the loans); **Schedule E** for creditors with unsecured property claims (such as credit cards and personal loans); **Schedule F** for creditors with unsecured nonpriority claims (this includes all debts which aren't included in the other two schedules, and include such debts as unpaid student loans);   **Schedule G** for contracts and leases that

you are still paying on, and haven't paid off; **Schedule H** for what are called co-debtors, or people like co-signors or other people on deeds and contracts who aren't included in the bankruptcy; **Schedule I** to list your current income; **Schedule J** to list your current expenses; a **Summary Schedule** to put the totals of A through J; and a schedule in which you swear, under penalty of perjury, that everything you put in all of the other schedules is true and correct.

3. The third type of form is called a **Statement of Financial Affairs**. In this form you have to give a financial history of yourself over the last 5 or 10 years. The first entries are your family income record, next are payments to creditors, then law suits and things like that including the history of the cases and whether they came out for or against you. They even ask for gifts and other bankruptcy information. The last entries is your closed accounts and business records of partnerships and inventories. Of course most people will have no entries under these last areas, and if you do have complicated business dealing involved in a bankruptcy you are better off working with a bankruptcy lawyer than trying to do it yourself in any case. For most of us though much or all of this doesn't apply.

4. The fourth type of form is a **Chapter 7 Individual Debtor's Statement of Intention**. This form requires you to tell the court what you intend to do with the property you have put up to guarantee your debts. You have to list your properties and state whether you are planning to keep it or sell it to pay off your creditors. A description of the property includes an address and written description, and a list of any creditors you may still owe for it. This helps to determine how much equity you have in it. Equity is just a word to say how much of the value of property belongs to you and how much belongs to the people who loaned you money to buy it. Tax liens also decrease your equity since they are debts you owe and which must be paid before you can use the remainder to pay off other debts. Since you are listing all of your property and debts on this form you also must check off those properties which fall under the exemptions you have claimed.

5. The fifth form is called a **Mailing Matrix**, and it is used to list the names and addresses of your creditors. The bankruptcy court will use this form to prepare mailing labels and mail notices to your creditors. Some of these forms vary from court to court, but the basic type is just a blank piece of paper divided into squares. But the creditors need to be listed in a certain way'; they have to be in

alphabetic order, you have to include cosigners and other debtors listed on the sales contracts or deeds, if there is a law suit which concerns the property, and even information about a spouses' debts if you are in the process of getting a divorce. Once you have filled out this form you need to make several copies of it (make 10 copies to begin with unless you have been told to make either more or less by the court). Before you put down your alphabetical list of creditors list your own name and address in the top left hand corner, and then proceed with the creditors' names below. If you finish one sheet and have more creditors to list just add more sheets, but keeping them in alphabetical order when you assemble them for the court.

6. The sixth form is a group known as a **Bankruptcy Petition**. These are forms that are required locally, and will vary from state to state. Because these forms are different everywhere you will have to get them from your bankruptcy court or lawyer, or from a typing service in the area that prepares bankruptcy papers.

This completes the list of forms that every bankruptcy filing must have. What you are still in need of are a few general tips for filling them out: 1) Once you get the forms make Xerox copies of them before you start working. If you haven't bought legal forms for a while you should know that they can cost several dollars each, and copies can be substituted for originals if you make a mistake; 2) Before you try to type your entries in the forms, so that you can turn them in to the court, use some of your copies and make your entries in pencil. This will give you a chance to get all of your information written down in the proper form; 3) Doublecheck your entries to make sure that they are thorough, that you have answered every question, and that you are clear in your answers; 4) Now some tips on how to write your answers--when you are answering questions don't be afraid to put the same answer down more than once if that is what the question calls for, be honest or you could go to jail, add more pages if you need them and don't just stop when you run out of room on a page, go get help if you really can't do it yourself, and make sure to include business debts; 5) Now type your final drafts, that is the copies you are going to turn in to the court. Nothing is going to prejudice a court faster against you than if you turn in a big mess and tell them that it is your bankruptcy papers. Not only will that make them believe that you don't know what you are doing, but you may make some clerk or judge look for a way to get even with you for being such a fool. Get it typed if you can't do it yourself.

4. Filling the forms-- making copies, paying fees, and delivering your forms to the court.

Filling out the forms has gotten you ready to file so that you can get your bankruptcy moving through the legal system. To get this accomplished you are going to turn over the forms and schedules you have filled out, but the courts do not want just one copy of each form, and all of the bankruptcy courts in the United States do not want the same number of copies of the forms either. To find out exactly what the requirements are in your area write a letter to your bankruptcy court and ask how many copies of each form they require in a filing. To make sure that you get a reply include a large, self-addressed, and stamped envelope along with your request for information. While you might be able to phone and get the same information, having their requirements in writing will protect you if there is any question later on that you didn't follow court rules in filing a legal bankruptcy. Also make a copy of all forms and letters you fill out or send, that has to do with your bankruptcy. No one is going to have this information available for you later on if you don't keep your own copies. As a rule you should also keep copies of any financial or legal papers that you have to use at any time.

Once you have filled out all of your forms and made your copies they still must be filed with the court in order to get your bankruptcy under way. The fee for filing is the same for everyone no matter what their financial condition, but it is not an extremely high fee. While the fees may vary somewhat, and certainly go up, the fees a couple of years ago amounted to a $120 court fee and a $30 administrative fee. If you simply cannot come up with this much money all at once it is possible to arrange with the court to pay it in installments. However, do not let this debt become delinquent.

Actually delivering your forms to court requires that you assemble them in the correct order and format so that the court can process them. This requires a number of steps, which will be outlined here: **1)** Doublecheck your list of forms and copies to make sure that you have everything that you need; **2)** Put everything in order using the list given above as a guide; **3)** If you are filing your bankruptcy with someone else, such as a wife or business partner, make certain that you have their signature on all of the forms, and also that you have signed all of them yourself; **4)** Besides the copies required by the court have an extra set for the clerk of the court, and two copies of your Statement of Intention for each person who is listed on that form, as well as a copy for the trustee; **5)** Put a two hole punch on the top of all of the papers so they can be assembled, but don't staple anything together; **6)** You can now either mail or hand deliver your papers to the bankruptcy court, but you must also pay your filing fee at this time as well; **7)** The court will have assigned a trustee for your case and you need to ask the court clerk for the name and address, and then mail a copy of your Statement of Intention to them (that is your responsibility and not the court's, and you have to do it within 30 days of filing); **8)** Send the name and address of the trustee to all of your creditors. This should be done with registered mail so that you can get written proof back from the post office that each of these people was properly informed. Once that is done it will be up to them to pursue their claims for payment.

5. The court schedules a meeting of your creditors.

Soon after you file your papers for a bankruptcy the court will schedule a creditors' meeting. If you don't have enough non-exempt property to sell in order to pay your debts most of your creditors probably won't bother showing up. But if you do have enough to sell the creditors will have to show up and file claims to be paid. These two conditions are called no-asset cases, where there is not enough property to pay the debts, and asset cases where there is enough property. Once the meeting is held the creditors have 60 days to file a claim, or to contest the dismissal of their debt. To contest something, in legal terms, means to object to their debt being cancelled. The trustee named by the court is the one who will make the decision whether or not you have an asset or a non-asset bankruptcy case.

You should be anxious to see your creditors meeting called since once the trustee mails them the official notice they can no longer take any action against you to collect their debts. All collection agency actions will stop, they cannot file lawsuits, spouses can't sue you for past due support payments, you can't lose benefits like food stamps or have your electricity cut off, all lawsuits currently going on are stopped, your money can't be seized for debts, and no one can file liens on your property. None of these are permanent conditions, and any of them not cleared by the bankruptcy can be resumed afterwards, but this should give you a break of 3 to 6 months from dealing with creditors directly, which is the usual amount of time it takes to process a bankruptcy.

6. The creditors' meeting.

Whether or not you expect your creditors to show up, you make sure that you do. If you miss your creditors' meeting you could be fined $50, and have your bankruptcy thrown out of court.

At the creditors' meeting the trustee will ask you some questions about your entries on the bankruptcy papers. If you haven't gotten a bankruptcy lawyer contact the court clerk before the meeting and let them know that you will be representing yourself. Ask the clerk what records you should bring with you, and then bring copies of all bills, deeds, financial records, and even checkbooks and tax returns to support the information on your schedules.

If, for any reason, you have been dishonest in filling out your papers or have tried to hide anything, see an attorney before the creditors' meeting. Of course you can have one accompany you as well, but it shouldn't be necessary if you have taken all of the steps and been honest and complete in everything you've done.

Then take the evening before the creditors' meeting to read over everything you filled out. If you have left out anything, or have an incomplete answers to questions make an effort to complete them now, and bring that information with you as well.

In addition to everything you have already put on your schedules you will still be asked about your expectations of a tax refund, who your current employer is, why you got into financial trouble, have your problems ended, who helped you to fill out your forms and how much did they charge, and even whether or not you have destroyed your credit cards? All of these questions will be part of your creditors' meeting whether or not any creditors show up, so you should be ready for them.

Finally, if this is a joint filing make sure that your partner or spouse goes with you to the creditors' meeting as well.

7. Working with exempt and non-exempt property to get the best deal. What happens to property put up as security for a loan?

Normally the trustee will sell off all of your non-exempt property to pay off your debts, or at least as many as possible. However, there are exceptions. You can rescue non-exempt property if you find other money for debt payment. You can decide to sell exempt property and use the money to buy back non-exempt property. Say you have a motorcycle that you really love, but you have listed your car as exempt property because you thought it would be more useful. If you change your mind later you can sell your car, give the court the amount of money that was expected to be gained from selling the motorcycle, and maybe have the motorcycle and a little money left over to get another car. On the other hand if you suddenly started making more money at your job, or won some money in the lottery you could rescue the non-exempt property.

Property classifications can also backfire on you though if the trustee does not let you keep things in an exempt category where you think it belongs. You may consider yourself a musician and have a $1,000 guitar listed as exempt, but the trustee may decide that you only earn $100 a month from playing the guitar and it is really just a hobby. If you can't buy your guitar back for the court valuation you are going to lose it in the bankruptcy settlement.

Property used as security comes under some different rules. This includes any property that is financed, even credit cards. If you wish to keep your house, or car, or even your furniture when it is in this class you are going to have to work out a payment plan with the creditor within 45 days of your hearing or the creditor can ask the court to let them take it to satisfy the debt. If you are working with the creditor the court may give you more than 45 days, but if you ignore the creditor you will lose it. You cannot claim secured property as exempt.   You have to work out a payment plan with your creditor if you want to keep it, in all cases.

8. The discharge hearing.

Sometime following your creditors' meeting the court may schedule a discharge hearing. Not everyone who files for bankruptcy will have a discharge hearing since it is up to the court to decide whether or not to hold one. But if your case is scheduled for one of these hearings make sure that you attend. The discharge hearing is held so that the judge can lecture you about staying out of debt, and explain anything to you that he thinks is confusing in regard to the discharging of your debts. If you have agreed to pay off some of your debts, called reaffirmation, the judge will also bring this up and explain your responsibilities.   In fact you are not likely to have a discharge hearing unless you have already indicated in your papers that you are reaffirming a debt.

Then, within 4 weeks after the discharge hearing, you will receive a copy of your discharge papers from the court. While this form will not be as detailed as the ones you put into your discharge file, it is still a legal paper and you can mail a copy of it to any creditors who are giving you a problem after the bankruptcy by still trying to collect on discharged debts. In most cases the discharge hearing and getting the discharge papers will be your final act in filing a bankruptcy, but all may not be well and we will next look at some of the exceptions that can come up later on.

9. Filing an amendment when you aren't satisfied.

Amendments may be made to any of the papers you have filed if you haven't received your final discharge. After the final discharge it may still be possible to file amendments, but it is more complicated. The most common reason for filing amendments is that you have left a creditor off of your list, but it is also common to add or delete exempt property, or that you have changed your decision to reaffirm or give up property put up as security for a debt.

If you are filing an amendment you have to change the entries in all of the forms where the information needs to appear. To add or delete exempt property you use Schedule C, and you may have to use Schedule A or B depending on the type of property involved. To amend information on secured property use the Statement of Intention. To amend the list of creditors you will use any of several forms, but also include this new creditor on your mailing matrix so that they will be informed of the bankruptcy.

Whenever you file an amendment make copies of all forms for your records, along with one for the trustee and one for the creditor if you are adding creditors. By the way, whenever you file an amendment there will also be a $20 filing fee that must be paid at the same time.

10. After bankruptcy problems; new and non-exempt property, and new creditors.

If you come into the possession of property, whether exempt or non-exempt, withing 180 days after your discharge you have to notify your trustee. If the property is non-exempt and is valuable the trustee can choose to reopen your bankruptcy and pay off some more of your creditors. If the property is of little value in relation to your debts, even if it is non-exempt, the trustee will probably ignore it and leave your case closed. The types of property that must be reported includes inheritances, property received through a divorce settlement, and money from insurance for death benefits or injuries. Otherwise you are also required to report any non-exempt property that should have been included in your original filing. This information must be given to the trustee. Remember that you are giving the trustee all of this information to protect yourself, and not just be a good person. If you don't supply the court and the trustee with all of the information that they require your creditors can come back and try to collect debts on it since it was not protected through the bankruptcy.

New creditors are another problem. If the new creditor is found, or finds you, before the final discharge he will be handled through an amendment. But if it isn't found until afterwards, or has been left off of the notifications, he is still a creditor who can go after your income and remaining assets.

This is where the bankruptcy cases get a little confusing. If you had non-exempt property which was disposed off to pay off your debts the new creditor will be prevented from re-opening your case. But if you had a case in which there was no non-exempt property the creditor will be able to re-open your case, but only after some non-exempt property is found in your possession so that it can be disposed off for debts. The reason you can file late for some of the money when there are assets is that it would be considered unfair to the other creditors who got in on time.

11. Re-opening your bankruptcy case.

Once your case is closed the only reason it will be re-opened is if new assets are found that can be sold to satisfy some of your debts. If such assets do turn up the trustee will make the first judgement as to whether the case should be re-opened. Of course you can argue that it shouldn't because the original discharge was too long ago, or that the assets aren't worth enough to justify it, but the judge has the final say. if the judge wants to, and believes that there is enough money involved, he can re-open your case even a year or two after it was originally closed. Still, in spite of the risk, report your assets truthfully to the court as you are instructed or you risk losing a lot more than some money or a piece of property.

12. Can they revoke your discharge?

Now that's a terrible thought, 6 months or a year after you had your debts discharged you start getting letters from some of your creditors trying to collect the debts on your closed accounts. What should you do? Do you have any obligation to pay debts that were discharged in a bankruptcy? And exactly what's going on if a bankruptcy doesn't protect you from creditors? Ordinarily when a debt is discharged you are protected from lawsuits by creditors, as well as efforts at collecting consisting of letters, phone calls, seizing of your interest or income, or even of filing a lawsuit against you.

The answer to all of these questions is that any creditor who tries to collect a debt that has been discharged in a bankruptcy is violating the law, and can be sued or held in contempt of court. Your first action, if one of these creditors contacts you, is to write them a letter and cite your bankruptcy case as proof that the debt has been discharged. Normally this is all that it takes since any creditor can make a mistake, and they should all know that they can't collect debts that have gone through bankruptcy.

If your creditor is more persistent, however, you will need to hire a lawyer to write a follow-up letter explaining the same thing. If this doesn't work then you bring a lawsuit against the creditor for harassment . Even if the creditor sues you first, countersue. Since a discharged debt is not an obligation, any attempt to collect it constitutes fraud on the part of the creditor. Courts do not look kindly on this type of activity, and you are likely to receive a substantial settlement for humiliation and embarrassment, as well as all of your attorneys and court costs. However, amongst this rosy picture there is a thorn, there are certain conditions under which your trustee can get the court to revoke your discharge: if you participated in fraud at any time by misrepresenting the information given to the court; that you received non-exempt property at any time within 180 days of the discharge; or that you refused an order or instruction of the court, including simlpy refusing to answer questions given to you. Normally the discharge can be revoked for up to one year after it is closed. If your discharge is revoked you again become liable for all of those debts you thought had been discharged, and the only break you get is that the trustee will credit any payments you have made to your creditors. This is not a pretty picture, and if you face a revocation of your discharge it may be a good time to consult a bankruptcy lawyer.

HOW TO WORK OUT PAYMENT PLANS

While we have already looked at some of the ways to handle your creditors after they have started sending your accounts to collection, it is often possible to stop the process much earlier than this if you contact your creditors as soon as you see that your credit is getting out of hand. While you still may be forced into bankruptcy or end up with a bad credit record you can often avoid all of that if you handle your creditors in the right way..

First, you need to understand that so long as your payments are coming in on time and you have a nice healthy level of credit your creditor will pretty much ignore you. If there are no problems creditors don't bother contacting their people about problems--after all, they don't want to create any negative thoughts, such as what will happen if I quit paying this bill every month.

Now, let us suppose that you lost your job one month, and it took you 6 months to find another one. What happens to your bills? Do they stop along with your paychecks? Not quite, they just go on and on coming in every month, and the creditors continue to look for your payments each week as well. However, if you stop sending in the payments, because you have stopped getting paychecks, the creditors will begin to get very excited. For a one month late payment they will just put a note in your payment, but if it gets to be much over one month you will probably get a phone call. They will be very polite, but will strongly suggest that you send the full delinquent payment now. The emphasis is on the now. If you indicate that you do not intend to make your payment it is likely that the creditor will then suggest that you work out some sort of payment plan to "keep your good credit."

This is your opening, and you should take advantage of it whether or not you consider your financial condition to be permanent. What you want to do is work out a payment plan with your creditors that will decrease the amount of your payments, and still keeps your credit record clean. Of course if you set up one of these with a creditor and then fall behind again you can expect notations on your credit record immediately, but that is another problem.

For now we will say that you have gotten your creditors to agree to give you reduced payment plans, and that you want to know just what that really means. The first thing that it means is that you are going to have to continue sending payments to your creditors each month--just not as much money. A payment plan does not mean that the creditors have cancelled any of your debt, or that they have decreased your credit. On credit cards you can still be paying 18% to 20% on the unpaid balance, and not the 8% or 9% you might like.

Normally credit payments include all of the interest due, plus an amount extra which is sufficient to pay off the principal in a certain number of years. If you decrease your payments you are going to be paying less than is necessary to pay off your debt in the number of years you originally expected, and in some cases you may be paying less than the amount of interest charged. When you pay less than the interest on a debt the balance of the debt actually gets bigger each month and not smaller. Thus you could pay on a reduced payment plan for your car for a year and then owe $500 more money on it than you did at the start of the year.

Nevertheless, if you aren't able to fix your credit as soon as it begins to go bad do hesitate to use a reduced payment plan to help get yourself back on track. There is at least one limitation you will come up against though, these plans have a time limit. When you set them up you have to tell your creditors just how long you expect to stay on them. If it is too long the creditor may file some sort of foreclosure on your property, or just sue you for his money.

In general these plans are not only useful, they only require that you deal with the individual creditors and not with courts, collections agencies, or even credit bureaus. Also, this is one part of fixing your credit where you do not need a lawyer involved. If a creditor sees a lawyer when he is just trying to fix a debt that is a month late he may very well conclude that you are really planning a bankruptcy. This is one credit solution that you really need to approach on your own. But be confident, creditors don't want their clients to fail, they just want them to pay up for their entire lifetimes.

CAN YOU GET CREDITORS TO CANCEL PART OF YOUR DEBT?

This is a much more difficult plan to sell to a creditor than simply setting up a payment plan for you. For one thing, with a payment plan the creditor still believes he will eventually get his money, plus interest. With a partial debt cancellation he will lose part of his principal as well as some of his interest, which is what he might expect to happen if you filed for bankruptcy. Of course if you deal with him personally you can avoid the stigma of bankruptcy on your record, and he might come off in much better shape. To get any creditor to agree to a debt cancellation you are going to have to convince him that he will be better off than if you end up filing a bankruptcy.

Most creditors will ignore you if you go to them and suggest that they simply cancel part of your debt. After all, a home or auto lender will simply seize your property, resell it, and use the proceeds to payoff what you owe them. If the car or home does not sell for enough to cover the bills they may sue you later on anyway. In most cases this is not a problem, and rarely you might even get some money back if the sale raised more money than your debt, and the expenses of the sale.

That is pretty much what you will face with any secured creditor. But on personal loans and credit cards you might be able to get a deal. While there is still money involved, they would be competing with the secured creditors for the equity in your property in order to get their money. It would be your job to convince them that you are one step away from a bankruptcy. Many times these creditors will settle for any thing if they are convinced that you are serious about filing bankruptcy.

Debt cancellation, outside of the court system, is probably one of the hardest deals you can make with a creditor, but there is nothing to prevent you from offering to settle your entire debt for something less than you owe if you get into such a bad financial situation that you are not going to be able to keep up your payments anyway.

SHOULD YOU PAY EVERYONE OFF?

Of course that is what all of your creditors would like, and if you can manage it, paying everyone off is usually the best course. But like all things that look good on the surface it has both good points and bad points, and to make the best solution for you, you should consider both sides of the coin.

On the good side, paying off all of your creditors will lower the amount of money you need each month to get along. You will be able to write fewer checks each month, and your life as a whole will get   more simple. I can't fault any of these accomplishments, and they can be carried out by the simple expedient of just paying off all of your creditors.

The question arises as to where does the money come from that is going to accomplish this task. If you have a healthy income you could live very conservatively for 3 or 4 years and probably pay off just about all of your debts. Then, if you didn't get too fancy in what you were doing, you could increase your living standard more to what you would like it to be, and put some money in the bank each month to take care of those purchases that you were charging before. You could even save up for a car, should you need one, as well as furniture and appliances for your home. This would be a perfect life, in so far as managing your money, and you would never live in fear of creditors again.

All very well and good, but what if your income was on the low side, and your money came from a one-shot windfall such as a lottery winning, inheritance, or the sale of some property. This isn't quite the same thing since you still don't have the income to take care of your debts, and you also won't see that money again until some unnamed time in the future when you get lucky again.

While having an income which will support you makes it possible to pay off your debts and keep them paid, but getting enough money to do that once raises a lot of questions about what you should do with it. If you are of retirement age and you get some money paying off your debts is very reasonable since you will probably have a much lower standard of living in the future. But if you are young and ambitious, or you have a family, you may have a much higher need for that money than just paying bills. It could be used to start a business, or pay for a college education, or used to take a trip that you never thought that you could afford. Sometimes there are better uses for money than just paying off creditors.

This pretty well summarizes the downside of paying off all of your creditors, even if you are able to, and just for those of you who are still undecided I can bring up a few more questions. If you are someone with many plans for the future you are probably going to need a lot more resources in the future than you have now, after all, most of us do. So if you spend all of your money paying off creditors in a year or two you will probably owe just as much as you do now anyway.   That would make it rather useless to use what little resources you have gotten just to pay creditors. After all, if you have to use creditors for all of those purchases over the next years it just means that you will have to get someone elses approval before you can do what you were going to do anyway. If this seems to describe you pretty well then put your money into the bank and use it directly as long as it lasts to make your purchases. It may not seem like it at the time, but it is awfully nice to have some of the things you need without owing anyone for them. I guess that is my final advice--if you can see yourself making major purchases over the next 2 or 3 years, then leave most of your money in the bank and pay for the things you need as you buy them. But if you fall into one of the other categories, you are retiring or you have a good income anyway, than paying off your creditors will help your standard of living and make you happy for a long time to come.

TEAR UP MY CREDIT CARDS? ARE YOU MAD?

The ultimate revenge against the credit card companies, tear up the cards and send the little pieces back to them with a letter informing the hateful bunch of pukes that you can live better without their services. Now wouldn't that feel good to do to all of those companies that you have to send money to each month. I've done it one or twice, and I love it, but unfortunately it didn't cure me. No matter how many times I have made up my mind to live a pure life, without the sin and degradation of credit cards, I have failed.

This has led me to the conclusion that no matter how much we may want to most of us cannot get along without the occasional use of plastic to pay our debts and buy our luxuries. Necessities are another matter, but we can now use credit to buy groceries and gas as well as cars and homes.

I do not personally know of anyone who lives without the use of credit cards. I still think that using credit every day just because it is convenient is true madness, but that doesn't make it any more avoidable. It is just because credit has become so much of our daily lives that we can't get rid of our credit cards. Just think of it, if you take a long trip across the country would you feel better having a credit card with you that has a $5,000 credit limit, or would you like the feel of $5,000 in cash or travelers checks. The credit cards are there so we use them.

That is what is wrong with credit in the United States today, we can't really live without it unless we want to carry around wads of money that will invite robberies. Credit cards are a necessary evil, and for most of us they must be kept in our possession as we go out and about the town.

So what is the answer to my simple question? It is this, though you may take my credit cards from me, even by force, it is pure madness to think that I will go long before I get an offer for another one in the mail and agree to accept it on a trial basis. Of course I never intend to use it, but a year from now I bet that there is a $1,000 balance on it anyway, and I will still be making payments on it 5 years from now too. I'm afraid that I have given up the fight to get rid of all of my credit cards, and for most of you, you might as well save your energy and use it to keep from overcharging your accounts than to use it to get rid of something that just won't stay gone anyway.

HOW LONG SHOULD IT TAKE TO FIX CREDIT?

How long it takes depends upon the method used to fix the credit problems. Naturally that in turn depends upon what kind of problems you are trying to fix. A simple case of 30 day and 60 late payments can probably be taken care of within 6 months by talking to the creditors that you were behind paying. Your argument in dealing with them is that they make their money by keeping your good will, and by making certain that you keep sending them payments every month. If you have been behind in the past just contact them and explain the difficulties you are having because of the late payments on your credit record, and promising never to do it again and asking them to remove the late payments from your record. If you keep your part of the bargain most creditors will be happy to work with you. After all, it costs them nothing, and it keeps a bill paying customer at their store.

If things are somewhat worse, and you have a generally bad credit record you are going to have to go through the procedure for clearing up a credit record account. This could easily take you a year or more, and it may be impossible to clear some of the negative remarks in your record. Still, with a lot of letter writing and persistence you may be able to clear up even a very messy set of credit reports.

But if things are very bad, and you have a bankruptcy on your record, you are going to have problems for a long time to come. Normally a bankruptcy stays on your credit report for 10 years, and that is quite long enough. If you look closely at virtually all credit applications they ask you if you have ever had a bankruptcy--don't answer that if it was over 10 years ago. While you can be prosecuted for lying to obtain credit, you are also protected by the law from having to give information that is too old.

The reason that I am saying this is that most credit agencies will automatically reject anyone who has ever had a bankruptcy. This is illegal, but they will tell you to your face that this is their practice. Naturally they do this to protect themselves from people who they may expect will be likely to file another bankruptcy, at least that is what they say. I think they really do it to punish anyone who has had the gall to cancel a credit debt without paying it off. It's just their way of getting even. At least that is more understandable than the reasons they are likely to give you.

This goes for legal decisions and past due tax bills as well-- 10 years after one of these unfortunate happenings your credit should be clear, no matter how bad it was. To be certain get your credit reports from the credit reporting agencies and at least prepare answers to any questions that a creditor may ask of you the next time that you fill out a form requesting credit.

SHOULD YOU USE CREDIT TO FIX CREDIT?

Generally this is a bad idea. The most common method that people use is to borrow from one credit card to make the payments on their other credit cards. When you do this you usually pay a cash transfer fee of about 2%, the balance on the credit cards stays the same so you are also paying around 1 1/2% a month interest which adds to how much you owe each month, and the amount you have to borrow to keep this up increases each month as a consequence. If you begin by owing $1,000 on your credit cards at the start of a year, without even using your credit to buy anything more you might owe $1,500 by the end of the year with all of the fees and interest you are paying each month. Eventually you will run out of interest and go bankrupt, and you won't even get the benefit of improving your life style by using your credit in the meantime.

This is a most unpleasant view of things and you should avoid it. Never use credit to pay for credit over any extended period. If you are in a situation where this looks like the only way to go start looking at bankruptcies and debt consolidation loans right then and not after your debts have grown much too large for you to do anything about them.

As you probably already know, if you own a home, the interest you pay on it is deductible on your taxes. In fact it is almost the only interest deduction that the average citizen can take any more, and it applies to lines of credit the same as to 1st or 2nd trust deeds. This makes it a very attractive source of money to consolidate your debts. If you can bring yourself to destroy most of your credit cards it is even a good place to use credit to fix the credit you have that is in trouble. You will have to own a home to do it though, and that may be the biggest drawback for most people who are in financial trouble.

But I have one other suggestion that might just work for most of the rest of you. Most regularly employed people are eligible for membership in a credit union. The beauty of credit union loans is that they depend only upon how long you have been in your job, and your income. Furthermore, when you take a loan from a credit union you can arrange for automatic payments so that you never see the money, and loan rates are usually lower as well. So here is what you do; add up all of the debts you can't keep up with, go to your credit union and take out a debt consolidation loan with automatic payroll deductions, and get everything up to date. So long as you don't tell creditors that you owe money to a credit union your loans will never show up on a credit report, and because your overall indebtedness to your other creditors has just decreased you will now be in a much stronger condition financially.

Credit union loan interest is also no longer deductible, and the loan itself could take 3 to 5 years to pay off, but you can get your money in a month or two. The only drawback that I can think of is that there is a limit on the size of these unsecured, signature loans. I think that most of the time the limit is between $5,000 and $10,000, and you will probably have to tell the credit union what you are going to do with the money. On the other hand they will usually be very favorable toward a debt consolidation loan with automatic payments.

At all costs avoid using the easy credit home loan people for debt consolidation. They are easy to borrow from, but their interest rates are higher, and if you get a month or two behind they will have you out on the street. These people care for nothing except getting your name on a loan and then getting their payments for as long as possible. If you take out any loan, and make minimum payments it will take you 10 years or more to pay them off. I consider them a trap that should be avoided at all costs.

WHEN ALL ELSE FAILS, PLAY THE LOTTERY

The voice of desperation is in the land. You are out of all your options and no one will give you credit. Do you ever wonder why most of the people who win the lottery are broke and have poor jobs? It's because they are the ones who play most of the time, and who put up most of the money.

If you have any other option don't depend on such simpleminded games as playing the lottery to get on firm financial ground. The odds are still 20 million to 1 against you. Should you ever play the lottery, or gamble, then? While I believe the answer is no I still can't resist putting down a dollar or two when I go through Nevada, or buying a lottery ticket when the jackpots get big. But I always put a limit on what I am doing, and I never do it on a weekly or daily basis. Regular betting will only make you go broke. Playing occasionally probably won't hurt, and you might even win a big pot once in a while. After all, some people have done it several times.

My advice to you though, if you are down and out of options so far as you can see, play a dollar once or twice a week and hope and pray that one of them comes in with a win. If there is nothing else for you to do it can't hurt if you take a gamble once in a while and hope for a big win. But never spend your rent money, your food money, or the money you need for your baby's clothes. There is always hope, and sometimes that's all it takes to get us through the day. If playing the lottery gives you hope for a day, then play sometimes. It's sort of like the passage in the Bible: The Lord helps those who help themselves. If playing the lottery is your way of helping yourself, then maybe the Lord will help you too.

Good luck.

6 THE BENEFITS OF BANKRUPTCY

Chapter 13 is not a bankruptcy in which you just pay what you can and all of your debts are wiped out, it is more accurately called the Federal repayment plan. It is most useful for those who are still working and would like to pay their debts, but who are just unable to for some reason. With Chapter 13 you can meet your obligations and maintain your self pride, but under the protection and direction of the courts.

With a Chapter 13 plan you pay back part of all of your debts over a 3 year period. You are required to make monthly payments, and all of your debts will be wiped out at the end of the 3 years. Advantages over doing this yourself through a loan consolidation plan is, there is no interest or finance charges on the debts while you pay them off, you can participate in deciding how much you will pay each month, and you can decide what percent of the total debts you are going to repay. While you may not pay off all of your debts, you must be able to pay off most of them or you may not be allowed to file.

How does this compare with a regular bankruptcy? In a regular bankruptcy all of your debts are added together,and all of your assets are added together, except for those that are exempt, and the assets are sold and distributed to the creditors to pay for the debts. It is very probable that none of your creditors gets all of his money back, and most of your possessions are sold. In addition anything that you get in the immediate future may also be taken and sold to pay remaining bills.

In a Chapter 13 bankruptcy all of your debts are added up, and all of your income is taken into account, and you agree to pay as much as you reasonably can over the next 3 years on your debts, after which they are canceled. You get to keep most of your possessions in the Chapter 13, but you will have to deal with it for 3 years. In a regular bankruptcy you are through with it in a few months, but you are starting all over from scratch as far as what you own. Since getting credit after a bankruptcy is very difficult you will have to work very hard for a very long time to set up your home again so that it fits you. With Chapter 13 you will still have your possessions, and you will have already worked hard to keep them, but all of your debts will be gone. Besides self-esteem, Chapter 13 can leave a lot more of your life intact to help you out in the future.

Chapter 13 has one large advantage over a regular bankruptcy in that there is no time limit as to when you can file, or how often. With a regular bankruptcy you are limited to one filing every 6 years. You could file a bankruptcy one year, and then file a chapter 13 the following year.

The proceedings: The first step is to fill out and file a Chapter 13 repayment plan with your local bankruptcy court. The papers you file consist of a complete monthly budget with your income, regular living expenses, and an amount left over which can be applied to your debts. Filling out and filing these forms will vary somewhat around the country, but was recently noted to be $90.

How to figure out your Chapter 13 budget: This is an absolute necessity if you are going to file a Chapter 13. Your budget determines how much you are going to have to live on each month, and how much you are going to pay in debts. If you have never lived on a budget, now is the time to learn how.

The first step is to list all of your monthly expenses. Do not leave out expenses you have each year, but which you only pay some months and not other, like insurance. Your list should have categories, something like the one below, but with additional entries for other expenses you have but someone else might not:

> Housing (rent or mortgage payments)
>
> Home insurance
>
> Property taxes, if you own

Utilities

Food

Clothing allowance

Laundry costs

Medical expenses

Transportation and auto expenses

Auto insurance

Entertainment

Miscellaneous

Savings

Do not list your debt servicing expenses on your budget since they will be covered by the Chapter 13. However, you have to set up your budget so that you have 10-20% of your take home pay to make Chapter 13 payments to pay off your debt load. If this takes some reduction in certain categories of your budget that is acceptable. As a warning, don't figure your debt repayment at greater than 20% of your clear income or you will probably fail, losing the benefits of the Chapter 13, as well as much of the money you have put into trying to make it succeed.

Once you have 10% to 20% of your take-home pay budgeted for debt repayment you need to multiply this amount by the 3 years that you will be making payments to see exactly how much of your total debts you will be able to pay off. In 3 years there are 36 months, so you multiply the monthly amount by 36 to get your answer.

An example of a Chapter 13 budget: Theory doesn't help a great deal when you actually have to figure out how to do something you haven't done before so I thought that an example would be very useful. Take a look at the budget that John came up with and see how you might be able to make up a similar plan for yourself.

John has been in trouble with credit for the past couple of years and has gotten $11,000 of short term debt that he has trouble making the payments on. Minimum payments run a total of $220 a month, with $165 of that going to interest. With the principal going down so slowly ($220-$165=$55 a month), that each year finds John another $4,000-5,000 in debt. John can see a day in another 2 or 3 years when his only option will be bankruptcy, which he wants to avoid, and wants to consider Chapter 13 as a way of getting out of debt.

John's income is $2,400 a month from his job as a manager in a local restaurant. The first step to finding out if Chapter 13 is the right decision for John is for him to do a budget. This is John's monthly budget.

Housing (rent or mortgage payments)		$450
Home insurance		50
Property taxes, if you own		75
Utilities		225
Food		300
Clothing allowance		50
Laundry costs		25
Medical expenses		150
Transportation and auto expenses		250
Auto insurance	75	
Entertainment		150
Miscellaneous		200
Savings		100
Total		$ 2100

When we subtract John's monthly budget from his monthly take-home in come we get $2400-$2100=$300. John has $300 a month to pay off his $11,000 of debt.

Now would John's income and budget work out to a successful Chapter 13. If we take the $300 John has a month and multiply by the 36 months that there are in 3 years we get $10,800, which is very close to the amount that John has to pay off.

This gives John two options: he can go ahead and file a Chapter 13 with the budget that he has filled out, pay off $10,800 of his $11,000 debt, and ask for the remaining $200 to be forgiven, or he can modify his monthly budget to get another $6 a month out of his budget to pay off the other $200 and come out with a completely clear record.

Both ways of solving John's problems would work with a Chapter 13 plan, but since John is so close to being able to pay off all of his debts with a small adjustment in his monthly budget he would be better off making the extra effort to clear his record completely. Any forgiveness of debt that you get through any bankruptcy, even a Chapter 13, is looked upon very negatively by future creditors.

It should not be lost in this that the reason the Chapter 13 works for John is that he isn't paying interest on his debts over the three years of his repayment plan. If he were he would still owe most of the original $11,000 in three years because interest would take up most of his payments.

You should also note that while John is operating under the Chapter 13 he is going to have to find some other way to live than by adding $5,000 in credit debt each year. If he is not able to do this his Chapter 13 will fail. This is also something that you will have to think very hard about. If you can't change your way of life, live on a budget, and live without increasing your credit debt for 3 years, you would not be able to successfully complete a Chapter 13 repayment of debt.

What happens after you file: When you file these forms all direct payments to creditors stop, and all creditors and collection agencies must stop harassing you. They are no longer subject to wage attachments or automatic payroll deductions for debt collection. You do have to continue making payments, but you make them to your court appointed trustee, and he pays your creditors according to the information you have given him.

What the court will do: About a month after you file your papers the court will have you come in for a meeting with the trustee. You will be questioned in regard to your debts and your plans for payment. When the trustee has agreed that your plan is reasonable and that it can be successful you will meet with the bankruptcy judge. If he agrees with your plan he will confirm it, and you will be held to it for the next 3 years.

Limits and laws governing Chapter 13: While there are no limits on the number of times you can file Chapter 13, you are still limited by the total amount of debts that you have. You are eligible just so long as your unsecured debts are less than $100,000, and your secured debts are no greater than $100,000. If one of these is more than that you are ineligible to file.

We have already run into classifying property as exempt and non-exempt. Exempt property can be kept regardless of the type of bankruptcy you file, and in a regular bankruptcy non-exempt property must be sold off to pay creditors. In a Chapter 13 you must repay debts equal to, or greater than, the total amount of exempt property that you have. In the example which was given above, if John did not have non-exempt property worth at least $11,000 he could not use Chapter 13 to pay off his debts. Some of the rules for determining exempt and non-exempt property are given in the section on bankruptcy.

The treatment of wages under Chapter 13 is controlled by a Federal law. Under this law if you are still owed wages for work you have done in the last 30 days, only 3/4 of your wages are exempt. Since 1/4 of a month' s income could be non-exempt, and end up going directly to your creditors or have to be figured into your non-exempt property limit, you should file your Chapter 13 the day after you have been paid for your most recent work. If you have any vacation pay or options due from your job you should take these first as well or they will also raise your non-exempt limit.

The tools you use in your job are always exempt. This could be a computer, a car, carpentry tools, or a lawn mower if you had a job as a gardener. There is no value limit on tools of the trade.

Which debts cannot be paid off with Chapter 13?: Just as in a regular bankruptcy, you cannot cancel underpaid and past due taxes, and family obligations such as alimony and child support are unaffected.

Can my creditors veto my repayment plan?: Repayments plans are not submitted to creditors for approval. Your plan does have to be approved by the court, but the plan itself is yours. You figure out how much money you have available for debt repayment after you subtract your living expenses from your income, and that is all you can be held to.

Will a Chapter 13 filing show up on my credit report?: Yes it will, the same as a regular bankruptcy or simple overdue billings, but it is better than either of these. A regular bankruptcy shows that you cancelled your debts without paying most of them. A Chapter 13 shows that you made an effort to repay your debts over a 3 years period, and that you paid most of them off--these are points in your favor. The credit report will list how much of your debts you paid under Chapter 13, but creditors won't automatically dismiss your application for credit as being from someone who tries to escape the debts they owe through bankruptcy. Of course you will probably not be able to get new credit until your Chapter 13 is completed, but look at it as if you were a creditor: would you grant credit to someone who paid off their debts under a Chapter 13 before someone who had cancelled them under a regular bankruptcy? I think you would, and both types of bankruptcy will still show on your credit record for 10 years.

Do I need to hire a lawyer to file a Chapter 13?: You need a lawyer to file any legal action, and that includes a Chapter 13. When you act as your own lawyer the law calls it in propia persona, or in prose. This is just a Latin term that means acting in your own name. However, just because you don't hire a lawyer you should know what one would do for you so that you can do it for yourself. First, if you need legal advice you can go to a book called "Legal Research: How to Find and Understand the Law," by Elias.

What would a lawyer cost?: Of course trying to learn the laws about anything by reading may take a lot more time than you would have and it may be much easier for you to go to a legal aid bureau or lawyer to get legal advice. It may cost $50 or $100, but that is a lot less than having a lawyer handle your entire case.

If you fill out the forms you can hire a lawyer to look them over for mistakes. He will charge by the amount of time he thinks it will take to do this, or you can have a lawyer handle the whole Chapter 13 for around $500. Costs for a Chapter 13 will vary from place to place. Where there is a lot of competition costs may even be lower, and in a very upscale area they may be a lot higher.

How can I find a lawyer who will do a good job?: Finding a lawyer you can trust is more difficult then deciding whether or not you need one. A bad lawyer will cost you the same money as a good one, although with a bad lawyer you will probably be no better off than if you did it yourself and saved your legal fees. Legal aid groups, which help the poor for free usually do not handle bankruptcies of any sort. Asking friends can be effective, but only if you know someone who has gone through a bankruptcy or a Chapter 13. It's best not to depend upon lawyer ads to find legal help since every lawyer will tell you that they are the best one around to handle your case whether or not they are any good. I would advise asking your local legal aid or bar association for a list of lawyers who specialize in Chapter 13 filings, and then interview several before you make a choice.

7 STAYING OUT OF TROUBLE

Everyone who has gone through a credit crisis should want to stay out of trouble in the future. After all, there is no upside to having a bad credit record, being refused credit when you need it, or of being forced into a bankruptcy because you can't solve your problems in any other way.

Naturally I can't guarantee that you'll stay out of credit trouble just because you read this chapter. I can just guarantee that if you violate the ideas that are written here you are going to end up with the same problems you had before, only the second time around it will be worse because you can't use the same arguments with your creditors and credit reporting agencies to clean up your record. You can't even file for bankruptcy again for 10 years, and everything you have could be gone. Don't do it again. Be a good person and stay out of credit trouble. But in the meantime read over the thoughts discussed and see if there aren't at least a few that you can apply to your life to stay out of trouble and to maintain your good credit.

WATCH THE BALANCE OF INCOME AND CREDIT PAYMENTS

Much of the secret of keeping good credit is watching the balance of income and how it compares with your credit payments. When you get to the point that just making your credit payments each month is difficult, and you no longer seem to have the money you need for your daily living expenses, you are probably overextended on your credit payment obligations. Of course it would help to have some guidelines, based on your income, as to what your maximum credit obligations should be before you become worried.

Generally you are expected to have no more than 50% of your total income obligated to monthly payments. This includes your housing, car payments, all of your credit cards, medical bills, personal loans, and anything else that you are making monthly payments on. Obviously this means that people with the same income can have different amounts of credit. In fact the reason that you should limit your expenses to 50% of your gross income is that taxes will take most of what's left.

Suppose that you have an income of $20,000 a year, and that your state and federal taxes are $3,000. This is possible because smaller incomes pay less in taxes, and $20,000 a year qualifies as a low income. Now although you still have $17,000 left to live on, creditors still feel that you should have no more than $10,000 a year tied up in monthly credit and bill payments. While this sounds like a lot of money, all that you are looking at is about $800 a month. What can you buy for $800 a month today? You are doing well in most parts of our country if you can get housing for $400 a month, and a car for $200 a month. If you have no other monthly payments at this time, and you probably do, you have only $200 a month to work with for credit. What can you get for $200 a month. Most credit cards require a payment of 2% of the total amount that you owe. If you consider the $200 a month that you have to spend as 2% of the amount of credit that you are going to carry, then you can carry 50 times that amount of credit, or $10,000 total in credit card accounts. If you are confused at this point don't worry about it, because I am going to give you a little table, based on this 2% rule, and a few suggestions to help you check out your credit load.

Total Income	Total amt for payments	Pymts per month	Total credit
$20,000	$10,000	$ 200	$10,000
40,000	20,000	400	20,000
60,000	30,000	600	30,000

That should be enough to give you the pattern. The maximum credit you should carry is less than one-half of your total income. Unfortunately it is not that simple, however, because you can have self-imposed saving's plans that work the same way as debts to decrease the amount of cash you have for credit payments. If you have $5,000 a year taken out for a saving's plan, you should decrease your maximum credit by one-half of that, or $2,500 dollars.

Anyway this does get rather messy with all of the exceptions. As long as you keep your total monthly payments for all of your living expenses, plus bills and loans, to less than half of your monthly income there should be no problems. And any time that you see these payments go over that amount you need to take steps to decrease your bills in some way. You might use a debt consolidation loan, or a line of credit on your home, or even savings, but you need to keep your debt amount under control if you want to keep a clean credit record.

SAVING UP FOR BIG PURCHASES

It's almost un-American to suggest that you wait to make purchases until you actually have the cash to pay for them. After all, what would happen to our country if we stopped using credit whenever we felt like. MasterCard and Visa would go broke, we would need fewer mailmen since they wouldn't have to deliver bills every month, and millions of people in credit departments throughout the United States would lose their jobs. All that would happen if each one of us just waited until we could afford to buy the things we want and need until taking a credit card and doing it any time that we felt like it.

If that seems a little far fetched to you, well then you are right. Americans will never stop using their credit cards for big purchases, and they certainly won't do it for little purchases either. We are hooked on our credit cards, but we don't have to be as much as we are today.

While it may be impossible for most of us to ever save enough money to buy a home, and nearly impossible to save enough to buy a car, I still want to know what is holding us back from saving $500 to buy a couch. Why do we have to use credit every time we buy a piece of furniture. In fact it is even worse than that today. For many of us we don't even carry enough cash to pay for our groceries or gas for our cars.

There are also those of us who get suckered in using credit cards with the idea that we will pay off the credit card every month. This usually works for a period of time, but some month you will be short of money, or you will have to make an extra charge you hadn't planned on. When this happens you will end up carrying over your first balance to the next month. Later on this will get to be a habit, and you will have fallen into the credit trap.

If you must have a credit card, and I guess most of us must have at least one for emergencies, then never use it. If you never use it you will never have to send payments, and you will never have credit problems. Then with all of the money you save from monthly payments you can just make your payments in cash. Sound impossible, well it isn't. For at least 90% of the time, you can save up the cost of anything you will have charged in 3 to 6 months time. In fact, since you aren't paying 20% interest on everything you buy you will have that extra money to spend on the rest of your lifestyle.

Just look at the $10,000 in credit that I gave in the first example. For that you are making $2,400 a year payments, but 20% of $10,000 is $2,000. This means that you actually get to buy $400 worth of new merchandise each year, and the credit companies get the other $2,000. If you don't owe the $10,000 to begin with you can spend the whole $2,400 on yourself each and every year, and never answer to a credit company again.

I think that it is highly worthwhile to save up for as many of your major purchases as you can. I do it as much as I can, and I never regret it. What I do regret is sending too much money to credit companies each and every month of the year.

LIMITING YOUR CREDIT USES

This is advice to go against the trend in credit use. The credit issuers, mainly credit card companies and banks, are trying to get every one to depend on plastic for all of their daily needs, and to carry as little money as possible. They promote this through the proliferation of pay-point marketing in supermarkets and gas stations. Their other big seller is the Versatel machines through which you can get $20 to $100 on any given day. For most of our needs that amount of money, combined with a liberal use of your credit card, will get you through the day. While it is very tempting to use your credit in this way, it will also lead you into credit ruin.

There are stories of people who have run up $10,000 in credit debt in 6 months, and $30,000 in 2 years. If your credit record is clean it is so easy to get dozens of credit cards that there is an investment advisor who uses this method to raise money for real estate purchases. His argument is that he turns over the property so fast that he never has to pay interest or fees on his credit uses. I will predict right now that one day, not too far away, this investment genius will fail to make his deal and will be filing for bankruptcy.

But all of that is off the mark. Just because it is easy to get and use credit, there is no reason to depend on it to solve every single one of our problems. Credit should have a defined use in your life, and you need to be very strict with yourself about staying within the limits you have set.

The best and highest use of credit is an emergency money fund, but only for true emergencies. If there is a serious illness in your family, credit can solve problems more rapidly than anything else. Homes and cars are generally too expensive to be purchased for cash, and credit is a necessity if we are ever to live in our own homes or to drive a car. Credit may also be necessary for car repairs or clothes, but should not be used for these purposes on a regular basis.

That is pretty much all of the uses for which credit should be depended upon. Emergencies and purchases which are too large to be made in cash, and yet which are necessities to life in the United States. With these restrictions you will rarely get into trouble with your credit, and you should never end up with credit payments that are so high that you can't afford to live and pay for your credit cards at the same time.

STAY AWAY FROM THE LOAN SHARKS

Loan sharks come in many shapes and sizes, but they all offer the same same thing--easy credit. These people are so easy to borrow money from that they sometimes don't even require your signature on the loan, but they will always know where to find you.

Now in talking about loan sharks I am sort of mixing two different ideas: there is the back-ally gangster type of loan shark, and the easy credit guy who waves to you from your newspaper every morning. Now I don't see very much difference in these two people, even though one will break your legs if you don't pay, and the other one will only take all of your furniture and throw you into the street.

To be able to avoid loan sharks you have to be able to spot them, but the good news is that spotting them is not difficult. A loan shark can come in the form of a person that some casual friend knows, who will loan you any amount of money just so long as you agree to pay the interest that is asked. Any time that you hear of such a friend of a friend you need to run as fast as you can, because you can't win with them no matter how lucky you think you are.

The other loan shark seems to walk the streets in every neighborhood, and no one even attempts to lock them up. These easy credit people demand collateral, although the collateral you put up as security for a loan can be virtually anything of value. They will take your car, your furniture, even the gold teeth in your mouth. They will also give you the money you borrow an hour after you walk into their business. What they will also do is charge you 30% or more in interest. These people come under special laws that allow them to charge interest rates as high as they want in many states.

If you feel tempted to go to a loan shark, no matter what he calls himself, take another look at your credit cards and other credit sources. In all cases you will be better off getting credit from a more restricted source than from someone who makes up his own rules. Loan sharks specialize in loans to those who are least able to borrow, or who are in a hurry to get money. Never be in a hurry when you are borrowing money, or seeking credit. It will never pay off for you.

DON'T GET SUCKERED IN BY EASY CREDIT

This area is close to the loan sharks, but is wider and includes all of those furniture and appliance stores that offer to sell you the things you need to live, no matter what your credit history. The scope of these people is almost unlimited. Driving down the street there are ads on auto dealer lots that offer easy credit, no credit history check, and no money down. They even say low credit, but they don't say what low is. Low cost insurance programs, that usually pay even less, are in the same bracket.

If you know that you have had some credit problems and that you have had trouble getting credit at banks, and someone comes out and offers to give you anything you want if you will just sign your name, then you have to be suspicious. Unfortunately Americans want to trust each other, and no matter how badly we have been treated we want to trust the next person we meet to treat us honestly and with respect.

It is exactly this story that the easy credit people try to convey, and it is hard to resist. When someone tells you that they can just tell that you can be trusted by looking at you, you can be pretty sure that what they are really judging is whether or not they can get some money out of you before they re-possess the merchandise they have sold you.

The conditions they generally offer, and you can use this as a checkoff, is no credit check, and quick credit. Little or no money down, and immediate delivery, the faster the better. Low payments are always offered, but these carry the catch--at the end of the pay period you usually owe as much or more than you did at the beginning. In addition, the total of the payments will more than likely be greater than the cost of what you are buying. These stores are betting that you will wear out the merchandise before you pay it off, and they will just go to court on you or garnish your wages when you stop paying. Oh yes, there will be a balloon payment at the end of the contract period.

Not that every one of the easy credit people will use this system, but look at its beauty, to the honest person with poor credit. Because it is so easy to get hooked it will appeal to many of the walking wounded in the credit area. If you are down and out, and can't buy anything that is any good, then getting credit for a television set may seem like a big step up. Sad to say we often measure happiness by being able to buy something nice once in a while. Easy credit offers that opportunity, and that is while we fall for it.

Now what does it do for the merchant--it lets him sell a lot of merchandise that he could not otherwise sell, and at inflated prices. Whatever they say about the price you are paying, you are probably paying way too much for what you buy. If one of these merchants can sell a TV at a 100% markup, and then collect most of that money, and finally, in many cases, either get it back because you run out of money or you buy another of the same thing for the same reason, he is successful.

The overdependence on easy credit will always lead to financial ruin. What do I mean by overdependence, having any more than one of these contracts to pay on at one time. This is true no matter what your income or the health of your credit. It is ideal to have none of them, by all means never have more than one.

BECOME A CASH BUYER OF MOST EVERYTHING

This is my favorite way of managing money and surviving in the world. When you purchase by cash it does certain things for you that don't happen when you buy with credit: First and foremost you have to have the cash before you can buy anything. Next, since cash can buy anything, and your cash is limited, you are going to have to make careful choices before you spend your money; and finally, no matter how painful the original purchase is, there is never a bill waiting for you afterwards. But I would like to talk about each of these with you a little bit to give you a better idea of what I am driving at.

First: You have to have the cash before you can make the buy. For some things, as I have said before, this just isn't practical, but there is no reason to go into that again at this point. Saving up cash means spending less money than you have in income. As one money manager said, if you always spend more money than you make you eventually go broke.   This means that everyone would have less cash obligations than they have income, and that goes for you who are rich as well as for those with much more modest incomes. So, now all of you are spending less than you are making means that you now have little cash to work with every week or every month. You can save it up, or just wait till sometime in the month and spend it on dinner or a movie, but you do have cash.

Second: Having cash now means that you are going to have to decide what to buy with it. Being primarily a cash person myself I will give you some of the plans I have used to make the kind of budget you can live with.

There are some expenses in your life that are fixed, and that must be paid each month. These include your rent or house payments, car payments, credit card payments, utility bills, insurance payments, and tax payments. These are inescapable, and it seems to be the job of the government agencies, utility companies, and insurance companies to find out if you have a free dollar left after paying their fees. If they do decide that you have a dollar they will all raise their rates and try to get it all from you. What this usually means is that if your income goes up one dollar, your set bills go up three dollars. There is nothing you can do about this directly, and so you have to outsmart these agencies.

Now, these bills, plus your credit payments should be less than 50% of your income - if it is, you are fine. But now that we have taken care of all of the set costs we have to look at the variable costs of the necessities we use - specifically food, gas, entertainment, clothes, and things we would like to upgrade. Some of these more or less necessary costs can serve as places to save money, and they are really the only areas that we can directly manipulate to stay on a cash basis. Of course, in my plan all of these should be cash payments.

The way that I do it is to figure out a rough monthly budget, and then adjust my expenses from week to week to take care of things as they come up. While that does not give me more money, it at least gives me a pretty good gauge as to whether or not I have money available for some extra expenditure that I would like to make. I also know that if I have all of my basic expenses covered, and I have the chance to earn some extra money I will be able to spend it on an extra purchase. Other than just making extra money I always have enough play in my budget that I can make a small lay-away if I want to. Sometimes I am forced to increase the amount of cash I put into my weekly budgets, but if that has to be done nearly every week then I know that I have to enlarge my monthly and weekly budgets.

This may seem like a very complicated way of doing things, but it is sufficient to manage a family budget over a long period of time. I don't worry much about yearly budgets, I limit what I am doing to the schedule on which I get pay checks.

That, in a capsule, is a household cash based budget that I have found to work over a period of years. Because it is cash based it is easy to expand, should you have the opportunity, or to shrink down to half its size should that be necessary. But if this system isn't right for you go ahead and use trial and error to work out one that fits your lifestyle. Start with a plan, and just change it from month to month until you get it into a form that is just right for you. It might not guarantee that you will never have credit problems, but it will sure help.

Third: This is the most unpleasant part of living on cash -when you have gone to a great deal of time and trouble to save up some money to buy something you have to make the choice to buy it, and then face starting all over again.

I always regret it when I have spend 6 months hoarding money, getting it wherever I can, and putting it away without telling anyone, and then spending it all on a single purpose. Of course it also has its good points since you aren't going to make very many impulse buys you will spend a lot less money anyway. If I see something that interests me I may think it over for a month or more before I decide that I am going to buy it. That gives me time to compare costs and to do a lot of shopping. And once I have made a careful choice I rarely regret it and feel that I made a mistake.

Now, afterwards. Afterwards is great! You never get a bill later on, and your only costs are upkeep and operations. When you buy on credit it is less painful making the choice to buy since you aren't actually spending money, just plastic. But afterwards, and usually for years, you are paying that 20% interest. When you do that no matter how good the buy originally you usually end up spending a lot more than you would have on cash. Cash saves you all of these later costs, and you don't have to factor in the payments in buying anything, once you have the money and make the purchase its over. Its yours to do with as you wish. Do you know that when you take a loan to buy a car the loan company will keep your pink slip until you pay off the loan, and will even tell you what kind of insurance you have to carry. That is control, and with cash you are in control of yourself. No one can tell you what to do after you have made your purchases. Anyway, go to cash if you can, you will be happier for it.

8 SURVIVING CREDIT BOONDOGGLES

Because it is not always possible to stay out of trouble with credit it is desirable to have some plan of how to live when credit goes bad. Now I don't want you to think that this means you should give up trying to clear your credit and get into the mainstream. But suppose that it takes a year or two to clean things up, or even 10 years from a bankruptcy, you still have to live in the meantime. This can't be a complete guide to living without credit, but it is an appropriate piece of information to have when you are dealing with credit. While some of you reading this are looking for credit for the first time, most of you are more interested in cleaning up credit problems.

Now I should say a word or two about what I mean by credit boondoggles. An example of such a state of life would be when you have accepted all of those pre-approved credit cards that seem to come in the mail every week, and then you start to use them without keeping track of what you are buying or what you are committing yourself to in payments. If you want to get $20,000 in debt to credit cards in a hurry this is a good way to do it.

Another appropriate example can be taken from the use of a line of credit on your home. These quick approved plans will give you credit on up to 80% of the value of your home, and $50,000 in total credit. Can you imagine having a credit card with a $50,000 limit when most bank cards have $5,000 or $7,500 limits. The idea is just overwhelming, and you can spend like there's no limit. Unfortunately some people do, and you can easily run up a credit card bill on a line of credit that is more than your 1st trust deed. Of course when you let this kind of credit get out of hand they take your house from you.

You can probably come up with some other ways to totally ruin your credit and let it get out of control, but that is not what I want to teach you. I want to give you some ways to get by after these things have happened. Credit is only a very useful tool to living our lives, it isn't the only way to live. Until a very few years ago most people got by with very little credit, and there is no reason that you can't do that again for a period of time if you try. Read over the suggestions I have here and see if there are not a few that you can use. There are always choices to make and alternatives to every choice. Living without good credit doesn't have to be something you do for the rest of your life, but it is certainly something that you can do for part of your life.

WHAT TO DO WHEN YOU CAN'T FIX IT

This is sort of a worst case scenario, at least so far as credit is concerned. But assuming that your credit can't be fixed, or at least that you can't see how to fix it, what do you do next. You could follow one of the suggestions that I have used before and go to a cash economy. Just save up and pay cash for pretty much every thing. You will probably have to do that anyway to some degree, and you could make it the main strategy that you use to live.

Now when you are in credit trouble, unless you have already filed for bankruptcy, you are going to have collection agencies and credit companies after you all of the time. In fact it is not so much owing the money that kills your spirit, it is being constantly harassed by all of these creditors wanting what little money you do have that makes things miserable. Until you get court protection there is no way to stop these actions, and if they get judgements against you they can garnish your wages as well. If you think it is hard living now just wait until half of your check is taken by creditors before you get the money. These actions are probably some of the major reasons that people file bankruptcy anyway. Even if you can live with the debt, you just get fed up with dealing with angry creditors.

While it may not be possible to escape these people completely, it is often possible to increase your income off the books so that the creditors can't get the money before you do. While they are entitled to their money, so are you. Oh, by off the books I don't mean that you should do anything illegal, just get involved in some form of labor where you get paid directly and without withholding. This is called 1099 income by the IRS, and you will still owe taxes on it, it's just that your creditors won't have any way of seizing it before you have a chance to spend it.

Some of the forms of 1099 income are handyman work such as helping your neighbors paint or repair their homes, or do yard work. Freelance writing qualifies, and even working for one of these temporary employment agencies. In fact the largest source of 1099 type jobs are temporary agencies. Because you are only signing up for daily labor you can go to several of them if you want to. Pay is atleast minimum wage, and sometimes higher, and you can take days off whenever you need to. You won't work every single day anyway. Of course you can use this to find a day here and there of moonlighting jobs if you have a regular daytime job.

Seasonal work can also help to tide you over as well. Some of the favorites I see, and these are most common in city areas, are county fairs, seasonal Christmas work, income tax preparation from the first of the year through April, yard work in the spring and summer, and temporary sales jobs around every holiday. None of these jobs will make any real money for you, but if your creditors are taking most of your money these days what you can earn on temporary work can make it possible to live from day to day.

SURVIVING BANKRUPTCY

Unlike what many credit agencies would like you to believe, bankruptcy is not a fatal disease. No one ever died from bankruptcy, or even went broke because of it. If you are worried about what you will do afterwards, if you file bankruptcy, focus your attention upon what you do it for. Bankruptcy is the legal solution to an otherwise insoluble problem of excess debt. The largest bankruptcies are for business, but it doesn't mean that those who file can never go into business again, and just because you file for bankruptcy it doesn't mean that you will never have a credit card or a credit account again.

Let me tell you a few ways that you can build your credit after bankruptcy. There is nothing mysterious about them, but for some reason most people don't think about them: Begin by building a saving's account. There is no time limit to this, but the more rapidly the better. Have your money in a bank that offers credit cards and loans, like Bank of America. Once you have at least $1,000 in the account, and more if possible, it is time to talk to the bank. Offer to put your money into a timed savings account, and then ask to get a loan or credit card from the bank based on the money of yours that they have on account. Tell them exactly what you are doing, explaining that you have had credit problems in the past, have filed bankruptcy, and now you are trying to build a new life and would like their help. You are dealing with people so you are likely to get sympathy, and besides they already have your money.

Using a guaranteed credit card, or taking a guaranteed loan, is one way of earning a good credit record at any time. Just pay back any amounts that you use as rapidly as possible, and never get behind. Because you already have the money in the bank there will never be an overdue notice and you will get no 30 day notices in your credit report. That is no excuse to give up paying on time. Even though you will only be building credit with one bank, if that bank gets to trust you it will mean a real credit account. Now just one other suggestion, take a secured loan from another source when you get the chance. One of these loans can be secured with a car or furniture, and the size of it doesn't matter.

What I am trying to tell you is that you should live on cash, and build your credit on your security. Take no chances with your credit at this point or you will simply end up with the same problems you had before your bankruptcy.

BUYING WITH BAD CREDIT

This is a way of buying with bad credit which doesn't really use credit. It was a lot more popular before everyone had credit cards, but it is still offered by most stores. It is called a lay away. A lay away is similar to credit in that you secure your purchase at a specific price, and then you make payments on it until you get it paid off. It is different from regular credit purchases in that you don't get to take your purchase home until you have finished paying for it. Usually there is no interest on the purchase, and that is an advantage over the credit account. The drawback on it is that it is usually limited to 3 or 6 months. Large purchases may go to 9 months or a year, but they never seem to go longer than that these days. You have to make payments each month, and it is best if you can do so each week. You are also required, by most merchants, to make a 20% down payment. The other major drawback is that many purchases cannot be made with lay always. No one will sell you a house or car this way, and you will probably be limited in the furniture or new clothes you can buy. Nevertheless, always look into buying on lay away if you have credit problems. After all, if you stop making payments, or don't pay it off on time, the item can be resold as new since you didn't take possession of it.

LOOKING FOR PRIVATE SOURCES OF CREDIT

Private sources of credit come in many shapes and sizes, but in every city you can find people with cash who are willing to lend it to those with something as security. I guess the key to surviving a credit collapse is to have some property of value that can be put up to secure loans or new credit. Of course buying some things can provide its own credit as well. But in addition to going to the stranger now may be the time to go to your relatives and friends. If any of these special people have money, and feel that they can trust you, they are often the best path to take for temporary relief from a lack of credit.

Objects of value can also be converted into cash through a pawn shop. Pawn shops will give you some of the value on your property, though no more than half of what they can sell it for, and you will have a certain number of months to redeem your property at a premium. If you borrow $100, it may cost you $120 to get your goods back. Pawn shops are very conservative though, and just because an object has great value to a collector, if it is not something that a pawn shop thinks it can sell easily it will not give you a loan.

Pawn shop credit does not go on your credit report. After all, if you fail to redeem on time the pawn shop just sells off the goods to make their profit. But this is just one idea, and there are probably a few more that you can come up with if you think about it for a while.

SHOULD YOU JUST CHANGE YOUR NAME AND RUN AWAY?

Yes, by all means yes. If you have gotten yourself into such a financial mess then run away and change your name. This violates all that the credit agencies try to overcome. You will lose your entire credit history, and no one will give you an open ended line of credit, but who cares.

It is possible to get in such a state that there is no hope of getting regular credit. Let us say that your credit record is full of negative statements, you have a bankruptcy against you, the IRS has a judgement on you, and you have just gotten out of jail. All of this information will be on your credit record, and no creditor in his right mind would give you a credit card or a loan.

This is a good time to find a new identity. First, there is no law against you changing your name. Second, you can move anywhere you want in our country, and most anywhere in the world. Third, the only way to change your credit report is to use a new Social Security card.

A problem arises in that it is unlawful to give false information in order to obtain credit. While they may not catch you right away, when they do they will send you to jail.

So I don't really recommend this method of dealing with conditions of bad credit. No I don't, because you can't do it without getting into trouble. Legal trouble you don't need on top of credit trouble.

Nevertheless, go onto a personal cash economy, use secured credit for as long as you need to, and play the lottery on occasion for a chance to bail yourself out all at once.

Good luck.

9 CREDIT ADVICE FOR WOMEN ONLY

Why should a chapter be devoted to the credit problems of women? After all, isn't that giving women a special advantage over men in dealing with credit? I don't see it that way. For most of the credit decisions we make men and women face the same conditions. But women also face some questions that men never have too, and just to give women an equal chance to use credit it is only fair that they get a little advice which is for them only. Naturally men can read this chapter if they want to, perhaps to give them an idea of what women are up to, but all applications are meant only for women.

THE SPECIAL PROBLEMS WOMEN FACE IN GETTING CREDIT

In America women tend to have credit problems largely because of the way in which they are thought of in society. There are two processes working against most women, that work in favor of men: women earn less money than men on average, and women tend to marry men who are older than they are. Why should these two rather unrelated facts of life have anything to do with the problems of women and credit?

Since the second is the more serious I will deal with the first at this time. In all surveys of work and pay, women earn less. They earn less over their life times, and they earn less in the jobs that they hold even if they work the same number of years. Face it, women have a lower income than men. The relationship of credit to income is very close. If you have less income you get less credit. You simply cannot qualify for many home purchases, or to buy some cars, or for many of the better credit cards. Consequently women on their own simply have less access to credit.

But what does women marrying men older than they are have to do with them getting credit. For one it means that the experience of women with credit is often cut off after they have worked only a couple of years. When men marry they already have 5 or 6 years credit history and experience, and couples then rely on the husband's credit history in the future.

After marriage the experience of women in dealing with credit often stops. Married couples usually on the husband's credit, since he is making the major part of the family income, and the man often pays all of the bills as well. As you can see women start out with less credit and less credit experience when they marry, and then progressively lose most of whatever skill they had acquired in dealing with credit throughout their married life.

Of course not all women marry, but for at least 90% of the women in our country this is a fairly accurate picture of the way in which women are set up for credit trouble. Women have to consistently assert themselves in their use of credit and dealings with money. It may not always be pleasant but women have to take on this lifelong task the way most men do, and the way all members of a family should take on the raising of children.

DO CREDITORS GIVE WOMEN A HARD TIME?

AND WHAT TO DO ABOUT IT

According to law there should be no discrimination against women from creditors. However, this does not mean that creditors won't give women a harder time then men based on their own prejudices. If you assume that credit organizations are controlled by men you will be making a safe assumption. Women may show up in positions of influence, but to depend on women to help other women in getting and dealing with credit is not going to let you function as a responsible person in credit.

According to the federal Equal Credit Opportunity Act creditors cannot deny women access to credit because of their sex, and there are provisions to help women develop the credit history that they need to have all credit privileges in our society. Before this act women could be denied credit in their own name, and creditors could require the signature of a husband or parent on the credit application of adult working women.

The act helps you to develop a credit history by requiring creditors to list both marriage partners in their credit records. Of course this can work against you if you separate from your husband and he files for bankruptcy without telling you, but that is another problem.

In spite of this act some creditors will not make the effort to put a wife on a credit account when they only deal with a husband. To check up on your credit status you need to get copies of your husband's and your credit reports from the major credit agencies to see if the same creditors are listed. If there is any discrepancy contact the creditors and remind them that by law they must list both of you as creditors of your accounts. This should probably be done once a year throughout a marriage.

Creditors seem to overlook the presence of women, and unless it is a place of business that deals extensively with women they are often treated in a demeaning manner. While credit unions treat everyone very fairly as a rule, many banks have trouble in giving credit to women that they readily give to men on the same salary. Some of the excuses you may hear, should you be turned down on a credit application, is that women your age often get married, or pregnant, and for that reason they do not receive the same consideration that a man would for the income.

Women are not as often discriminated against these days, as a result of the credit act, but you can still run into a reluctance to grant credit. The discrimination some women face can be just as serious today as in the past. In some of our smaller communities the risks are much greater because they may not be alternative credit sources available in the area. In all such cases where you have trouble getting credit when you need it cite the credit act in writing to the creditor, and if you fail to get satisfaction look into filing a law suit, with damages, against the creditor to get his attention.

WHY YOU SHOULD HAVE CREDIT IN YOUR OWN NAME

Having credit in your own name is not the same as simply being listed on joint credit accounts with a husband or parent. You need to have your own credit accounts for which you are responsible partly to be protected against any credit problems that they may have. If all of your credit is joint with your husband and he files for bankruptcy, your credit will have the bankruptcy on it for 10 years, the same as his. If you have your own separate credit accounts and your husband files for bankruptcy your own line of credit would remain clean. This could be credit that you could live a normal life on over the years that it might take your husband to clear his credit. This makes your family stronger than if all of your credit is joint.

But of course you may not be married, in which case you have no option but to build your own credit history. Or you may become divorced or widowed at some time in your life. In any of these cases you will need to have credit in your own name or you will have no credit at all.

If you have married young, without a decent chance to get credit accounts in your won name, it is still desirable that you build your own credit. In these cases you may be forced to apply for joint credit accounts initially. However, once you have joint accounts you can start applying for accounts in your own name. This is much easier to do if you are still working, and since most women work after marriage these days it should be less necessary to get joint accounts. As a general rule you need to keep your joint accounts to a minimum, and to always stress building separate credit.

HOW YOU SHOULD MANAGE YOUR MONEY FOR A GOOD CREDIT REPORT

Money management is tied very closely to credit, and most people have a very poor understanding of either one. Of course you can learn about money management through a community college or night school course, or even from the YMCA, but you do need to gain an understanding of them for your own good. Some of the basics of money management I can give you right here.

The first rule of money management is that it depends upon establishing a budget. Most families, and singles as well, do not like to live on a budget and only use a very informal budget plan to get through each month. This means that if you can establish a budget and live on it you will have much greater power than those who have not taken the trouble to gain this skill.

Your first step in setting up a budget is to list all of your sources of income and all of your regular expenses. In your income you need only list your clear pay, but also include sources such as tax returns. While it's nice to have a little pocket of cash for special purchases and events, this should only be set upon after you have taken care of your necessities. Now that you have all of the funds listed that you can expect in the coming year you need to break this down into a monthly income level, since that is how most of us pay our bills.

Now you need to take your list of regular expenses and add them all together. Regular expenses for utilities need to take into consideration the variations you have at different seasons of the year. Insurance costs, which may only be paid a few times a year, must be included, as well as property taxes if you pay these. Make an effort to be as complete as you can. Your object will be to have a budget that doesn't require you to use credit to cover regular expenses since you aren't getting any benefit from this kind of credit use. If you are a college student, or have students in the house, include their expenses as accurately as you can also. Now, as you have just added all of these set expenses together, divide this total by 12 to get an average income level necessary to pay these bills.

If your average income level is less than your average budget requirement you are in trouble, and something will have to change. Either your income is going to have to go up or your bills are going to have to come down. Other alternatives, if you have a major expense such as college expenses, that are pushing you over the edge, is to use credit to pay for the college in the expectation that your income level will increase when you are through and you will then be able to pay back your debts. While I would do that for training, I would not use credit to make utility payments since there is no way that such an investment would allow me to make more money.

In the unpleasant event that you are caught in this bind, and no easy solution presents itself, you will have to examine ways of cutting down on your expenses and/or of increasing your income. Telephone bills can often be reduced by using one of the special plans that the telephone company offers, by changing carriers for your calls, or just by restricting the time of day you call and the number of minutes you talk. Insurance may be decreased by changing the type of coverage you have. After all you don't need collision insurance on a 10 year old car with 100,000 on it. Car payments can be reduced by getting rid of the car you have and getting something cheaper. The idea is to look for any method possible to decrease the amount of money you have to write in checks through the year until it is less than your income, and it has to be less than your income for you to be credit worthy.

When you have cut out all of the expenses you can, and you still have less income than you need, it is time to look for ways in which you can increase your income. The most direct solution is to take on an additional job. Such 2nd jobs pay notoriously badly, and you may be in better shape if you can find some way of getting overtime at your current job. If you don't currently work you may have to go to work. It is my philosophy that even if you don't have to work you should do something for which you are paid, even if it is at a minimum wage, so that your can build your own credit history later on.

On to the next step. You have now established an average monthly income level greater than your average monthly payments for your regular expenses. The income that you have available at this point is what you are going to use to set up a savings account, and to pay for those things which you want, but which are not absolutely necessary for life. While you will have to make these decisions according to your own needs, at least 10% of this money must be put away into a savings account to take care of emergencies. Without an emergency account you will always be subject to having a great need arise in your life, and not being able to take care of it. Putting off tuneups on your car is going to cost you in the end when your car breaks down, so having money in the bank for tuneups, as well as repairs, is actually a necessity and not a choice that you are free to make or ignore.

In this portion of your budget include money for recreation, since everyone needs to have fun once in a while. Vacations if you take them, gifts for Christmas and Birthdays, and anything else important in your life. If your budget is very close you may not have much money to put toward each of these uses, but at least you will know what you have and be able to make adjustments accordingly. Included in this phase of your budget should also be new credit needs. If you need a car you should budget the $200 a month that it will cost. Of course it may be more or less than that amount, but that is up to you and how much money you have to work with. If you are looking to buy furniture, budget that, or to outfit yourself for a new job or your children for school, allocate money toward those areas. Leave as much flexibility as you can in your budget, but make sure that you cover all of the important points so that bills don't pop up each month that ruin your budget. If this happens once or twice go back to the top of this section and start your budget all over again. Your budget should be sufficient to cover all of your expenses 11 months out of the year, with enough extra available to finance or pay any emergencies that come up.

Buy now that you have a budget, and some money to work with, you are ready to go about building your own credit history. Go on to the next section and we will see what we can discover that will help you along the way.

TIPS ON BUILDING YOUR OWN CREDIT HISTORY

We will begin with the steps to building a credit history to be taken by the married woman. In order to get credit you need to have assets, and if you are married and do not have assets in your own name make sure that all of your joint assets are listed in both your name and your husband's name. Every time you apply for credit in your name you can then list your joint assets. Assets of this type will include your home, cars, bank accounts, stock, boats, motor homes, and even vacation homes.

Request a copy of the credit records for you and your husband from each of the three credit reporting agencies. The list of the big three is included in this book along with their addresses. Examine these reports carefully to see which ones are keeping a separate credit file on you. If you have a credit file look it over carefully for negative statement, and to see if all areas of joint credit that you have with your husband is also included in your record. If there are inaccuracies go through the steps that were laid out in dealing with credit reporting agencies to clean up reports.

If you are married check the reports to see the credit you had established beforehand is included. Since you will have changed your name, the credit reports may have missed the change and started you all over with a new record. This can be very damaging to you if you had maintained a healthy credit report up to that time. If your single credit history information is not included in your credit report write to the credit agencies and instruct them to add it. A fee may be charged, but it should be minor.

Now that you have a credit record in your own name it is time to start building a current credit history. The most direct, and one of the most useful ways to go about building your credit is by getting a small cash loan from a bank in which you have a savings account. The money in your savings will serve to secure your loan, and obtaining and paying back this loan will establish you with the bank for future loans should you have the necessity of borrowing in your own name. If you are single this is a good way to start build a good credit history, and even if you are married you can never tell when you might be single through divorce. You may even get the idea to buy something that you don't want your husband involved in, and this would make it possible for you to get the money without regard to your husband's credit record.

If you do not already have a bank that knows you personally, you will need to shop around. Go to two or three banks, if that is necessary, and explain that you are looking for a cash loan. You can use any purpose you want, and keep the amount small - either $500 or $1000 are nice round figures. Talk to the loan officer, and if you get favorable answers to your request for a loan open a savings account and a checking account to establish yourself. In this way the bank will get to know you through your contacts of making payments and maintaining the checking and savings accounts. The better they get to know you personally the more cooperative they will be if you approach them for another loan or a credit card.

Depending upon your assets the bank will be making you either an asset secured loan or a cash secured loan. With an asset secured loan you may be putting up a car or household furnishings as collateral for the loan. It is usually easy to get car loans from banks because the car acts as security for the loan, and can be seized and sold if you default on your payments. To get a cash secured loan you may even have to put the loan amount in an account. In this case you won't have direct use of the money until you pay off the loan, but that should be acceptable if you are not borrowing the money to make a purchase. If you default on the loan the bank keeps the money, and if you make all of your payments the bank gets the interest while keeping the money locked up in its own vaults.

Now if you need the loan for something other than property that can act as collateral, like a vacation, the bank may ask you to get a co-signer. Since you are trying to establish a credit history which is independent of your husbands do not ask him to be your co-signer. Find another friend or relative to be your co-signer instead.

When the loan is paid off get a copy of your credit record to see that all payments are accurately reported. Also check with the loan officer to see if your loan has been reported onto your credit history. Should you default on your loan do not approach this bank for another loan. You need to start over with a new bank and try to carry out the loan and repayment without problems.

Once everything is free and clear on the first loan you will have to make a decision on what you wish to do next. You can apply for a second loan, or for a credit card at the same bank, or from some other source using your credit record at the first bank as evidence of your responsibility. In all such cases make all of your payments on time, and never charge more than you can handle. Especially when you are first starting to use credit and haven't yet built up a track record, banks and other credit issuers will cancel your credit much more rapidly than someone who has made payments to them for 20 years, and has only recently made some late payments.

WHAT TO DO IF YOU ALREADY HAVE GOOD CREDIT

AND GETTING MARRIED

Not all women enter marriage as credit novices. Today, in our liberated world, women in their later 20s and 30s are getting married for the first time after having used credit for several years. These women may have just as productive careers as the men they marry, as well as have purchased homes and cars on their own income.

If you are one of these women you know all of the basics about credit. You have your own credit cards and charge accounts. You even have a well established credit history at the credit bureaus. But in getting married your credit is going to be subject to stresses and strain that it has never faced before.

Are you going to maintain all of your own lines of credit, or are you gong to combine them into joint accounts with your husband.

Some credit will become joint no matter what you want. If you decide to buy a house it will probably take both of your incomes to qualify for the one you want.   And most of your purchases in the future will be joint just because the decisions will involve both of you.

Now, some good advice. If you have good credit when you get married do everything that you can to keep it. Keep your own credit cards, as well as bank account. You should   probably keep both a checking account and a savings account in your name. While you may have to use joint credit for many of your purposes there is no reason to merge all other credit sources that you have.

No men change their name when they marry, but if you do, notify your creditors immediately, to report your credit to the credit bureaus in your married name from then on. Wait a few months and request copies of your credit report from each of the credit reporting agencies.

Of course if you have no credit history when you marry start taking the steps to establish it. There is a whole section on this so I will not go into detail here on how to establish your credit history.

HOW YOUR HUSBAND'S BANKRUPTCY AFFECTS YOUR CREDIT

If your husband files for bankruptcy you need to know how you are going to be affected, and basically since marriage is considered a legal condition of joint responsibility your assets are going to come under the same laws as those of your husbands. Of course in marriage most of your assets will be jointly owned, and most credit accounts will also be joint. It is really impossible to come out of a bankruptcy with good credit if your husband has entangled you in credit problems.

But there may be relief if you are divorced. Of course you may still have joint assets after a divorce, and it is these that will affect you in the case. If an ex-husband files for bankruptcy you may lose property that was coming to you as a part of the divorce settlement, and he may not be able to obtain the credit he needs to maintain his obligations to you and your children. Bankruptcy does not affect your right to alimony or child support, or back taxes that are owed.

However, in most states property acquired during marriage is considered to be community property. If you later divorce and your spouse files bankruptcy, your creditors can come after any community property that is still left from the marriage on the grounds that both parties are equally liable for debts incurred during a marriage even it was principally the fault of one member that the debts were not paid.

In such a case you do not have to just go along with the bankruptcy and lose your property. While you can file for bankruptcy protection as well, if you have the money you can offer to pay off the back debts. If that is not possible at this time, but you still want to avoid bankruptcy, contact the creditors and try to work out a payment schedule that will let you avoid bankruptcy. You are going to have to talk to each creditor directly, and only write it you aren't able to talk to a representative personally. Tell them that you are involved in a divorce and that you want to avoid the bankruptcy even if your ex-husband goes ahead with his filing.   Let them know what your income is and what you have available to debt repayment. Since creditors will be better off with a slow payback of their money than with a bankruptcy they will usually cooperate in giving you a monthly repayment plan that you can live with.

If you do not feel up to carrying out this negotiation yourself contact the Consumer Credit Counseling, or CCC, office in your area. These are consumer groups set up to assist citizens who have gotten into credit difficulties that they can't handle. Just check your local phone book for a representative near you.

That is about all of the advice I can give you should you be caught in a bankruptcy action which is not your fault. Try to protect your credit and work things out with your creditors.   Perhaps community property isn't all that its cracked up to be sometimes, but if that is state law than you are just going to have to deal with it.

HOW DOES DIVORCE AFFECT YOUR CREDIT?

Frankly, it depends upon how well you have planned for your divorce. If you came into the marriage, as many women do, with very little credit history and then let your husband handle all of the money and credit through most of the marriage you are probably very poorly prepared for what you are about to face. In the first place you may have no independent credit history, and even if the credit agencies are required to have listed you on joint accounts, they may not have even known that you exist. In such a case you are a non-person so far as credit is concerned.

This problem could have easily been avoided if you had planned for the possibility of divorce while you were married. Since around 50% of all American marriages end in divorce it is foolish to think that it could never happen to you. Divorce is more common at all ages below 60 than is being widowed. And the fewer years that you have been married the more likely you are to have a divorce.

There is one factor of American life that makes this little scene much less likely, most married women work today, where they did not work a few years ago. With the women's movement and the poor economy of the past 15 years women have not only had the opportunity to go to work in more jobs, they have been forced to work in order to support their families. Most middle class families cannot live on a single salary, whether from a man or a woman. It is only the truly wealthy who can afford to have the wife follow other pursuits than making money.. Unfortunately this trend to have working wives results in less time together for couples, which mean less reliance upon one another to give and receive comfort or to share their lives. Naturally this results in more divorces since many couples who have been married several years barely know each other any longer. The tendency of the American workplace to keep wage levels as low as possible has resulted in fewer families and a greater likelihood that a woman will have one or more divorces in her lifetime.

But enough of this. Your problem is how to prepare for a divorce, whether or not you anticipate getting one in the future. Think of this as a guide to protecting yourself in case the worst happens. If it doesn't happen you will not have hurt yourself by knowing what to do should be suddenly be called upon to handle your own credit responsibilities.

HOW YOU CAN PLAN FOR A DIVORCE

If you are anticipating a divorce in the near future, or just want to take precautions for your own protection, there are 5 steps you need to go through in order to plan for a divorce. A divorce is often seen as one of the great failures of our lives, but if it is considered just another trial of life through which many of us must go through you can forget about trying to place blame on one side or another. Even if the divorce is entirely the fault of your husband, it is no reason to ruin your life with hate and regret while you can plan a new life and treat it as a learning experience. Learn what is offered here to protect your credit when you divorce and you may come out stronger than when your were married.

Step 1: Establish your own credit history. This must be separate and distinct from your husband. The method is given in a previous section. Getting your own credit history is basic to everything else you are going to do to prepare for your impending divorce. If you should be questioned about this by your husband never admit that you are doing it because you are planning to get a divorce. Just state that getting your own credit is a way of strengthening your families finances since if anything happens to his credit then you could still use yours for needed expenses. Of course it is better if your husband does not find out since he may not believe your story, and your divorce could come about before you are ready for it.

Step 2: As long as you are married use joint funds to pay for joint responsibilities. Unless you have a source of income that you have kept separate throughout your marriage you will need to use the income you receive, and the income your husband receives, to make payments on all joint credit. This would include mortgage payments, joint credit cards, loans you have taken out in both of your names, and even cars if both of your names have gone onto the pinkslip. The reason for paying these down as low as possible while you are married is that joint debts may be split at the divorce and become your exclusive responsibility afterwards. Half of the debts may prove to be a bigger problem then it sounds if your income goes down by more than half when you get divorced.

Step 3: This is something discussed in terms of building your own credit history. Get copies of your credit record from each of the three major credit reporting agencies. Even if you already have credit in your own name get the credit report for you and your husband as well. You need this report in order to clear up any problems you find. All problem remarks on your own record need to be cleared, and as many of those on your joint accounts as well. Since this may take several months it is best to undertake it while you are married. Again, try not to involve him, but if he finds out what you are doing just explain that you are trying to clear up any negative information on your credit record.

Step 4: If you have negative statements on your joint credit record that you can't clear up before your impending divorce comes about write out a detailed explanation of the reasons for the poor report. Of course you are going to blame everything on your husband, unless something is clearly your own fault. Then, after you have filed for divorce, send your explanation to each of the credit bureaus and ask that it be placed into your credit record. Keep a copy of your explanation available and give the same information on any credit applications you make until your credit is clear. Creditors appreciate honesty much more than they do someone trying to hide negative information from them. Do not put this into the credit record before you have filed for divorce or your husband may find out.

Step 5: Find a lawyer or financial advisor you can trust and discuss your approaching divorce with them. You are interested in anything they can tell you in regard to protecting yourself financially. You should do this discreetly. After all, your husband will meet your lawyer soon enough anyway without him doing it while you are still together.

However, if you husband gets wind of what is going on and files for bankruptcy while you are trying to get your divorce the divorce proceedings will probably be halted until your creditors are taken care of. This would be a smart move by your husband since any property which is joint could be taken to retire his debts as well as yours. If this happens immediately see a lawyer and sue any legal methods possible to protect yourself financially. Even if there is nothing you can do during the bankruptcy, have the lawyer help you prepare for your divorce as soon as it is possible to proceed.

WHAT HAPPENS TO YOUR CREDIT WHEN YOU BECOME A WIDOW

This may be the worst thing that can happen to many women. After all, what do you do if you had not handled the family finances for many years and your husband dies. You are suddenly thrust into the role of money manager and responsible for dealing with all the bills and bookkeeping of living. This is a time when you seek advice from many people, and having something here to serve as a guide to get you started is very useful. There is no reason that you can't learn those things that you must know to manage your money. You will not only have control of the bills and income, but may have to make decisions regarding large sums of money from insurance and pensions. Look this over even if you are not a widow, and keep it in mind should your need be for more than just information.

Preparing to manage your credit after becoming a widow is much like preparing for a divorce. The steps are given in detail in the divorce section, and consist of building a credit history for yourself, getting copies of your credit record and removing or explaining negative information, and consulting with a financial advisor as to future management of your assets and income.

The great fear of any happily married woman is that she may be suddenly widowed. Besides the grief and disorientation in the world that this produces, it also prevents any preparation. In such a case you may well be caught without a credit history, have a credit report that you have not seen, and which contains negative statements that will injure you in the future. Creditors that you were not aware of may begin sending overdue notices, and may even require that you apply for credit in your own name if credit was originally granted to you based on your husband's income. If you had credit accounts in your own name, and based on your own income, it is unlikely that you will be required to apply again for the same lines of credit.

In the case of such a sudden death you can gain some time by delaying the reporting of your husband's death to your creditors for 2 or 3 months. It is not wise to wait longer then this or you could be charged with fraud for withholding information in order to gain the use of credit. But a delay of up to 3 months should be no problem. In this period of time get all of your families finances in order. List all of your debts and obligations, sources of income and assets. Find out how you stand financially, and get your credit records from the credit reporting agencies. You should do this as rapidly as possible and then inform all creditors directly of the death of your husband. Put it off no longer than you can help since your future use of credit may be prejudiced against you if creditors find out in some indirect manner that your husband died some time before and that you have been withholding information from them.

Some widows make the mistake of simply continuing to use joint credit account for years after a husband's death, and then find that they cannot borrow to buy a car or even an appliance. In a routine check the credit company finds out that your husband has died and that you have no credit history. They then make the decision that you are financially unstable, and feel that they can't trust you to give them truthful information in your credit application.

On applying for your own credit you may have trouble qualifying for the amounts you want based on your income. You should be sure to include income sources such as annuities, pensions, social security payments, and disability payments. You may have other sources of income as well as a result of your husband's death. Creditors must take all these into consideration, although it is generally true that a widow's income level will be less than when her husband was alive. Creditors are allowed to weigh these sources of income according to their reliability. Thus, if you are getting a supplementary social security payment for minor children a creditor could discount most of this money on the basis that you would not be receiving it for a time sufficient to cover your use of credit. The same may be true of an annuity if it had a life, and some annuities have lives of only 5 or 10 years. Lottery winnings have 20 lives, and if you were in the last 5 years of this source of income a creditor would be justified in ignoring this income in making a credit granting decision.

In addition, when you apply for credit in order to build your own credit history, any information in your joint credit accounts that applies to you as well as to your husband should be included in your new credit history. If you were working at the time that you qualified for a form of credit, point this out to the credit agencies, as well as to creditors to whom you are applying. It may be difficult to justify the inclusion of this information in your favor so gather any documentation that you can including tax returns or pay stubs that would show your contribution.

When a husband dies it often takes a month or two before insurance proceeds are received or bank accounts are made available where you were named as a beneficiary. And even before the processing begins you are going to have to file a claim. The claim must be accompanied by a copy of the death certificate as well as any claim forms required. Because all that you may have in the meantime is your husband's last paycheck or pension check, it is important that you have your own credit established long before an emergency occurs. While having money in a private bank account may be best it is not always possible, and having a line of credit to help you out for that critical first month or two can be vital. There are enough decisions to make at this time without worrying about buying food and making your house payment.

Most deaths result in a process called probate, in which your husband's obligations and assets are placed. His debts will be paid out of this probate proceeding and divisions of property will be made between heirs. For the most part this will pay off your obligations. However, property debts, such as car and house loans, will not be paid off, and debts that are in your name will not be affected. You are going to have to continue to deal with these just as you did when your husband was alive.

The amount of credit you need to have in your own name to get you through this period is up to you. It can be as little as $1,000, or as high as $10,000. I would judge that, for most women, a line of credit of $5,000 would be sufficient to cover expenses for a month or two, until all benefits were received and probate was completed.

10 HOW TO SLASH YOUR INTEREST RATE

If you are like millions of Americans, you are carrying a balance on your credit card. The higher the interest rate, the more difficult it will be for you to pay off your balance and crawl out of your personal, self-created nightmare of plastic debt.

Carrying credit card debt is bad enough, but credit card debt with super high interest rates of 18 percent and beyond is plain ridiculous. If you cannot pay off your entire balance in a very short time, you can, at the very least, slash your interest rate, so that each time you make a payment a bigger portion will come off the principle, rather than be drained away by the high finance charge

So how do you do it? Will your credit card company simply lower your credit rating because you ask them to nicely? You may surprised to know that the answer can often be "Yes!" Give it a try. Call your credit card company and give them your best story. Tell them that you simply want to catch up on your payments, improve your financial situation and continue to be a good customer. Many credit card banks will view this attitude with respect. After all, they are interested in doing business with you. In any kind of business, all is fair in love and war. Sometimes a lower interest rate is yours for the asking.

BUT NOW FOR THE MORE LIKELY REALITY:

More often than not, when you ask for a lower interest rate, the answer will be "Sorry, can't do that." Credit card companies have a certain fear that if they give one guy a break, they'll have to give everyone a break. Therefore, you'll have to provide them with some incentive to deal with you.

Fortunately for you, there is plenty of incentive at your fingertips.As credit card distributors get ever more competitive, more and more companies are seeking to attract customers with lower interest rates. And they don't stop there. Many credit companies are actively seeking to "buy out" their competitor's card holders.

You can take advantage of this growing competition. Your first step is to simply find a competing credit card company that has an interest rate lower than your current card company. From this point, you can proceed in one of two ways:

1. Call the company with the lower rate and tell them you want to transfer your current account to them. Most credit card companies will be glad to take you on. You may even get a super low introductory rate that will slash your interest rate to a 6 percent or lower for a limited period of time. This will make it even easier for you to catch up on your balance, and even pay your total in full.

2. Another way to lower your interest rate is to locate a card company with a lower interest rate, and then call your current card company. Tell them this: "Look, I want to remain a card holder with your company and continue to give you my business. But the XYZ Company offers all the same services as you, but their interest rate is 6 points lower than yours. Now, I have contacted the XYZ Company and they have agreed to take me on at their lower rate. I am calling you to give you the opportunity to match their rate. Can we do business?"

Most of the time the answer will be yes. Card companies know that sometimes they either must compromise, or loose their customers in droves to the competition.

Try this method of lowering your interest rate. You have nothing to loose but bigger payments on your balance.

SLASH YOUR PAYMENT IN HALF

Is it possible to cut your current credit card payment in half? Yes, this is possible 100 percent of the time, but you may have to make a sacrifice of your own, although some would not consider this action to be a sacrifice.

If you are having trouble making your current payment, your best bet is to contact your card company directly and just be honest. Tell them: "I'm getting into a bit of trouble here. I want to pay my bill in full and in a timely manner, but my current payments are so high, I just can't handle them anymore. I would like to cut my payments in half for the next six months (or year). In exchange, I will forgo further use of my card while I catch up and bring my balance under control."

Most often, the card holder will agree to this prudent action. They may add a stipulation, however, that your interest rate will be higher during the period of lower payments. While this will offset the benefit of cutting your payments in half, this will give you some breathing room until you get on your feet again. It will also break your habit of debiting. Six months from now, you may be more than ready to make bigger payments, and get back to your former lower rate of interest.

This strategy, then, is designed for you to give a little so that you can get a little. It may be painful for you, but it's a sensible strategy for those who want to get off the destructive bandwagon of credit card debiting.

11

HOW TO BUY A HOME WITH NO MONEY DOWN

I want you to strongly consider buying your own home. Why? Because nothing puts you in better financial standing than being a home owner. The entire credit community will look at you differently if you own your own home — even if you are buried under 35 years of payments!

A home is equity. Unlike rent, which goes out the window and out of your financial life every time you pay it, a house payment is an investment in your own life, and in your own ability to borrow and earn money. If you buy a house for $50,000 today, chances are it will be worth $100,000 before you finish paying for it. Of course, there are a lot of variable that come into play — interest rates, neighborhood, type of home, city and state, etc. But generally, a home almost always increases in value, and most often, increases greatly.

Most people never consider buying homes for the oldest reason on earth — money! Or lack of it, to be more precise. But now the good news. There is no reason why you can't buy your own home right away without paying a penny for a down payment. Not only is this easy, there are more than a half dozen ways to do it! Let's look at some of the best:

THE GOVERNMENT

First of all, the U.S. government is one of the biggest holders of private property in the country, and much of it they can't wait to get rid of.

HUD, the Department of Housing and Urban Development, has many programs designed to help people buy homes with guaranteed loan programs, grant programs, very low-interest rate programs — and HUD even has a program in which they will sell you an entire home for $1!

Forget the mortgage or the down payment, you may be able to buy your own home from the federal government for a buck.

HUD as a program called Urban Homesteading. Under this program, single homes that have been abandoned for one reason or another, and which were insured by Uncle Sam, can be sold for $1, rather than letting the home stand empty.

The houses are turned over to local communities, which in turn must sell them to low-income families, or other qualified buyers for $1.

To find out if such a house is close to you, write or call:

HUD

451 7th St. SW

Washington, DC 20410

Phone: 202-755-8702

But HUD has other programs as well, such as the program under Section 203(b). This allows anyone to apply for an FHA-insured loan, which may lower the amount of the down payment you must put up to nearly zero. The ceiling for this program is $125,000, which will still buys a decent home in just about any city or state of the USA.

Another way you can get a home without a down payment through HUD is to take over payments on one of their assumable FHA loan programs. In this case, HUD has houses for sale, which for whatever reason, the original owner was unable to make payments. All you have to do is agree to assume the monthly payments and the house is yours without a down payment.

Again, you can contact HUD at the number given above to find out more about these programs.

DON'T FORGET THE VA

If you are a veteran of military service, you almost certainly can get a house without a down payment through a Veteran's Affairs Housing Program. But here's good news for the rest of you — the VA also offers this program to many non-veterans!

As it happens, many veterans themselves default on homes they obtained through the VA. These homes are in turn offered to any buyer who can take over payments — often without a down payment.

For more information on how to get a low-cost, no-down-payment, or low-interest loan house through the VA, call or write:

Veteran Administration

810 Vermont Ave. N.W.

Washington, D.C. 20420

Phone: 202-393-4120

Try This Little Known Method to Defer a Home Down Payment:

If HUD or the VA fails you, there are still some excellent and workable strategies for buying a home without a down payment. Follow closely now, and I'll explain a way:

You can buy a home and include the down payment in the overall sales price. This method works best with homes that have been on the market a long time, and thus have owners that are willing to engage in creative financing techniques to unload them.

How do you find a home that's been on the market along time? Well, you may already know about a few. Some of the houses in your town or neighborhood may have had "For Sale" signs in front of them for months on end. If you try, I'm sure you can remember where one or two of those houses are right now. But a truly reliable way to find homes that haven't sold for a while is to check back copies of your local newspaper a the library. There you'll easily spot homes that have been sitting vacant and without buyers, possibly for years.

Also, try to find a house that is being sold by directly by the owner or a building contractor. Because they have not been able to unload their property for a long time, they will be willing to work with you in the way I am about to describe.

Arrange a meeting with the home owner. Tell them that you have scoped out several homes, that you have never bought a home before, and that you are extremely interested in closing a deal. Tell the owner that you want to confirm the sale of the house by signing a contract which states that the down payment will be included in the contract, and that the owner will pay all closing costs.

If you are still a bit confused, I'll take you through the process now step-by-step:

1. Have the owner state in the contract that the entire down payment is to be paid at the final closing of the house purchase.

2. When the contract is signed, you give the home owner a check for $500, which is a necessary deposit on the house. (Which will later be refunded to you — read on).

3. When approval comes from the mortgage company for the sale, arrange a time and date to close the sale with the seller. That may be in his home, or possibly at his or your attorney's office.

4. At the time of the settlement, the attorney will ask for your down payment, usually 5 percent of total house value. A $50,000 house will fetch a $2,500 down payment. You give the attorney a check for $2,500. After the settlement is complete, the seller then gives you a check for the same amount.

5. The house is now yours. The seller is happy because he has sold his house and has his money from the mortgage holder. He doesn't care about the down payment because it has been included in the total purchase price of the house. The bank is happy because it has sold the house in a proper way, down payment made, and everything else in order. You are happy because you have bought your home with paying a hefty down payment. You did pay a $500 deposit but that can be taken off the total purchase price, or you can arrange to have it refunded by the seller if the money is included in the total purchase price.

There are several variation on the above method, such as the "secured trust method." In this case, you get the seller to hold a second trust for the down payment. This will help the seller because it can help him avoid paying taxes on profits from the second trust until the next year.

DON'T FORGET ...

Don't forget one this common method of owning your own home: "Rent to Own!" This gives you the best of both worlds. Renters don't like to buy because they like the freedom to pick up stakes and move whenever they want. Home owners like the financial advantages of owning their own home. You can find a rent to own home situation in just about any city. This means no down payment — you just start paying rent like you would for any rental property. At some point, however, you can decide to buy. At that point, all your rental payments become house payments.

Disadvantages of rent-to-own may be higher interest rates, so be careful. Still, this is a super easy way to own your own home with no down payment.

12 WAYS TO CREATE, MAKE AND RAISE YOUR OWN CREDIT

One of the most hackneyed phrases about money is still one of the most true: it takes money to make money. It's far easier for people who have money to make more money because they can take advantage of investment strategies that require large chunks of up-front cash. If you don't have it, you can't play the game ... or can you?

The truth is, there are many ways to make money on investments, even if you don't have a single sickly upfront dime to spare. The answer is to leverage easy sources of credit, put the money into high-yield enterprises, collect your profits, pay back the money you borrowed — and keep the return on your investment.

First, a little common sense math. The easiest way to borrow large sums of money with no collateral and a minimal credit rating is through credit cards, which are as easy to get these days as bottled water. But even at an introductory rate of 6.9 percent, which many card companies offer, you will not be able to find an investment that returns a greater percentage in a short period of time. Remember, a 6.9% rate usually last only 6 months to a year.

Therefore, you must find those situations in which you can turn the figures around, that is, borrow money at low interest rates, and invest it in places that will earn very high rates of return. It's not as hard as you think. What follows then are five ways that you can make money with borrowed money. First, we will name five ways to borrow money at little or no interest. Then we'll follow them with five investment strategies that will help you make a profit on the money you borrow.

1. FORM YOUR OWN CORPORATION

Forming your own corporation is actually quite easy. It's a matter of filling out the proper forms and filing them with the proper offices. (See xxx on how to form your own corporation). In many cases, you can hire an attorney, or better yet, a paralegal to do the job for you, often for less than $200.

But once you have formed your corporation, you have given yourself several advantages in your ability to leverage credit. One of the best ways is to sell private stock in your own corporation. In most cases, you do not need permission from the Securities and Exchange Commission to sell private stock in your own corporation, but you should check with your attorney or ask your banker to make sure. You must not exceed 25 people, or it will be considered a public offering.

This is the way wealthy people make money with the money of other people. Instead of risking their own piles of cash, they simply shelter themselves with corporations of their own creation and then entice ordinary people like you to stick their money into it. This way, they literally make money by using other people's money.

Rich people do it, and so can you!

Offer your stock at whatever people will pay. You may have to guarantee a certain percentage of return, but that percentage can be volumes lower than in what you will invest the money in for your own purposes.

2. SEEK PERSONAL LOANS

Instead of borrowing from a bank, borrow from a private individual, and cut your own deal. This is done a lot more often than you might think. To find people willing to borrow you money from their private account, place a classified ad in the "business opportunities" section of your newspaper or a money-oriented magazine. Some common ads of nature read like this:

Silent partner wanted to invest capital in promising venture. Call: xxx-xxxx

Seeking investors to establish new business.

Call xxx-xxxx.

Need $10,000 immediately for crystal import venture. Double your money possible. Call xxx-xxxx.

3. BORROW FROM UNCLE SAM

The U.S. Small Business Administration will borrow anyone up to $15,000 without a dime of collateral. You get the money on your name and signature alone. The drawback is that the SBA usually attaches a lot of strings to what you do with the money, but that doesn't mean you can't reap huge profits anyway. After all, the SBA is interested in helping you succeed in a small business.

Many Other U.S. Agencies provide more direct financial support in the forms of guarantees, loans, leases, and grants.

Some of these agencies are:

DOA/ASCS. Department of Agriculture/Agriculture Stabilization & Conservation Service.

DOA/FmHA. Department of Agriculture/Farmers Home Administration.

DOA/REA. Department of Agriculture/Rural Electrification Administration.

DOC/MA. Department of Commerce/Maritime Administration.

DOC/NOAA. Department of Commerce/National Oceanic & Atmospheric Administration.

DOE. Department of Energy.

DOE/ICP. Department of Energy/Innovative Concepts Program (ICP).

DOI/BIA. Department of the Interior/Bureau of Indian Affairs.

DOI/GS. Department of the Interior/Geological Survey.

Ex/Im. Export/Import Bank (although independent, finances U.S. Company exports and imports).

NIST/ATP. National Institute of Standards and Technology/Advanced Technology Program (ATP).

NIST/ERIP. National Institute of Standards and Technology/Energy-Related Inventions Program(ERIP).

NIST/MEP. National Institute of Standards and Technology/Manufacturing Extension Partnership (MEP).

NIST/N-ERIP. National Institute of Standards and Technology/Non-Energy Related Inventions Program (N-ERIP).

OPIC. Overseas Private Investment Corporation.

SBA/SBIR. Small Business Administration/Small Business Innovative Research (SBIR) program.

SBA/STTR. Small Business Administration/Small Business Technology Transfer (STTR) program.

NTIS. National Technology Information Service,

5285 Port Royal Road, Springfield, VA 22161

4. SEEK VENTURE CAPITAL

Many individuals and companies deal in venture capital. Venture capital are funds invested or available for investment in business plans which carry considerable risk of loss, but also have potential for enormous profits.

To find sources of venture capital in your state, contact your state department of commerce and they'll tell you where you can find venture capital sources.

Before you decide to seek venture capital, decide just what you want to use it for. Here are the most common uses of venture capital:

STARTUP FUNDING

Use this for earliest stage of business, starting from scratch, etc. In this case, you will get your money based on your business plan. The more detailed and credible your business plan, the better.

FIRST ROUND FUNDING

This is money for growth in a business you already have. Funding is often in the form of a loan or convertible bond.

SECOND ROUND FUNDING

Money for an established company where a future buyout, merger or acquisition by another company is a possibility.

LATER STAGE FUNDING

For an established company where money is needed to support major expansion or new product development.

EQUITY LOAN

This is a situation in which you offer the venture capitalist an ownership position to induce the loan. Also, is can be a loan that has an option to convert from debt to equity.

MEZZANINE FUNDING

This means your company has made enough progress to sell stock to the public and venture capital is needed to support his effort.

MERGER AND ACQUISITION

This sounds like what it is — joining your company with another. Yes, this still qualifies as venture capital if it means building up your company's assets. If one company survives it is a merger, if both survive it is an acquisition.

WHAT'S THE BEST APPROACH

Once you have decided what kind of Venture Capital situation you are in, how exactly do yo work with a venture capital firm? How should you approach and evaluate a firm and any financing it might provide for your company?

As you might have guessed, venture capital firms are as different as entrepreneurs. There's a wide variety among these firms in terms of their industry expertise, business experience and, most importantly, their ability to work effectively with you.

Your selection of a venture capital firm is more about "How much money will this firm make me?" rather than: "How much money can I borrow?" That's because your venture firm, if used right, will most likely be an influential element in the ongoing decision making process of your company.

The venture capitalist can add a whole new level of experience to your corporate problems because such a company has most likely been involved in a wide variety of other ventures with other firms. You not only get their money, you get their expertise — (even if you don't want it sometimes!)

The experience of the venture capital firm enables it to recognize patterns within your company that may have been may be invisible to you.

When you select a venture firm, expect almost a partnership that will last five to ten years or more and which can be a pivotal factor in turning your company into a major enterprise. Because of the rate at which a high growth venture company encounters new challenges, decision making times can be greatly shortened.

A good venture capital firm will reinforces what's good about your company, and shore up the areas in which your company is weak. The less experience you have in some matters, the more you may need to rely on your venture firm's advice. The more experience you have, the more you will appreciate the quality of the advice.

Remember, a venture capital firm only makes money when you make money. Therefore, they will be vitally interested in helping you succeed. Because of this, a key question to ask yourself is: "Do I believe that I can develop a relationship with this firm that I can have confidence in, which will help me solve problems, and help me grow?

If you can easily answer yes to all, you've found your venture capital firm. Most likely, you will want a venture capital firm that will just give you your money and then go away! There's nothing wrong with that, but I encourage you to look at all the positive aspects of letting the venture capital firm help you become better, and using the often excellent advice and expertise they have to offer.

5. MONEY FROM YOUR HOUSE

One of the easiest sources of money is a second mortgage on your home. If you have been making payments on your current home for a number of months, you have already built up a considerable equity. Also, you home has likely increased in value since you bought it.

You may be able to receive as much as 80 percent of the value of your home, less the amount you still owe on the first mortgage.

Many firms advertise home equity loans with "no credit check." This means that no mater how bad your credit has been in the past, you can get a loan against your house if your house payments are current.

The downside, of course, is that fact that you are betting your home on your investment. If your investment pays off big, you're doing great. If it flops, you could lose your home! Hey, I never said all sources of credit are without risk! Just keep in mind that some of life's greatest rewards go to the boldest ... but that doesn't mean you should be stupid!

Now that you have five methods of raising fast, low-interest money, here are five dynamic investment strategies that could help you strike in rich.

1. THE BEST INVESTMENT — YOURSELF

When many people think of investment, words like bonds, mutual funds, and stocks immediately come to mind. You can money with all of the above, but bonds and the rest all take something you may not have a lot of — time. Even the highest yielding bonds and mutual funds take months and years to get results. But you want to turn the cash you have borrowed into profits within days or weeks.

Therefore, I suggest that you first invest in yourself — that is, in your own business, in your own ideas, in your own ability to work and take risks. Make a commitment to use the money you have borrowed, not just to pay bills and buy the things you want, but to start the profit-making enterprise of your choice.

2. REAL ESTATE

One of the fastest ways to make huge profits in almost no time is to buy real estate at rock bottom and sell it at premium prices.

Fortunately, it is almost too easy to get your hands on houses and land for just pennies in the dollar of what it's worth. You do this by attending tax delinquency and lien sales. These sale are made to recover unpaid taxes on property. Check with your county assessor for times and dates of such auctions in your area. It is not uncommon to buy a $60,000 home for as little as $3,000.

This investment strategy has not only worked for thousands of people, but it has made many people filthy rich. I can't think of one reason why you should not look into this and give it a try.

3. INVESTING IN DISCOUNTED MORTGAGES

Another real estate oriented investment strategy which can yield you up to 30 percent return on your money involves discounted, or second mortgages.

The reason this is such a great opportunity for investment is that many mortgage holders do not like having their money tied up for 20 to 30 years. Most people like the idea of having ready cash on hand, instead of receiving monthly payments for what seems like forever.

Your job is to offer the mortgage holder a price which is below the face value of the mortgage. Usually, you should begin negotiations at 60 percent of the face value. You can then work up to 75 percent and still make a 25 percent profit on your investment. Sometimes, when the holder of the mortgage needs cash fast, you can obtain the mortgage for as little as 35 to 40 percent of the face value.

Here's an advantage: Often, the real estate for which you have the second mortgage, is sold after 10 or 15 years because the owners died, divorced, or just could no longer make the payments. While the first mortgage holder is guaranteed payment for his investment before you are, most of the time the property is sold for a high enough price to pay everyone off.

Before actually getting involved with a second mortgage, check the credit history of the person who will be paying the bills. If the person has a good track record of paying all bills completely and on time, chances are they will be a good risk. Being a discounted mortgage buyer is especially good for investors who have some capital—at least $15,000—to play with. You can find second mortgages available for as little as $2,000 or as high as $50,000, and the returns can be significant.

As with any major investment, being successful at buying real estate for profit hinges as much on knowing the market as it does on luck. Understand what you want in an investment, and know what the market will bear, and you can end up with a lucrative, long-term investment in real estate.

4. BEAT THE DOW WITH THIS INVESTMENT STRATEGY

A sure fire strategy to beat the stock market has yet to be invented — or has it? The following investment strategy comes extremely close to being flawless.

Here is what you do:

At the beginning of the year, look up which 30 stocks had the best year. Out of those 30, pick the top 10. Hold your stocks for one year. Next year, look at the best 30, and buy the top 10 again. Try to spend at least $1,000 on each stock category. Also, buy the stocks yourself as opposed to hiring a stock broker. On 10 stocks, this will save you about $500.

The results? Those who have tried this strategy over the past 20 years have realized an average 19 percent return on their money. Some have gained whopping profits of 40 to 60 percent. This is an extremely low-risk investment strategy, and it's almost "can't lose!"

5. FRANCHISING

I have to include franchising as one of my top five investment strategies for one simple reason — it's one of the fastest ways I know of to generate enormous sums of money.

After you have made the investment is establishing your own business, you can multiply the value of your business thousands of times by issuing a franchise license to other people who want to start the same kind of business. You make money on the franchise fee, which can be anything from $50 to $5,000! Also, there is no limit to how many you can sell.

You can franchise just about any kind of business, from dog groomer to home health care to daycare to landscaping.

For example, if you establish a successful dog grooming service called "Doggie Nice," you can allow other people to benefit from your success if they pay a fee. In exchange for their fee, they get instant name recognition, and the instant legitimacy of an established business — and any other benefits you may choose to offer as part of your franchise package.

Make a trip to your local library and find out more about franchising. It's a fast way to very large sums of money.

There you have five ways to raise fast low-interest cash and five ways to transform your borrowed money into pure profit in your pocket! What are you waiting for?

MAKING MONEY WITH CREDIT CARDS

Most people use credit cards to get themselves in a heap of trouble with debt. But you can use credit cards to do just the opposite — make of heap of money for your savings account.

How? By using the easy and fast financing which credit cards can give you to "buy low and sell high."

Just what am I talking about? Perhaps a true story will help illustrate what I am talking about. Read the following story carefully, and then I'll discuss making money with your credit cards in more detail

Marlin L. of North Dakota was a carpenter, making a decent living at his trade. But Marlin had always longed for more than just a living. He had often entertained thoughts of "working smarter, not harder." By that, he meant making money through some kind of clever investment strategy. Rather than working 10 to 12 hours a day to earn his $15 per hour wage as a carpenter, Marlin wanted a situation in which he could land large sums of money with the mere flicker of a pen across a few credit application forms, and through some savvy buying and selling plans.

A famous scientists once said, "chance favors the prepared mind." And because Marlin had his mind open and prepared, it wasn't long before an opportunity cropped up right in front of him.

One day while taking on supplies at a local lumber outlet. Marlin learned from the lumber yard foreman that the yard had over-purchased a large amount of plywood, and that they wanted to liquidate it as quickly as possible. They were asking $14,000 for the lot of it.

As it happens, Marlin knew of a major construction project for a series of large low-income apartments which was about to get underway in another city, ad that the supply order for the project included some $30,000 in plywood.

Marlin saw clearly before him a golden opportunity. If he could snatch up the plywood for $14,000, he could almost instantly turn around and sell it to the apartment complex project for some $30,000 — and pocket a $16,000 profit almost instantly.

The problem: Marlin had nothing like $14,000 just laying around. He had a couple thousand dollars in savings, a few other bucks here and there — but all of it together didn't come close to Fourteen Large.

Although he did okay at his day job, he wasn't exactly in the Bill Gates League. Marlin spent his day off visiting eight or nine banks, seeking funds to buy up the plywood, and all politely told him the same thing — no.

The banks considered Marlin's venture a bad risk, but he believed firmly that he could pull it off.

He decided it was time to take a risk. Marlin knew that his VISA card had a $10,000 limit, and that just about every other week, other card companies were writing him letters telling him he was "pre-approved" for a new card.

Marlin went down to the library, got a copy of Consumer Report, and looked up the names of all the major credit card companies in the U.S. He searched for those cards which offered

$10,000 limits, and gave them a call, asking for an application.

Although Marlin already had his own card, he found it easy to be accepted by two more card companies because he had kept his balance paid. Before long, Marlin had two more cards with a $10,000 credit limit each. With his existing card, he now had nearly $30,000 at his instant disposal. His wife also applied and was accepted for two cards, and they soon had $50,000 in credit.

Money in hand, Marlin approached the lumber yard and told them — to their considerable surprise — that he'd take that plywood off their hands, and he'd pay them cash for it. Marlin used $14,000 from his new multiple card credit fund.

The very next day, before any of the card companies could so much as say 18 percent interest, Marlin sold the lot of plywood to the apartment complex for just over $32,000 — and pocketed a neat $18,000 in profit. He paid back each card company before they could collect interest, and the rest is history.

THE MORAL OF THE STORY

These days, it's incredibly easy to get large sums of instant credit in the simplest of ways — with ordinary credit cards.

What Marlin did was obvious, but in a way, ingenious. What allowed Marlin to be successful was his willingness to take a big risk — plunging himself into $14,000 in plastic debt.

But he tempered that risk with an intelligent plan, and a reasonable expectation that he could turn his sudden debt into sudden wealth. Marlin new he had a solid customer that was eager to buy. He had a solid source of product that could be purchased at an attractive price.

Furthermore, Marlin shattered the paradigm, or "closed thinking" that ensnares most people on most days. Credit cards are for consuming, not for swinging major business deals, right? Marlin's answer was: who says!

Marlin's story illustrates one way that a simple intelligent plan mixed with a bit of luck and the courage to take a risk can result in a money windfall.

No matter who you are, or where you live, you can do the same. No matter how bad your current credit, or how lowly your economic condition, you can find a creative way to leverage the cash you need.

Thus, credit cards can be used to make fast cash. You must simply keep you eyes open for opportunities to "buy low and sell high."

A great way to increase your chances of doing so it to attend bankruptcy auction where you can often buy top-notch office equipment for pennies on the dollar. Buy the stuff with your credit card, then sell it off as fast as you can.

Always be checking the classified ads for "desperate" sounding sellers, such as ads for automobiles that say: "must sell!" of "take over payments." These indicate a person in dire financial straights — contact them and make a hard deal — as long as you come away with a deal in which you can easily turn around several hundred or several thousand dollars in profit.

You CAN make money with your credit cards — just keep an open mind, and open eye, take a few risks, and be smart!

13 MORTGAGE INTEREST REDUCING

One of the most simple thing in the world that you can do to save money is reduce the interest on your mortgage, and save $50,000 to $100,000. In the U.S., the average mortgage is amortized for 30 years, and you pay interest not only for the original loan, but you also collect interest in arrears and compound interest. At the end of 30 years, your lovely $100,000 home can end up costing you three times its original purchase price!

An alternative to the normal U.S. mortgage is what is known as a bi-weekly mortgage. With this, you pay every two weeks for 21 years instead of every month for 30 years.

By paying every two weeks, you get the equivalent of 13 monthly payments. This cuts down the total amount of interest you pay, and a typical homeowner can save as much as $50,000 to $100,000 on the final cost of the home! In other parts of the world, such as Canada, the bi-weekly payment is the standard way to handle mortgages.

Now the downside to this seemingly easy plan. Most banks will make the bi-weekly payment difficult for you. They will very likely charge you a higher closing cost, which may saddle you with a higher interest rate.

Another drawback: many people find that making a payment every two weeks is just more difficult that issuing a check just once a month. That means late fees and penalties. It takes a lot of planning and discipline to keep up with a bi-weekly payment schedule — but if you can do it, you WILL save big.

TRIM A LITTLE, TRIM A LOT

The subject of saving money on your mortgage is so interesting and easy, it bears a little further examination. The above plan of going to a twice a week payment system may not appeal to everyone for the reasons I gave. Let's assume that you need further a better way to save big money on your mortgage. Is there a better and and easier way. Absolutely, my friend, and here it is:

Consider the following: If you were to make an additional $5 payment on your mortgage each month, above and beyond your regular payment, you would save about $10,000 on a $60,000+ house. That's $10,000 in your pocket!

If you were to bump up that $5 to a $10 payment per month, you would save $18,000! An extra payment of $20 each month would save a whopping $30,000!

My question to all you home owners out there is: "Why on earth would you not want to save this kind of money for so little pain?" I find it amazing that so many people strongly resist paying even an extra five bucks a month, yet 90 percent of all people do. Even after they learn that they can save $10,000 on their house payments, 90 percent of people will not part with that puny $5 a month. Amazing, isn't it!

NOW THE REAL KICKER

I don't want to stop with saving you $30,000 on your mortgage with this easy plan. Let's go a step further. Because you are prepaying your mortgage, the equity in your house is building faster than it would be if you were making your regular payment only.

By prepaying your mortgage, you can have sooner access to a second mortgage on your existing home — and easily get enough money from the second mortgage to buy a second home — either the vacation dream home of your choice, or perhaps a home that you can re-sell for a large profit!

So you see, just a few extra dollars a month paid on your regular mortgage almost gets you two home for the price of one! Yes, it's true and its that easy! Why are you not doing this right now with your current house payment!

14 NON-BANK SOURCES OF CREDIT

When it comes to credit, some people are their own worst enemy. They are limited by their own thinking. When they think "credit," they automatically think "bank." But banks are by far not the only source of credit, nor are they generally the easiest source of credit — or the source with the lowest interest rates.

Let's look at five other common and creative sources of credit.

1. THE GOVERNMENT

Before you go to a bank, go to the people whom already work for you — your own government!

The Federal government, your state government, and even your county or city government have literally hundreds of sources of credit, and government terms are almost always more pleasant that those offered by banks.

You can get a government loan or grant for just about anything, including money for:

- Starting a new business
- A college education
- To explore for natural resources
- To help poor people
- To recycle trash in your neighborhood

- To not farm your own land

- To start your own import/export enterprise

- To pay for your personal health care

- Buy a vehicle for your non-profit cause

- Buy computer equipment

... and the list goes on. The point is, before you look anywhere for credit, you should look to where your own tax dollars are going every day.

Some of the more common sources of government credit are:

THE SMALL BUSINESS ADMINISTRATION (SBA)

The slogan of the SBA is: "To help people get into business and stay in business."

Thus, if you have always wanted to be self employed and need an easy source of credit to start the business of your dreams, why not contact the SBA? They will give you a loan for as little as $200 to as high as $100,000. As I have said elsewhere in this book, the SBA will even give you a loan without collateral. In fact, you can get up to $15,000 in SBA money on "you name alone."

For an SBA loan, contact your local bank, or call the SBA answer desk toll free at: 1-800-827-5722

FARMERS HOME ADMINISTRATION (FMHA)

This is another government agency that loans millions of dollars each year to American citizens of all sorts, and not just farmers. You can also get money from the FmHA if you live in a small town of population 25,000 or less.

Contact the FmHA at

Farmers Home Administration

U.S. Dept of Agriculture

14th and Independence, SW

Washington, DC 20250

Phone: 202-447-7967

THE MINORITY BUSINESS DEVELOPMENT AGENCY

If you are a member of a minority group, such as African American, Native American, Hispanic or some other, you may have access to funds through the MBDA.

Contact the following for further information:

Minority Business Development

14th and Constitution Ave. NW, Room 5099

Washington, DC 20230

Phone: 202-377-1936

THE OVERSEAS PRIVATE INVESTMENT CORPORATION

If you are interested in starting your own business on foreign soils, you may be able to get a loan from this organization. Contact them at:

Overseas Private Investment Corporation

1615 M Street, NW

Washington, DC 20527

Phone: 202-457-7200

EXPORT-IMPORT BANK OF THE UNITED STATES

The U.S. Department of Commerce is very eager for millions of American to start a business which imports American made goods to foreign countries. Why? Because the more American goods sold to other countries, the better the balance of trade, and the better the balance of trade, the healthier the American economy gets.

The Export-Import Bank, known as Eximbank, will lend you money not only to get your business started, but also to produce your product or idea from scratch. This is a very help and easy source of low-low-interest credit.

Contact:

Export-Import Bank of the United States

Working Capital Guarantee Program

811 Vermont Avenue, NW

Washington, DC 20571

Phone: 202-566-8819

THE SMALL BUSINESS INVESTMENT COMPANY (SBIC)

This is a subdivision of the Small Business Administration. It was formed in 1958. They make long-term loans or corporately invest in the borrowers company. It's kind of a cross between a government loan and a venture capital situation. The SBIC may be right for you, For more information, contact your local bank and ask them about the SBIC program.

Don't forget your state government, or your local government as sources of credit, start-up money or money for other uses. All you have to do is ask. Pick up the phone book, look up the number for "information" and start asking questions. After just a few phone calls, you will have uncovered a ton of literature and potential sources of easy-to-get, low-interest credit.

2. VENTURE CAPITAL

Here is another common source of credit that does not come from a bank. What is venture capital, who has it, and who gives it?

Venture capital is simply money held by private firms which are interested in investing that money so that they can make even more money.

Venture capital firms provide money for all kinds of unsecured ventures, many of which would scare the be-jeepers out of any banker. Venture capitalist will take great risks if they think they can make great profits. It's up to you to convince them that you have a good idea, and that they will make a profit if they lend you the money.

Venture capital firms are interested in new, ground-breaking ideas, so don't hesitate to cail them. Where do you find them? Call you state's Department of Commerce for a list and they will provide you with one. If you live in a larger city, check the Yellow Pages under "Venture Capital."

3. START YOUR OWN INVESTMENT CLUB

One of the hottest trends in private investment strategies today is the Investment Club.

An Investment Club — some call them "inner money circles" — is simply a group of people who come together, pool their money, and then use this group fund to buy and sell stocks. Each member shares profits based on the amount of money they put in. Some members of investment clubs put up as little as $10, while others float $10,000 or more.

Today, there are more than 13,000 investment clubs in the United States, and they have an extraordinary rate of profit and success.

An Investment Club does not have to be limited to playing the stock market. As long as you get all members to agree, you can plunge your money into any kind of enterprise you choose, whether it be a small business, or an oil well in southern Mexico.

In effect, your own investment club is like having your own bank, or starting your own Venture Capital firm. Perhaps the only drawback to this approach is maintaining a consensus among members.

Human beings, being what they are, tend to see things differently. If one person see a glass as half full, you can bet another will insist it is half empty. Therefore, when you form your investment club, strive to get as many like-minded people as you can. The more compatibility you have from the beginning, the smoother sailing you'll have in the future.

4. A SILENT PARTNER

Many people choose the finance their dreams by taking on a silent partner. What is a silent partner? Simply a private individual who has some money to invest, but who prefers to stay in the background, for whatever reason.

How do you find a silent partner? Simply take out a classified ad in the "Business Opportunities" section of your local paper, or in a money-oriented magazine. You ad can read something like:

"Seeking silent partner for terrific investment opportunity — double your money in less than one year."

An ad like this will produce a lot of calls, most of which will listen to your idea, and say. "no thank you." Others, however, will be interested if your idea sounds promising and capable of producing a profit. It's up to you to sell your silent partner on your idea. It's up to both you and your silent partner to determine the level of risk vs. the level of probably gain. As in any investment situation, the higher the risk, the more money you will make — or lose!

5. BORROW FROM PROFESSIONAL PEOPLE

This idea is similar to the Silent Partner plan above, except is seeks a more specific kind of investor — professionals, such as doctors, lawyers, dentists, business owners, and so on.

Many of these people have high incomes and thus are in very high tax brackets. That means they are hungry for tax shelters, and one of the best way to avoid taxes is investing in new money making opportunities — one of which could be yours!

Put together your idea for what you will use the money for, and then approach the professionals you have dealt with in the past, meaning your own doctor, dentist or attorney. Very often the answer will be "no" but just as often, they can name a fellow professional who might be interested. You may have to do a bit of legwork, but that all part of the game and joy of finding the credit that will make your personal financial dream come true.

15 GETTING BANKERS TO BEG FOR YOUR BUSINESS

Now let's talk about that vile beast — the banker. Let's face it, when you are seeking credit, your banker is your enemy. He has what you want and he knows it. Because he holds all the cards, he gets to dictate terms to you. If you don't like the terms, you can take a hike. Furthermore, the banker is very fussy about who he will do business with. If you don't make the grade in his eyes, you are so much pocket lint. Finally, a banker wants to use you to make a profit for himself. He does not care about your risk, he only cares about his own.

In a very real sense, a banker does not live in the real world. I can say with 100 percent certainty that a banker is not a business person. A banker MAKES money because he HAS money. He knows nothing about developing a product, putting together a marketing plan, pleasing customers, buying low and selling high. The banker focuses like a laser in one thing: are you paying back the money on time and at a hefty rate of interest?

A banker cares not a whit that you are out in the street — in the trenches — struggling to make a profit with your business, so the banker can make his own profit.

The banker gets to sit back in the comfort of his office pushing papers across his desk, while you slug it out in a good economy or bad economy, in a hot market or a cold market, in a bustling city, or in a city on the slide — it's all the same to the banker — he says: "just pay me what you owe, and on time!"

Banker are obsessed with time. Did you ever wonder why banks all display large clocks on or outside the building? It's because time serves the goal of the banker. Time truly is money. Interest accrues on a loan over time. Bankers use time as their whip. If you are a day late with your payment, the banker will slap a penalty on you with faster than yo can say overdraft. Sure, a banker will act all bothered and wounded when you are late with your payment, but deep down inside he is happy because this helps him make more money. Fines and late fees are a major source of income for bankers.

My whole point is, don't waste a second feeling sorry for banker. Just the opposite, so everything you can (legally) to gain an advantage over him.

There is no reason for you to give in to banker-master, you-slave situation. In fact, if you take a different perspective on this, you can turn the master-slave relationship on its ear.

THEY NEED YOU

From this point on, I want you to keep one thought in your head: The banker needs you more than you need him! Repeat this phrase to yourself 100 or 10,000 times if you have to. Internalize it. Thoroughly condition your mind into believing that you need not be a slave to the mighty master banker. Before you even enter into negotiation with a bank for a loan, you should carry the deep-seated conviction that YOU have the upper hand.

The fact is, a banker cannot make a dime unless you either deposit money in their bank, or start a business that will produce profits which they can leach from.

To help you understand how important you are to your bank, consider what they do with the money you deposit in their coffers.

These days, a saving account will pay you less than 3 percent interest on your money. If you put $5,000 in a savings account, you might ear $200, or $250 on that over the period of one year.

But while the bank pays you a paltry 2.5 percent, they turn around and lend out your money at rate of 18, 19, 20 — even as high as 24 percent! That's an incredible deal for them. They take your money, toss you a tiny 2.5 percent scrap, and then go wild. The money rolls in for banks, and God help anyone who forfeits on a payment.

Knowing this is important for the psychology of dealing with bankers. When you visit with your banker, make sure he knows that you are aware of how much interest they make from you versus how much you get from them. Be diplomatic, but attempt to establish a certain atmosphere of mutual respect.

WHAT ABOUT BANKER LOSSES?

Yes, bankers sometimes get stiffed by the people to whom they have lent money. But it's all a numbers game. Bankers know that from the beginning that x-amount of loans will go bad. To counter that, they push their lending rates as high as the government will let them. In the end, the banker always makes a profit. Those who successfully repay their loans make up for the dead beats many times over. The banker, however, will moan and groan pathetically over the small percentage of losses, and will never tire of reminding you of how they were burned by this person, or that corporation.

The point is, don't feel sorry for them. They've got their butts covered, and covered nicely.

Now that you understand the psychology behind the lending game, let's cover some specific ways that will make any banker think of you as a top candidate for a loan.

THE APPLICATION FORM

You make think an application for is merely a series of straightforward questions about you and your current financial standing — but don't believe it. The fact is, there are many right ways and even more wrong ways to fill out a credit application form.

Did you know that six out of 10 credit application forms result in rejection? That means your chances of getting a loan are a mere 40 percent, at best.

A lot of the information on credit application forms are subjected to a secret point-rating system. That means that each blank on the application form has a number of points. Depending on how you answer, you could score high, or bomb out with zero points. Knowing which answers will give you the highest points per category, then, is essential to being accepted for a loan.

THE THREE CS

To the banker, the three Cs are of prime importance in terms of whether you will get a loan or not. The three Cs are:

CAPACITY — CHARACTER — COLLATERAL

1. Capacity. This refers simply to your current income, and your potential to keep earning it, and possibly earn more in the future. To determine this, they look at your pay rate, how long you have been at your current job, at your current residence and if you are likely to continue to be employed? How does a banker find out if you are likely to be downsized or not? They ask. It is not uncommon for a banker to call your place of business and ask if you are likely to be employed their for the near or distance future. If they answer is yes, you get good points. If no, you lose big points. Of course, the higher your salary, the better off you are.

2. Character. Are you an upstanding person who would never run away from a bad debt, or will you slink out of town in the middle of the night and leave behind a pile of unpaid bills? The banker wants to know. How do they find out? From examining your credit record, which they can get from a variety of credit bureaus, as you learned elsewhere in this book.

They also determine your character by looking at whether you own a home, or if you are a "mere" renter. If you rent, you lose points. If you have only been at your current address for less than a year, you lose points. Did you make your past payments on time? If not, you lose points. Remember how obsessed we said bankers are with time? Many lender reject on the basis of lateness alone.

3. Collateral. This is something you have that a banker can take away if you fail to repay your loan. Collateral can be just about anything, but more and more, banker are getting fussy about what they will accept as collateral. Land, for instance, is not a top choice, and neither is a mobile home. A car that you have no loan on, or office equipment is more to their liking. Surprisingly, bankers

consider computer equipment good collateral, which makes little sense, because nothing depreciates faster than a new computer. Jewelry, gold, antiques, painting works of arts with a true appraised value all make top-notch collateral.

The better you sit in terms of the three Cs above, the bette your chances of getting the credit you want.

THE SCORE

All application forms vary somewhat, but all contain a few core questions that have specific point ranges attached to them. The most common categories are:

Your occupation

Your Annual Income

Length of Employment

Your Age

Length of Stay at Current Residence

Do you own or rent?

Home Phone Number

Home Ownership

Bank CRedit Cardholder

Checking and Savings Account

College Graduate

Married

Single

Using a Finance Company

Banker use certain numbers for each category, depending on your answer. Here is how banking insiders score in the categories above:

OCCUPATION

Professional or CEO	+50
Management or Foreman	+30
Service Employees	+20
Technicians	+15
Clerical or Sales workers	+10

ANNUAL INCOME

Under $15,000	+5
Between $15,000 - $25,000	+10
Between $25,000 - $50,000	+15
Over $50,000	+25

LENGTH OF EMPLOYMENT

Less than 2 years	0
3 years	+5
4 years	+10
5 years or more	+15

AGE

Under 30 years	+10
Between 30 and 40	+20
Between 40 and 50	+15
Over 50	+25

LENGTH OF TIME AT CURRENT RESIDENCE

Less that 2 years	+0
Between 3 and 5	+5
More than 5 years	+10

HOME PHONE

Yes	+70
No	0

OWN YOUR HOME

Yes	+60
No	0

HAVE AND BANK CREDIT CARD

Yes	+50
No	0

BOTH CHECKING AND SAVINGS

Yes	+40
Only checking	+25

COLLEGE GRADUATE

Yes	+15
No	0

MARRIED

Yes	+10
No	0

USING A FINANCE COMPANY   -20

When you look at the point scoring system, you discover some amazing things. Having your own phone number, for example, scores you a mighty 70 points — a far bigger category in the eyes of a banker than whether or not you are a college graduate! Go figure!

What valuable about knowing the above scoring system is that you can easily control many of the high scoring ones. I mean, you can't just get married solely for the purpose of getting an extra 10 points, but you can easily get your own phone number for a whopping 70 points.

You can also easily start a savings account, even if you stick only $25 in the thing. As long as you answer yes, you get 40 points instead of 25.

If you are going to apply for a loan, you can't lie (that's a federal offense), you can't change your age or get a college degree over night, but you can make sure you score high in those categories which you can easily control.

GET CREATIVE

Why not beat bankers at their own game? Since they give so many points to professionals and executives, why not bill yourself as one. Am I talking about lying. No! I'm talking about positive spin. If "spin control" is good enough for the President of the United States, it's sure-as hang-fire good enough for you.

What do I mean by positive spin? Well, if you are a handyman, why not call yourself an engineer, which qualifies as a profession. Sure you are a "mere" maintenance engineer, but so what? Your "profession is just as valuable as anyone else. After all, no doctor could keep his clinic open, and no lawyer could keep his office open without a maintenance man to keep all things in running order.

A garbage man is a sanitary engineer. A nurse's aide is a health care professional. A secretary is an administrative assistant. You get the picture?

WHAT IF YOUR ARE SELF EMPLOYED?

If you write "self employed" into your occupation box, you are slitting your own throat. (Pardon the vulgar expression.) Banker really get the willies when they see someone who is actually bold enough to build something of their own, using their own smarts, experience, labor and initiative. Than banker is more comfortable with a corporate drone or an assembly line worker who is taking few risks in life.

If you are self employed, simply state the job title you carry within your own company. If you own your own landscaping firm, call yourself: Executive Director, Greenleaf Landscaping.

WHAT IF YOU LIE?

Now the ordinary person might reason: "Millions of applications are processed every day. So what if I fudge my age or lie about having a college degree? Are they actually going to check? Are they going to demand a copy of my birth certificate or call the college Listed as ny alma mater to see if I am on their books as a graduate?"

Most often, the answer is no. You application is certainly not going to be screened by a senior vice-president of the bank. Rather, your application will be processed by low-paid clerical drones. They simply read your answers and add up the score. At times, they may check your phone number or verify your job or place of employment, but they do not do that in every case, and by far, they do not do it inmost cases.

But your application will also be checked against your credit history report, but if there are no major differences or no glaring contradictions, you will either be quickly approved or rejected based on your score alone. Yes, in the eye of the bank, you are a number. You see, the bankers greatest strength can also be his greatest weakness. They are so obsessed with numbers, they often fail to look beyond numbers. If your numbers look good, you get the loan. If you lied to get those numbers up there, they may not even know about it.

So should you lie on your credit application, or not. I say definitely not, and in case you don't understand me, I say "No!" — do not lie on your credit application form!

I can't in good conscious or legally encourage anyone to break the law. All I'm saying is that, if you do lie, chances are you will get away with it. On the other hand, if you actually do get caught, you are in a pile of legal trouble. If that happens, it will be by your own head, and not as the result of anything you read in this book.

MORE CREDIT APPLICATION FORM TIPS

• Do not list yourself as a dependent. The more dependents you list as having, the more points you lose. Also, if your spouse works, you do not have to list him or her as a dependent. You can get away with this because most credit application forms ask about dependents in a vague way. MOst simply include a box that says OTHER — and you can take that to mean "dependents other than you."

• If you have an unlisted telephone number, you may want to give it to the banker anyway. Remember, a phone number can be worth up to 70 points.

• Open a number of accounts in a number of bank. When bankers see that you have a half-dozen accounts in a half-dozen banks, they'll think you have a lot of money. The trick is, privacy laws permit you to conceal how much money you have in each account. You might have $10 bucks in 10 banks, but the banker will never know that you savings total a might hundred bucks!

• List your "potential" income. You can make your income look larger if you list the amount of money you would earn if you were working a second job — even if you aren't. If they ask you about it, you can say: "At the time I filled out the application form, I had just been hired for the second job, but it fell through the day after."

Is this a lie? Maybe, maybe not. You could make it true by applying for a second job and accepting that job before you fill out your application. You don't have to tell them that the reason the job "fell through" is because you decided not to take it!

• Some accountants, for a small fee and a pledge of secrecy, will make a false IRS form for you that lists you income as being anything you want it to be. Banks are not allowed to check the form you give them against the real thing because of privacy laws. Once again, you would being doing this at your own risk.

• Combine your spouse's income with yours. There is no reason you can't do this, especially if your spouse co-applies with you. The higher the number in your income box, the more points you get.

• Don't list "other income." Amazing as this sounds, listing other sources of income can actually cause you to lose points. That's because a banker may think that you are so desperate for money you have to work a second job or have a monthly garage sale. Rather than calling extra money "other income" call it a "dividend" or a "royalty."

• Don't fill out your application by hand, have it typed. Nothing says "honesty!" like those perfectly formed little letters. A banker is far less likely to think you have been dishonest if you put things down in such clear and indelible type.

A FINAL WARNING

You must understand that lying to your mother or wife or husband is not nice, and can get you in some hot water, but lying on a credit application form is called "fraud" in the eyes of the law. Commit fraud and you will be in more than hot water, but, in the worst case scenario — jail!

Also, if you default on your loan, you may not be able to get bankruptcy protection if a bank can prove that you made false statements on your credit application form. If you are guilty of fraud, you have waved any other rights you may have under bankruptcy protection laws.

16 17 BUSINESSES TO START WITHOUT MONEY OR CREDIT

ASSOCIATION MANAGEMENT

There are literally tens of thousands of associations across the country and around the world representing professional and grass roots organizations, special interest groups, and just about anything you can think of that brings people together for a common mission.

Although they may start out small, the administrative duties of managing the association's day to day business may soon overtake the ability and time of volunteers. In cases where an association cannot yet justify hiring a full-time administrative director, they often turn to people that contract professional administration services.

In addition to providing needed administrative direction and support, the association management service provider frees up volunteer time to focus on the mission, policies, and program strategies for which the association exists.

That's where you come in. It becomes a cost effective, smart business decision for an association's boards of directors, and a good opportunity for entrepreneurs with administrative and management skills, and the desire for a home-based business.

Association management service providers can charge up to $35 per hour and earn up to $52,000 per year working 30 hours a week!

The duties association management service providers may perform range from simple filing to public speaking or lobbying. The job description includes just about anything it takes to serve members and keep an organization well-oiled.

The scope of the work needs to be defined with your clients and agreed upon between you and association leaders to which you will report. Expect to talk about things like:

1) member services and development — collecting dues, keeping membership lists, coordinating newsletters and other literature about the organization, answering phone calls, receiving, distributing, and responding to mail, organizing meetings and conventions, booking speakers or personally doing public speaking on behalf of the association,

2) fundraising — helping with events, coordinating fund drives and mailings,

3) good business practices — bookkeeping, ordering of supplies, maintenance of equipment, office cleanliness.

If all this sounds like a lot, don't fret. Today's technology will be your greatest office assistant. Most business records and project coordination can easily be done on a computer, and by establishing a few communication links with frequent users or sources you need, can be done from home.

Along with a basic set of office management skills, a computer (preferably with modem and fax capabilities), and a phone, it is very important in a business like this to be skilled at dealing warmly and patiently with people. Remember, associations live and breathe because of the dedication of volunteers who lead busy lives outside their involvement in volunteer tasks. It is not uncommon in volunteer setting to see egos clashing and conflicts of interest causing rifts within groups.

At times like these, your ability to be a gracious and respectful employee is important. The same goes for interaction with association members association members — you may often be the first person they come in contact with in the organization and how you deal with them can make or break their willingness to belong.

Finally, once you've done all these things right, your organizational skills — or lack of them — will be the clincher in the level of your clients' satisfaction and will help you win or lose your business with them.

What can you hope to personally gain out of a business like this besides a earning a good income? Well, you may have the opportunity to do some traveling to interesting places, attend stimulating meetings and conventions, and meet prominent people within the industry. And with the variety of tasks you may be asked to perform, boredom should be the last thing you run into.

Because most volunteers are contributing from the heart, they can be highly appreciative of a job well done that saves them extra time and hassle they don't have. Be prepared, however, to be on the same schedule as volunteers — on call as needed, working evenings and weekends, and brushing up against organizational politics.

To get going in your new businesses, you'll need to start by finding a way to tap into an industry either you know something about or can learn something about to get started. Ask a knowledgeable friend, read up in an area of personal interest, and find out everything you can about the issues the industry faces and the specific types of associations that serve these industries. Become familiar with the dynamics of how the industry operates.

Then start contacting. Call presidents of professional or trade associations. Join a gout or two and network. Volunteer to do a workshop for association teams on how to manage their project. Read and respond to classified ads regularly.

And what if you discover a special interest group without an association — and it could use one? Start your own. The same duties and skills apply. With all the new technology and fields of interest popping up all over the place, the opportunities to band people with like interest together is almost unlimited.   Do some targeted marketing to recruit members. Send direct mailings. Find out what trade magazines they read and advertise in them. It may be the beginning of your new association.

Running an association yourself could earn you up to $30,000 per year for membership dues alone (400 members at $50 yearly dues). Stack on top of that the sale of ads in your association newsletter, and you've got yourself a healthy business!

For more information, contact:

American Society of Association Executives,

1575 I Street N.W., Washington, DC 20005;

(202) 626-2723.

Institute of Association Management Companies,

104 Wilmot Road, Suite 201, Deerfield, IL 60015;

(708) 940-8800.

BILL AUDITING SERVICE

With over 5 million businesses in the United States needing the products and services of other companies to keep their own operations running, there's a lot of bills passing through business mail rooms each day. And with that kind of volume comes an equal chance of error. In fact, telecommunications experts have estimated that 70 to 80 percent of all bills contain errors.

The bottom line is that companies may be losing money unnecessarily. In the hubbub of daily business, bills simply get paid without a thorough audit for correctness, particularly utility bills, which are among the most complicated and hard to understand.

For the budget-minded bill detectives of the world, there's an opportunity to get into business for yourself as a bill auditor and recover what would otherwise be lost money.

Your job is to find the errors in billings by verifying their accuracy against different kinds of information. It might be as simple as an incorrect meter reading, a misplaced decimal, or an overlooked discount, but your search won't always stop there.

The verification process will include things like checking bills against purchase orders, checking receiving documents to see that products were delivered, and checking for overcharging against contracts, tariffs, applicable laws, tax rate rates, and other data that insures the company is getting billed fairly.

The incentive to do a thorough exploration when verifying bill correctness is high, because the bill auditor's fee is directly tied to the amount of savings he or she recovers. Usually the bill auditor and the company will split both the past and future savings of an uncovered overcharge. Often the bill auditor will negotiate a split on savings for three years out. What that means is that a one-time find can pay off each year for three years without any additional work.

With auditors typically charging 50 percent for past and future savings, each discovery can earn a bill auditor between $1000 and $3000 on the average. Experienced auditors can process one to two claims a day, while bill auditors new to the business may take a week to do the same. At those rates, even a rookie can make between $100,000 and $300,000 per year!

It's true that experience will breed speed and a keen eye for potential error spots, but there are some basic skills that any bill auditor needs to have to be successful in a business like this.

The payoff is truly in the detail, so the better you are at leaving no stone unturned, the greater your chances for success. It is necessary to have a solid set of math skills. A calculator may become your best friend!

An analytical mind paired with the practice of keeping up on all the laws, tariffs, and regulations that apply to each of your client's businesses are also prerequisites for becoming a successful bill auditor.

Finally, some tools of the trade like a computer with spreadsheet and word processing software, and a printer, will be essential. Also, your personal letterhead, envelopes, and business cards will secure a professional image.

The easiest way to get the experience you need to become a bill auditor is to work for a company, like a utility or insurance company, whose bills you will eventually audit. At the very least, learning the laws and tariffs that apply in several industries from which bills are regularly generated is a must. It may take three to six months or more to get up to speed on the rules and regulations for the industries you choose.

What types of clients need these skills? Commercial and industrial businesses with utility bills totaling at least $2000 a month should be the primary target. With de-regulation of utility companies in this country, billing by these organizations has become complex. Many companies simply assume the bills are correct and pay them rather than sort through the maze.

Clients may include businesses like hospitals or hotels that consume a lot of energy, water, and phone services. Besides a great opportunity for finding billing savings, you may discover creative ways to cash in on more efficient use of these services that the company has never explored. Finding a way to save a company $200 a month on their electric bill, for instance, can generate $7200 of found income over three years. That's $3600 for the bill auditor!

You can get clients like these by directly contacting a manager in the accounting department. Direct mail is another route — be sure to follow up with phone calls. Networking can also be key to finding clients. It may include making contact with people employed by the businesses you are targeting, or getting to know professionals like lawyers, bankers, accountants, and others who can refer their clients to you.

Any kind of publicity you can generate will also help you get noticed. Consider giving seminars or speeches on the cost savings of bill auditing. Try to get some press in newspapers or trade publications read by people in the businesses you are targeting. Suggest to an editor an article on bill auditing, or write one and submit it yourself. Advertising in these same publications may also help gain you clients.

The advantage a bill auditor has in selling him or herself is that the savings pays your fee. And what company wouldn't want to listen to an idea that generates cash and lowers overhead, especially if a recession or other conditions are causing the company some financial difficulty? The company does not spend anything additional to have you on board. And the percentage you received can be spread out over a three year period rather than a one-time charge.

The competition is relatively low, however, bill auditors need to be prepared for 60 to 90 day lags between the time they discover a savings and actually receive payment. And you don't get paid unless your client saves money — your paycheck is dependent on your own ability to find billing errors for the company.

The payoff can be big for the bill auditor and their clients. With sleuth-like instincts and a firm knowledge of laws, rules, tariffs, and regulations for the biggest "billers" around, the bill auditor can begin an on-going process of generating cash that pays both the bill auditor and client for years to come.

For more information, contact:

Auditel Marketing Systems

12033 Gailcrest Lane,

St. Louis, MO 63131; (314) 567-1980, (800) 551-9282.

Utility & Tax Reduction Consultants

1280 Iroquois

Avenue, Naperville, IL 60563; (708) 369-3072,

(800) 321-7872.

BUSINESS BROKER

In the same way that real estate agents hook up buyers and sellers of homes, a business broker's job is to find a match between sellers and buyers of businesses. Many states even require business brokers to have a real estate license.

And like real estate agents, a business broker can either represent a buyer or a seller of a business. Most brokers represent sellers, and their job is to find a buyer. Finding the right match between a buyer and a business is the key.

Most brokers are involved in sales of businesses with assets under $300,000, excluding real estate. Brokers will often focus in a specific industry, like sporting goods or entertainment clubs, or within a geographical area.

Business brokering is growing in the United States. The U.S. Department of Commerce estimates that 20 percent of the approximately 18 million businesses in the U.S. change hands every year. Ninety percent of these businesses are valued at $300,000 or less in assets. Inc, magazine even predicts that buying rather than starting businesses will continue to grow because of the reduced risk of failure.

Business brokers, says Tom West, owner of the Business Brokerage Press, spend about 40 percent of their time calling on prospective sellers, 40 percent dealing with buyers, 10 percent working with attorneys, and 10 percent doing analysis.

Brokers typically make between ten and 12 percent of a sale, with a minimum of $10,000. At one sale a month for ten months, a broker can earn $100,000 a year, and much more if he or she stays busy.

Staying busy depends on having several selling clients for which to find matches. Although a typical ad in the business opportunities section of the newspaper can yield between 6-12 inquiries, the sales cycle for business brokers may be long. Finding a match can happen quickly, but the time in closing the deal may take several months to a year.

With that in mind, perseverance is probably a business brokers greatest asset. The ability to read and interpret financial statements and other business documentation is also necessary, as is familiarity with the legalities of buying and selling businesses.

Good sales and communication skills are also key to this business. Often, business owners need coaxing to make the decision to sell. Then, they need to understand that you are trustworthy and can help them. And buyers need to understand why a business is a good fit for them.

Once both parties agree to the sale, a smart business broker will continue to listen and monitor the relationship between the seller and buyer. It's a good way to guarantee that the deal is structured in a way that is satisfactory to both parties.

Negotiating skills will also come in handy along the way — between seller and buyer, and when dealing with the attorneys, accountants, bankers, and other players that will be involved in the sale.

As a business broker, you will need a computer, printer, and a few software packages — bookkeeping, spreadsheets, word processing, and business analysis. Professional letterhead and business cards will also be necessary.

Before starting a career as a business broker, check first with your state real estate agency to determine whether licensure is required. Then start contacting business owners directly. Give them a call, send them a letter, or make an appointment to see them in person.

Begin networking within the industry you are choosing to specialize in. Find associations and other organizations where these business owners gather. Contact lawyers, bankers, and accountants for referrals.

You may even choose to purchase lists of franchises and other businesses from throughout the country that are currently for sale.

Becoming a business broker may be just up your alley if you have a knack for understanding business and putting deals together. The thrill of the sale and intricacies of business transactions can pay off personally as well as be financially for a true business buff.

For more information, contact:

Business Brokerage Consultants, 1998 County Road

427N, Suite 6, Longwood, FL 32750; (407) 331-8133.

International Business Brokers Association, Box 704, Concord, MA 01742; (508) 369-2490.

GRANT WRITING

Grant writing is an excellent home business idea for any one with a high school education or better, and for those of you who did fairly okay in your English classes.

Your first notion may be to just disregard grant writing as a possibility for you. Don't! Writing grants is not nearly the high art or difficult science that many people believe it to be. The fact is, thousands of grants are written successfully every year by nonprofessional writers, such as social workers, day care providers, church members and other people who need grants to further their goals of helping their community or helping people.

Just what is grant writing? Well, you know what a grant is. It's a sum of money which a government or private foundation grants to an organization or an individual for a specific purpose. A grant is not a loan which needs to be repaid. It is a gift, or sorts, given for a worthy cause. As we mentioned, a grant is very often given for nonprofit community or charity projects to help people and make a town or neighborhood a better place to live.

But grants are given for many, many other purposes as well. Individuals, such as artists, scientists, educators and students often apply for grants. Private businesses both large and small apply for grants to be used as venture capital for entrepreneurial projects.

Who gives grants? There are two primary sources of grants — government and private foundations. The federal government hands outs literally billions of dollars in grants each year. In addition to government sources of grant money, there are thousands upon thousands of private organizations, called foundations, which were established with the specific purpose of giving away money to worthy causes.

That's where grant writing comes in. In order to get a grant, you must make a pitch — in writing — to the government agency or the private foundation you want money from. That pitch is a written document, which is called a proposal, or grant. Thus the need for a person to write that document — a grant writer.

That's where an opportunity for you comes in. You can hire yourself out as a professional grant writer. Because hundreds of thousands of people are organizations are seeking grants all the time, you may find yourself plenty of business no matter where you live.

HOW DO YOU WRITE A GRANT?

As we said, writing a grant is more simple than you might think. The fact is, many grants are as simple as filling out a lengthy questionnaire which is provided by the granting institution. Most other grants follow a certain formula, something like: Introduction, statement of need, description of project, outline of the budget and conclusion.

It is a good idea to take a couple of grant writing classes, which are often available through community education programs, or as night courses at local colleges. Generally, you can learn everything you need to know about grant writing at one weekend seminar. Some programs, such as that offered by The Grantsmanship Center of Los Angeles, are week-long, intensive seminars that prepare you extremely well for this business.

Once you have written your first couple of grants, you will fall into a groove. Also, many granting institutions provide you with specific guidelines and points to cover when you make a request. In that case, it's simply a matter of covering all the points mentioned. When you give all the information asked for, you're done!

To get started in this business, you need to get the word out that you are a grant writer. In most states, you do not need a license or any special qualifications to set up shop.

The best way to get started is to approach a local charity organization, such as a food shelf, a homeless shelter, YMCA or YWCA, community center — and tell them you want to write a grant for them, and that you will do it for free. Doing a few grants for free will teach you how to write a grant, and will give a potential grantee incentive to give you a try. Start small with easier grants of perhaps $5,000 or less. The smaller the grant, the easier it will be to write, in general.

Even if you can successfully obtain a $500 grant for someone, you will have passed an important milestone. You will have proven that you can write a proposal that brings in money.

Having a few grants under your belt is important because the first thing potential clients will ask you is about your experience, and what grants you have obtained successfully. If you can claim even one small success, your position will be greatly enhanced.

Once you have cut your teeth on some of the smaller grants for local charitable institutions, you can begin to charge for your service. Obviously, what you need to start making money are clients. That means you have to market yourself. There are several ways to do that.

The first is advertising. We recommend you start with a small display ad or classified ads in your local newspapers. Be persistent and consistent about running your ads. Don't expect a one-time ad to bring you any clients or results. Most ads take 6 to 8 appearances to catch people's attention, and encourage people to call you.

It is a very good idea to buy a Yellow Pages ad as well. Some 80 percent of all people use the Yellow Pages when they look for a specific service. A large part of your calls will be generated by a Yellow Pages ad.

When people begin to call you, you must be prepared to answer their questions and put forward a professional image that projects confidence. That means you need a professional looking business card, letter head and envelopes that will identify you as a grant writer.

Surprisingly, though, one of the best ways to drum up business as a grant writer is to do it in person, and by word of mouth. As we said, you should first approach local charitable institutions and offer your services for free. Once you do that, however, you will have your foot in the door among the social services community. In most cities, the local providers of human services — from churches to food shelves — will most likely keep you busy for as long as you want to be busy.

HOW MUCH SHOULD YOU CHARGE?

Some grant writers work on a percentage basis, such as 5 to 10 percent of the total grant award. For example, if you land a $10,000 grant for someone, you get 10 percent, or $1,000. Sounds simple, but in general, working for a percentage is not always a good idea. The reason is obvious. Most grants, now matter how well written, are turned down. If you fail to get the grant, you will have nothing to charge a percentage on.

It's better to work for a flat fee. That way you get paid whether your grant is successful or not. You should make it clear to your clients that applying for a grant is never a sure thing — far from it. Even the best, most sophisticated grant writers have a very small success rate. But you still need to get paid for you work. Just as a lawyer gets paid whether he wins or loses, you as a grant writer get paid for you efforts, no matter what the outcome.

Some grants writer have a flat fee of $1,500 per grant. Obviously, you cannot charge that much for a grant of less than amount. Just use common sense. If you are trying to get a small grant of $1,000 or less for someone, you should charge about $200. That's okay money because small grants will generally take just a day or two to complete. Just make sure you size up the job, the complexity of the grant that will be be required, and charge accordingly. Remember, some grants can run up to 100 pages in length!

For a grant that big, you should earn big bucks — perhaps $5,000 to $10,000 — at least!

For more information on grant writing and how to get started, contact:

The Grantsmanship Center

P.O. Box 6210

Los Angeles, CA 90014.

World Class Grant Writing

P.O. Box K

Greenbush, MN 56726

Phone: 1-218-782-2631

PUBLISH YOUR OWN NEWSLETTER

Many hundreds of people have found that publishing a 1-to-8-page newsletter each month earns them more money than any full-time job they could ever have. Newsletter publishing is BIG business. More than one enterprising housewife have gotten filthy rich by publishing a newsletter in the past decade.

For example, housewife Mary Hunt began publishing a small, rather crudely designed newsletter called "The Cheapskate Monthly." Not only did subscription sales to the newsletter clear away her family's $100,000 debt, it also earned her enough to buy a $150,000 house — with cash! — after just a few years of publication. Mary Hunt worked with nothing more that a typewriter and a healthy supply of typing paper. She combined that with a knack for coming up with clever ways to save money on ordinary household items — the result was a fast six-figure per year income.

Perhaps you can become the next Mary Hunt.

What is required to publish a newsletter is a high school ability to write clear, understandable sentences that the average person can read comfortably. You also need the know-how of fitting those words into the simple format of a newsletter, which we'll outline in just a bit.

It also requires a single topic that will have a great deal of appeal to either a very large audience, or a very small, limited audience who will pay a premium price for yearly subscription. It will also help if you have "inside information" or special knowledge in a certain field.

For example, one attorney who specialized in a certain type of law practice started a newsletter on that topic which he marketed to other lawyers throughout the country. In a very short time, he was earning $14,000 a month — far more than his services as an attorney brought him annually.

Just what is a newsletter? A newsletter can be a single sheet of ordinary paper printed on both sides, or 4-to-12 pages stapled together. Most newsletters have an 8 1/2" by 11" format, although some use a legal sized sheet of paper folded three ways. Most newsletters are between 4 and 8 pages long.

A newsletter is something in between an informational brochure and a full-blown newspaper or magazine. A newsletter is highly focused on a speciality topic. That topic can be anything — from how to save money on groceries to how to have an out of body experience. The choice of topics is truly unlimited. That's where you come in.

Just about every person has a special area of interest, a hobby or a talent that they know something about. Or, if you have a knack or interest in a particular topic, you can delve into into research-wise and to come up with material to fill a newsletter.

Once you have your topic, you need to begin marketing your publication. That means selling subscriptions. Amazingly, the subscription price for a newsletter can be many times that of a popular, full-color magazine. That's because newsletters are viewed as "inside information," available to only a select few. When people subscribe to a newsletter, they want specific information that is highly valuable to them. Because of that, they will pay yearly subscription prices of $25, $50, $100, even as much as $150 to $200! Couple that with the fact that your cost to print each newsletters will be less than $1, and you get an idea about the astonishing profits that can be made.

You can search for subscribers to your newsletter in two primary ways — by advertising it in magazines that are similar to the topic you have chosen, or by buying direct mail lists of people who are known to have an interest in your topic.

You get lists from list brokers. To find out where they are, consult the Mail List Directory, published by Standard Rate and Data Services. Ask you librarian for this book. Most libraries have it on the shelves, or can get it for you.

You can publish your newsletter on whatever schedule you want — weekly, monthly, bi-monthly, or quarterly. Obviously, the more frequently you issue it, the more you can charge. But frequency of issue is often not the main determinant of price. Rather, it is the value of the information within the pages of your publication that truly makes it attractive.

These days, home computers are making newsletter publishing easier than it ever has been before. There are literally dozens of choices among "desktop publishing" software you can choose that makes writing, design and layout so easy, it almost feels like cheating.

Before we finish our discussion of newsletter publishing, let's briefly examine another angle on making money in this business. Instead of publishing your own newsletter, you can hire yourself out to produce newsletters for other businesses or individuals. This is also a well-paying occupation. Freelance newsletters writers easily earn up to $1,000 per 6-page issue. Most savvy newsletter writers can finish an entire issue in just one week. That means you can earn $1,000 a week or more by writing and putting together publications for other people who supply you with topic and information.

Especially with the availability of modern computer equipment and desktop publishing software, newsletter publishing and writing is one of the best bets for people who want to strike out on their own.

World Class Publishing

137 4th St. N, Suite K

Greenbush, MN 56726

Business Marketing

220 E. 42nd St.

New York, NY 10017

212-210-0187

PRINTING BROKER

This is a great job that you can get into with a bare minimum of start-up costs. What you need is a healthy dose of knowledge, and in this case, a thorough knowledge of the printing business.

Printing is a mystery to many people. There's a lot more to getting something printed than you might imagine. Getting words and pictures printed onto paper is a process that involves dozens of decisions and variables. What paper stock should be used? What color or shade of paper. How many colors should the publication have? What dimension of paper is best? What kind of binding? What typestyles should be used? How many copies should be run, and at what price? How do you obtain a printer's bid? How do you find the best deal? Who will do the typesetting? Who will do make-up? Will the publication be camera ready, or must the printer prepare the publication, partially or completely?

We could go on, but you get the picture by now. But please note: while the printing process involves a lot of decisions, it is far from rocket science! Learning the ins and outs of how printing is done is not only easy, but fascinating.

Even so, most people have no desire or time to deal with all the questions involved in having something printed. That opens up an opportunity for you. By becoming an "expert" on the printing process, you can act as a go between for client and printer. As such, you will perform a number of tasks for your client.

For one, you will seek out the best deal for your client. You do that by getting bids on each project from as many printers as possible. This helps your client because you will be able to save him or her money with your "inside" knowledge about who will do the job for the best price. You can also save them money on materials, once you learn about which paper looks best for the least cost, how money can be saved on ink, and so on.

Next, you will save your client time and anxiety by handling all the details — by providing the answers to all of the questions we listed above. With a thorough knowledge of how printing works, that will be a snap.

To get started, read a small book called the "Pocket Pal," which is available in your library or from the International Paper Company, P.O. Box 100, Church St. Station, New York, NY 10046. This paperback-sized books describes the printing process in detail, and will provide everything you need to know.

You will also be consulting with your client about what they have in mind for their publication. Most people have a general idea about what they want. It is your job to take their general idea and make all the specific decisions.

So how do you make money at this? Mostly by taking a commission on each project you broker. Doing so can make the money ad up quickly. Most printing jobs run into thousands of dollars. You can easily take a 10 percent commission. A $10,000 printing job may take you only a day or two to arrange, and that could net you $1,000. You could easily broker several jobs per week.

Often, a client will order additional press runs of a publication. In that case, make sure they go through you, and not directly to the printer. You can make a commission on each additional printing for doing no extra work beside giving the order for more.

Obviously, the more you know about the printing process, the better you will be at your job. Learn all you can, not only about printing, but about graphic art, design, paper stock, binding processes and more.

Of course, you must market yourself aggressively to garner clients. Get a business card and letterhead, and send them to every business you can think of. Direct your letters either to the top public relations officer, the CEO or even the accountant — that is the person most interested in saving money. If you emphasize that you can save a company significant money on printing costs, you'll get their attention — and a job.

International Paper Company

P.O. Box 100, Church St.Station

New York, NY 10046

RESUME WRITER

Writing resumes is fast, easy to learn and do, and good money — very good money. A resume writer can easily earn $150 to $200 a day.

As you know, a resume is a sheet of paper, often just one-page in length, which provides and outline of a person's qualifications for employment.

The vast majority of resumes are simple documents used by young people looking for non-skilled or minimum-skill jobs. They list education, past job experience, special talents or abilities, references, and contact information. An experienced resume writer can complete such a document in 15 to 30 minutes, and charge $15 to $20. From this, it's easy to see that a resume writer can earn $50 an hour or more.

Some resumes get much more complex as the educational level and experience of the client grows. But the more difficult the resume, the more you can charge. Some resume writers command from $150 to $200 for a top-notch, multi-page resume. Either way, simple or complex, you make decent cash as a resume writer.

These days, anyone can learn to write excellent resumes. For one thing, there are many excellent book on resume writing and resume styles. You do not have to be a skilled writer to prepare a resume. It's more a matter of following a format, and plugging in all the pertinent information in the right places.

Second, there are many computer software programs available which practically write resumes for you! It's true. All you need to do is open up the program, type in the information your client gives you, push a button and out pops a professional looking, high-quality resume. Then it's time to collect your fee!

Even though writing resumes is easier than ever, many people still don't feel comfortable with tackling the job themselves. Perhaps the most time-consuming aspect of resume writing is listening to people, and making sure that you get all of the important information you need. This is where listening skills can help, and also some knowledge of employment counseling.

To gather business, place an ad in the "Business Services" section of your local newspaper. Posters or flyer at busy bulletin boards are a good idea, too. College students are huge users of resume services, so be sure to place an ad in the student newspaper of your local college, and place your posters on the University hallway information boards.

Another "insider' tip: approach your local quick print shops and ask them for referrals. In exchange for a referral, tell them you'll send your client back for printing once you have written their resumes.

Your best resource is your local library, bookstore or computer software dealer. Ask for resume books or resume writing programs. Within just a few days, you could be earning a $30,000 per year, or more, with your own resume writing service.

For more information try:

Mariwhit Communications

P.O. Box 811

Xenia, OH 45385

BUSINESS PLAN WRITER

For almost every new idea, it seems there's an entrepreneur out there willing to take the chance and turn it into a viable business venture.

Small businesses continue to spring up around the country. And that good news, since its estimated that small business provides people with their first two out of three jobs.

Because of the nature of small business — getting by with just enough people and barely enough hours in the day to do everything — creating a thoughtful business plan often gets pushed to the side.

That might not seem like too much of a problem. However, research indicates that a well thought out business plan sets a direction for the company and increases its chances of success. Taking the time to project the company's expenses and revenues, consider a healthy organizational structure, and develop a market strategy are exercises too valuable to skip.

A business plan can also be a tool to help companies attract financial investors. It can be help convince them that the business is a solid venture poised for growth and success.

It is in a company's best interest to develop a business plan. And that's the message you need to send to potential clients as you develop a career as a business plan writer.

Your most important role as a business plan writer is to listen and interpret. Your clients have all the ideas and data you need to write the business plan — your job is to organize it all in the most clear, concise, and direct format possible.

And today's almost unlimited menu of computer software makes it easy for you. There are several business plan writing software programs available that prompt the author into creating a well structured, thorough business plan.

Another plus is that the competition for business plan writers is small. And with good writing and organizational skills, a background in business operations, and the people skills to communicate clearly with your clients, getting into this business may be a cinch.

The earnings from a career in business plan writing can range from $20,000 to $60,000 for 10 plans a year. Business plan writers typically charge between $2000 and $5000 per plan. The more plans that a business plan writer creates yearly, the higher the earnings.

Sometimes clients may simply want you to prepare an outline for them, or edit a plan they've written. There's opportunity to charge a few hundred dollars for services like these and create a referral base at the same time.

In addition to great earning potential, a business plan writer can look forward to working with a diverse base of businesses. You get involved in helping set the direction for success. You may even find a hot investment for yourself, taking an equity interest in a client's business as part of your fee.

At the same time, be aware that start up businesses represent risk. They are subject to economic swings, and there may be times when it is difficult to get work. Also, because new businesses often operate hand to mouth, paying for your services may end up low on the priority list.

To get going as a business plan writer, you'll need a computer with a printer. You'll also want to purchase business planning software. Letterhead, envelopes, promotional material, and business cards will also be necessary in creating a professional image.

Having a sample of your work will be a powerful sales tool that you should develop as well. If you're not familiar with business plans, you'll need to study business planning first. Then try out the software. You may want to consider writing a business plan free of charge to gain experience and to have a complete plan to show clients.

Networking through your personal contacts and business associations is a great way to begin the search for clients. If you don't belong to an association, joining one or two is a good idea.

You may want to create alliances with educational or governmental institutions that provide training and assistance to start-up businesses. Banks that fund small business could also be sources of client leads.

If you have enough business experience, you may even choose to teach courses on starting a business or entrepreneurship and get to know potential clients.

Just as the number of start up businesses is growing in our country, so are the opportunities for business plan writers. Maybe it's just the career opportunity you've been looking for!

Resources:

The Business Plan: A State of the Art Guide, by Michael O'Donnell, Lord Publishing, One Apple Hill, Natick, MA 01760; (508) 651-9955, 1988.

How to Prepare and Present a Business Plan, by Joe Mancuso, Englewood Cliffs, NJ: Prentice-Hall, 1983.

CREDIT CARD MARKETING TO COLLEGE STUDENTS

Would you like to make extra income by making sure credit card applications are correctly filled out? You can, if you market credit cards to college students.

There once was a time when college students were considered a bad risk by credit card companies because they don't usually have a regular income, a credit history, or any personal assets.

Within the last 10 years or so, credit card companies have changed their minds when they discovered students are a large potential market. When the money runs short, college students tend to use their credit cards for buying anything from books to pizzas.

Your job as a credit card contact is to sign up as many college students as possible for the various participating companies. In any given day, you might handle applications for cards from American Express, Visa, Discover, Sears, or more local gas company cards.

Because many college students are eager to sign up for cards, it is quite simple to find clients. Your first step is to talk to college officials about setting up a table in a good location like the main entry areas of busy student union and administration buildings.

Once you have a table with all of your material set up, your job is to let students know they can qualify for credit cards. Then stand back and watch the applications roll in!

Most credit card companies will pay you $2.00 to $2.50 for properly filled out applications. As long as all the information is in the right place, you get paid whether or not the student's application is accepted. You might process as many as 100 applications or more per day.

Once you get your business going, it pays to expand your market by training college students to assist you. With additional staff, you eventually can have tables set up in different locations at a number of universities.

To take full advantage of the student market, it's worth advertising your service in student newspapers and magazines, and distributing fliers to bulletin boards in dorms and fraternity/sorority houses.

A good source of information for starting up your own credit card marketing business is Financial Planning Associates. For a fee, this company will send you training manuals, introductions to lenders, and the instructions you need to get your business off the ground.

Contact Financial Planning Associates

210 Fifth Ave.,

New York, NY 10010.

LOAN MARKETING TO HEALTH CARE PROFESSIONALS

With its ever increasing demand for services and technology, the health care industry is one of the major industries in this country today. And the number of doctors, nurses, dentists, and other health care professionals continues to grow.

You can cash in on this booming industry without ever having to take one day of medical school. Simply set up a business loaning money to health care professional, and you can make a tidy profit.

Loan money to doctors? Aren't they filthy rich as it is? In fact, doctors and other health care providers are generally not as rich as you might think. The average doctor in America grosses around $125,000, and they are among the higher paid health care people!

Because of liability insurance, competition from other doctors, and the high cost of new technologies, many doctors find they have to take out loans to pay for all of these necessities. That is where you come in.

Several lending institutions are very willing to lend money to doctors because they are seen as a low risk, guaranteed income. Of all the people in the U.S., they are among the least likely to default on loans because they have to protect their reputations in the communities where they practice.

Your job is to match doctors with money sources. There are four basic types of loans doctors are looking for. They are accounts receivable financing, equipment sale/leaseback financing, unsecured loans, and 20-year amortized secured loans.

You receive a commission for each loan you arrange, with your commission being around four to five percent of the total loan. And many health care professionals have a credit rating of up to $1.2 million. This means you could make $5,000 on one $100,000 unsecured loan!

A great way to find customers is to visit the doctors personally. Depending on your area, you may be able to see 15 to 20 doctors in a week. If you arrange even one loan, you might make $2,000 or more for just that one week.

A good source of information on starting your own loan business for health care people is:

Financial Planning Associates

210 Fifth Ave.,

New York, NY 10010

INDOOR ENVIRONMENTAL TESTER

The things we are exposed to everyday within our homes and offices may literally be making us sick. That is a growing theory of several health professionals not only in this country but around the world.

The dangers of chemicals that make up our household surroundings are slowly being discovered, tested, and documented. More and more studies are being done on the effects of electricity, magnetism, and gases that we're obliviously exposed to on a daily basis.

With several hazardous household substances identified as likely culprits of depressed immune systems, instigators of allergies, and even causes of cancer, people are wanting to protect themselves by knowing more about the environments they are living in.

Indoor environmental testers can provide people with the facts about many potentially harmful aspects of the homes and offices in which they live and work.

Environmental testers look for several problem areas, like the levels of molds, bacteria, and dust. They also check on levels of toxic gases like carbon monoxide, carbon dioxide, and sulfur dioxide.

Electromagnetic radiation from nearby power lines, indoor wiring, appliances, televisions and video terminals, and other electrical sources is also tested.

They will examine toxic substances found in carpets, fabrics, wall coverings, furniture, and household chemicals. Insulation will be tested for asbestos. Sources of lead will also be checked, like within paint, dishware, and crystal.

As an environmental tester, your clients will often be people who are already ill of suspected environmental conditions. Their doctors often recommend as a part of their treatment a re-conditioning of their home to minimize the risks of further complicating the disease.

With our society becoming ever more health-conscious, however, increasing numbers of healthy people are having their indoor environments evaluated in line with illness-prevention and more healthful living.

Indoor environmental testers can expect to charge by the hour at $60 to $100, or by the job. An electromagnetic check, for example, may run a fixed income customer like a senior citizen $125 while the same test on a 3500 square foot home is $525.

Typical yearly earnings for an indoor environmental tester billing 20 hours a week at $65 an hour is $65,000.

An initial investment will be required to become an indoor environmental tester. You will need professional equipment with which to sample, test, and measure toxic and hazardous elements.

Most importantly, environmental testers need to be able to assimilate the broad amount of information that exists currently and that will continue to filter in about the potential hazards of indoor living spaces. You need the technical background on the chemistry or physics of potential problems. You need to understand the common and not-so-common sources of potential dangers. And you need to be able to offer viable, affordable solutions to homeowners on how they can minimize their risks.

Your own risks in the business include personal exposure to the very things you are trying to help your clients avoid. The work could be emotionally draining since you will be in contact with environmentally ill people a good deal of the time. A combination of sensitivity for your clients' conditions with detachment to preserve your own emotional state of being is a very helpful skill.

And because some of the testing you will be doing is still controversial, like exposure to electromagnetics, you may sometimes feel like you're under fire to justify your work.

Overall, however, the environmental field is booming and it's a great time be considering a career as an indoor environmental tester.

Start finding clients by networking with doctors and dentist who regularly diagnose environmentally ill patients. Some will even prescribe your services as a part of the patient's treatment and will contract you directly to perform the work. City planning departments and building inspectors may also be a source of referrals.

Get listed in the yellow pages as well as health and environmental resource guides. You might consider advertising in publications like these as well.

Generate as much publicity as you can about your expertise and services. Hold seminars on healthy indoor environments or write articles on potential hazards in the home.

If you aren't an expert in the field, plan to become one. Network with other environmental professionals. Research and keep up with the latest developments in your field. Practice your skills out on the homes of friends and relatives.

Your own desire for healthful living and a genuine interest in a fast-growing, ever-changing field may make you a perfect candidate for a career as an indoor environmental tester.

For more information, contact:

National Association of Environmental Professionals,
Box 15210, Alexandria, VA 22309; (703) 660-2364.

INFORMATION BROKER

This is truly the age of information. Technological advances within the last couple of decades have catapulted our ability to quickly generate information of almost every imaginable kind and in almost unlimited ways.

With so much information accessible on computer networks, libraries, through colleges and other institutions, and through private sources, finding what you need can seem like finding a needle in a haystack.

This situation has created the need for information "detectives", or brokers, whose job it is to track down specific pieces of information needed by their clients.

If it seems like a rather limited profession, consider this — information search and retrieval is a $13 billion industry and is expected to grow by 12 to 14 percent a year.

Information brokers work mostly for corporations and other professionals. A company, for example, may need information about their competitors. They might also need information that helps them make decisions — like the potential of expanding into a new market or introducing a new product.

Other professionals hire information brokers as well. Lawyers preparing for a trial may need to become experts fast on a particular case in which they don't currently have sufficient background. Almost any professional can benefit from the services of an information broker when working on projects requiring specific knowledge and expertise that's beyond their usual scope of work. And because information brokers are skilled in where and how to search, they can not only access hard-to-find information, but can do it more quickly and efficiently than the general public.

Although libraries are still important sources of information, computer communication capabilities like the Internet have minimized the number of information brokers found hiding out in the reference section. There are thousands of on-line computer databases, several news wire services, and now most major magazines, newspapers, and other publications can be accessed from your computer. Except for an an occasional interview with an expert to extract some necessary information, the only reason you may need to ever leave your house while working is to pick up the kids from soccer practice.

Information brokers need a love of the search. Hours might be spent looking and looking for what might be small but specific bits of information. You may shuffle through mounds of information on a particular subject you are researching — you need to be creative on where you look as well as a sharp eye to separate out what the client really needs versus all the "fluff".

The income for information brokers can range significantly. Hourly rates are from $35 to $100 or possibly more for highly sensitive or difficult searches. Given that, you may earn $17,000 for 10 hours a week at $35 per hour to more than $75,000 for 20 hours a week at $75 per hour. Because you typically bill by the hour or job, the more jobs you get and the faster you work will increase your salary.

A computer with on-line capabilities, a printer, and a budget for on-line services and time are necessary expenses of the business.

Information brokers need to find a niche in which they specialize. It might be in medicine, computers or other specific technology, law, business, international affairs — your own personal interests and background can help you decide.

Find your clients by networking within groups and associations that serve your particular industry. Promote your abilities and own expertise to potential clients. Write articles and give speeches on significant information you've discovered for clients like them. And since many people may not be familiar with your profession, you may need to do a little extra selling to convince them of your value. Explain how you do what you do, using your specific know-how and time, to get the right data they need.

If there's a natural investigator inside of you, being an information broker might be the perfect career for using your talents and being your own boss.

For more information, contact:

Association of Independent Information Professionals, 38 Bunker Hill Drive, Huntington, NY 11743.

Special Libraries Association, 1700 18th Street N.W., Washington, DC 20009; (202) 234-4700.

MEDICAL BILLING SERVICE

The state of our health care industry is one of America's hottest topics. The ways in which people receive care and the costs involved are topics being debated all the way down from the senate floor to the dining room table.

The health care industry has grown more complicated over the years, and in line with that have been increasing complications in the billing of medical services. Due to a 1990 federal law, doctors instead of patients are now required to submit claims to Medicare for reimbursement. The vast oceans of medical claims to Medicare, Medicaid, and private insurance firms requires a a full-time staff by medical providers like hospitals or long term care providers.

For smaller medical practices, however, the costs of a full-time billing staff may be too high. With a good number of physicians in private practices, there is a great need for the services of contracted medical billing.

Medical billers handle all the paperwork and phone calls it takes to process medical invoices and receive payment. Clients look to their billing contractors to be well versed in the almost overwhelming procedures and stipulations it takes to secure a check in the mail.

Medical billers often focus in an area of specialization, like orthopedics or radiology. They may also specialize in types of claims, like workman's compensation. In this way, they can become familiar with the medical diagnostics being billed for and the ins and outs of getting paid for them.

Medical biller need to be organized, have a sharp eye for detail, and knowledge on the rules and regulations for filing claims to governmental and private sources of insurance providers. Not only is this necessary to collect payment, but you can share what you know with patients who are more than grateful for your advise in sorting through the health care maze.

Good communication skills are an asset to medical billers since there will no doubt be several telephone calls to insurance providers in collecting. And since insurance providers typically pay a portion of the bill, you're left with the task of collecting the rest from the patient. The clearer and more diplomatic your communication, the quicker your success.

Medical billers may charge by the hour for their services at $10 to $25. They might also charge a fee per claim ranging from $5 to $100 depending on how complicated the claim is. Some also charge a percentage of the fees collected, usually from 3 to 8 percent. They may charge as much as 50 percent for collecting on overdue, difficult accounts. Typical annual incomes for medical billers ranges between $20,000 and $50,000 working 40 hours a week at $10 to $25 per hour.

A computer with medical billing software and a printer can get you going in your own business. Begin by calling on doctors with private or semi-private practices. Use a direct mail piece if you like. Check the classified ads and respond to those looking for billing help. You might even consider working in a hospital part-time to get exposure to physicians who could use your services.

If you don't have experience already, you'll need to learn about the medical field in which you choose to specialize. You'll also need to take courses on filing medical claims, which Medicare offers free through their local insurance agent contracted to process their claims.

The need for contracted medical billing services is growing. Now is a good time to begin your home-based business as a medical biller.

For more information, contact:

Medical Claims Processing Business Guide,
Entrepreneur Magazine, 2392 Morse Avenue, Box
19787, Irvine, CA 92713; (800) 421-2300.

MEDICAL CLAIMS PROCESSING SERVICE

Not everyone has the luxury of having all their medical claims processed by the clinic or hospital which they go to. Some clinics and hospitals are leaving the paperwork of filing insurance claims up to the patients.

Sorting through the rules and regulations of filing claims can be more than most people are willing to handle. It is time-consuming and confusing at best. At the worst, doing it wrong can delay payment and put a person in an uncomfortable financial position.

That's why many people opt to have their medical claims processed by an independent medical claims processing service. People in this business are familiar with the ropes to working with government and private sources of insurance. They can provide clients with the peace of mind that things will get done right and the benefits due them will be paid.

Medical claims processors need to be able to interpret the various types of policies available to people through insurance providers. They also need to be highly organized with a track record of accuracy. Communication skills are important — you need to be able to understand a client's situation as well as work with insurance staff to get paperwork pushed through as efficiently as possible.

Medical claims processors typically charge between $25 and $60 per hour. An average annual earning is $60,000 billing 30 hours a week at $40 per hour.

The general public is not overly familiar with this profession. It can be compared to other outside services they use, however, like tax preparers and lawyers. It's a specialized service that can make sure things are done right and save them time and money in the long run.

You can begin looking for clients in this business by contacting billing departments and social service workers who are in regular contact with patients' use of medical services. Ask to leave a brochure near their offices where potential clients will be likely to look.

Senior citizen populations are also a good market to target. Speak in front of organizations with high senior citizen memberships. Do direct mail to neighborhoods with a high senior citizen populations.

Small companies may also be a source of business. They often don't have the human resources staff to assist employees with medical claims. Your services can be contracted and employees can contact you directly for help.

Finally, there are simply some patients who are physically or mentally unable to file their own claims. Doctors and hospitals can refer these type of clients to you.

You may have medical background and are ready to get going in this business. If not, you'll need to understand medical terminology and become familiar with filing claims, reading and understanding policies, and working through the stipulations government and private insurance companies operate under. Medicare and other insurance providers often offer classes that you might take advantage of.

As the population ages, the number of medical claims needing to be submitted to insurance companies will likely grow. With the right qualifications, you can use your skills to start your own home-based medical claims processing services.

For more information, contact:

Medical Claims Processing Business Guide,
Entrepreneur Magazine, 2392 Morse Avenue, Box
19787, Irvine, CA 92713; (800) 421-2300.

MEDICAL TRANSCRIPT SERVICE

As a part of serving patients, doctors need to record and document their medical finding and treatments. These documents are often required by insurance providers in order to collect payment, they serve as legal evidence of treatment, and are sources of reliable data for research or statistical data collection.

Doctors verbally record the information verbally with a cassette recorder. It is the job of transcriptionists to listen to the tapes and turn them into typed reports.

There is currently a shortage of transcriptionists in the U.S. More hospitals and doctors than ever before are looking outside clinic walls for help in this area. Research indicates that transcriptionists working at home are more productive than those coming into the office every day.

With computers allowing people to transfer information back and forth with a simple telephone call, the medical transcriptionist can access hospital computers and digital dictation equipment. You need to have the discipline to sit for hours at your computer terminal with headphones delivering you the information to be transcribed.

It's easy to understand that quick and accurate typing skills are a must to do this work. So is the talent to listen and instantly translate what you hear into words on the computer screen. Given the medical field, you also need to recognize the words you are hearing and understand basic medical procedures of the field. If you don't have medical background, it will be necessary to take a medical terminology course or study up on terms on your own.

Editing is also a part of your job. Doctors are skilled in treating illness but not necessarily in grammar. And although you can develop this skill, you need to be able to persevere with your work through what might be difficult accents or dialects.

Medical transcriptionists have traditionally charged by the character, although with the advent of computers some now charge by the byte. Charging per page at $2 to $5 or by the line at 7 to 14 cents are more common. Hourly fees of $15 to $30 are also charged, particularly for more difficult work like interpreting a heavy accent or rush service, which is often the case.

Typical annual incomes range from $30,000 to $60,000 based on a 40 hour work week and making between $15 and $30 per hour. Let doctors, hospitals, clinics, and even attorneys with medical cases know you are available. Do direct mail and follow up personally. Drop off a business card or brochure if you can't get an appointment. Advertise as well in local medical publications.

Check the classified ads for medical transcriptionists. Describe your experience and explain the benefits of hiring a home-based contractor. You might also network with other transcriptionists and share referrals or overloads.

If you already have experience in transcribing, and can set yourself up with a computer, modem, printer, and transcribing equipment, and be ready to start your own business in short order. If not, you may need to contact a resource like the American Association for Medical Transcription (AAMT) or a community college which offers training to gain the skills for this career.

For more information, contact:

American Association for Medical Transcription, Box 576187, 3460 Oakdale Road, Suite M, Modesto, CA 95357; (209) 551-0883.

PROFESSIONAL ORGANIZER

Although still a relatively unknown profession, the professional organizer does just as the title says — helps people, and companies, get organized.

In this day and age of ever-accumulating tasks and "stuff", both individuals and organizations may feel overwhelmed by the amount of things that need their time and attention. As stuff mounts up, houses and offices become more disorganized, and feeling out of control begins to settle in.

It's the perfect time to call in a professional organizer. Professional organizers tend to specialize in one aspect of helping people and companies get organized — how to make the most efficient use of their living or office space space, managing their time according to goals and priorities, delegating work, creating a filing system for mail and paperwork, preventing clutter by having a place for everything, and maximizing use of storage and closet space.

Professional organizers may work on flat fees, charging one rate for a particular service, like organizing a work space. They might also charge a flat fee for training or a needs assessment. Hourly rates of between $25 and $125 are also common. And working on a retainer by contracting so many hours each month is often an arrangement made with corporate clients.

A typical yearly income for a professional organizer is $40,000 billing 16 hours a week at $50 per hour.

Although it's not hard to think of people or businesses we know that could desperately use the help of a professional organizer, the reality is there is a reluctance to pay for these type of services. It make take hitting crisis mode before the professional organizer is called in.

For these reasons, it's important for professional organizers to help their clients visualize the tangible benefits, the before-and-after picture, to assure them of the value of the service. The best testimony to the value of your work is your own demonstrated organization — being on time, meeting your commitments, stress-free and immediate access to what you need.

You should also be flexible to the needs of your clients. No one strategy is going to work for all of them. You should also have a broad enough base of knowledge on products, supplies, and strategies for getting organized that meets their particular needs and style.

Being a good listener and able to work with the varying degrees of disorder — and the different ways people react to the chaos in their lives — is an important skill. The professional organizer doesn't always have all the answers, either, and should be up front with their clients about that. Clients should be challenged to work along with you to come up with solutions that best fit their situation.

The rewards of your hard work are truly relieved and grateful clients. Getting them, however, may take a lot of up front time and energy. Unless you have several clients on retainer for repeat business, it's important to continually market for new clients.

Start by teaching classes, and speaking and networking at community meetings or business organizations. Also make contact with professionals in related fields, like interior decorators or consultants, whose clients are also businesses and can be a source of referrals.

Consider advertising in the yellow pages and getting as much free publicity as you can by submitting news releases and articles to trade and local publications.

You might even consider a regular newsletter with organizing tips to current and potential clients as a consistent marketing tool.

With the proliferation of more and more stuff making the homes and offices of Americans more complex, it's easy to see the need for professional organizers. The business is evolving, and if growing along with it sounds like a challenge you're up for, starting a career as a professional organizer now puts you on the ground floor.

For more information, contact:

National Association of Professional Organizers, 1163 Shermer Road, Northbrooke, IL 60062; (708) 272- 0135.

PROFESSIONAL PRACTICE CONSULTANT

Increasing numbers of doctors, dentists, and other professionals are going into private practice for themselves. Many are finding that running a business is at least as much a full-time effort as is practicing in their particular field.

That's why many private practice professionals are hiring practice consultants. Practice consultants handle part or all the tasks of running their business, from handling payroll, to hiring and training personnel, to billing and collections. Some are even taking on marketing responsibilities.

The majority of a practice consultants clients are in the medical field. And with the competition between private practice professionals growing, investing in a practice consultant is a wise investment.

In addition to just needing to stay current in their field, today's medical professionals have to practice smarter and run their businesses more efficiently in order to stay cost and service competitive. Professional practice consultants can bring organization and focus to running a tighter, more effective ship.

Practice consultants tend to specialize in a given field of medicine, like anesthesiology or dentistry, although some work as generalists. Experience and education ranges from MBA's and CPA's to years of working within a doctor's office.

Practice consultants charge by the hour for their services, ranging significantly from between $60 and $300 depending on experience and scope of the work being performed. They may also work on a monthly retainer. Average yearly earnings can be as much as the clients they're working for — $90,000 to $185,000 based on 30 billable hours per week.

Highly effective management skills to wisely manage not only your clients' businesses but your own as well are necessary to do well as a practice consultant. Your people skills must be sharply honed in communicating effectively with your well-educated clients and dealing with the many issues you'll face in running their business.

If you've been working in the medical field, you already have established contacts which to target as potential clients for your new business. Find new ones by networking within professional associations that serve your area of specialization. Join charities or community organizations in which your target clients are involved.

Generate publicity for yourself by speaking on management topics for the same professional associations and other related organizations. Work on getting articles printed in trade publications.

If you have the necessary management skills and experience, getting the equipment to set yourself up as a practice consultant is easy. Your investment will include a computer, printer, business software, a fax, a business card, and professional stationery.

As both a way to utilize your past management skills and make an above-average income, a career as a professional practice consultant might just be the perfect career choice.

For more information, contact:

Society of Medial-Dental Management Consultants, 6215 Larson Street, Kansas City, MO 64133; (800) 826-2264.

Society of Professional Business Consultants, 600 South Federal Street, Chicago, IL 60605; (312) 922-6222.

NEW LUXURY CAR FREE

For better or worse, most Americans still equate total success with owning a killer car. A Cadillac, a Lincoln- Continental, a Mercedes Benz. When you have a Corvette parked in your driveway, the entire neighborhood looks at you with unbridled envy. When you cruise briskly down the freeway in your $40,000 fully loaded Jeep Grand Cherokee, you get glances of wide-eyed longing from behind the windows of the rest of humanity, most of whom are driving some boring, ordinary Chevy, or worse, some battered clunker.

Don't you feel sorry for a person when you see them rattling along in a dented-up '78 VW Rabbit? The engine sounds like some geezer squirrel running along desperately in a tin cage, pathetically chasing a nut it will never catch.

If you are an ordinary human being, you frequently lust for the car of your dreams — either the plush luxury of a Cadillac, or the lightening power of an easy-to-maneuver Porche 944.

YOU CAN HAVE IT ALL!

Well, I'm here to tell you that owning the car of your dreams can become a solid reality for you — and you don't have to sell one of your major body organs to come up with a down payment. In fact, you can own any luxury automobile — FOR FREE!

This is not a joke. I'd never tease about something like this. There is a way to own the luxury car of your choice without it costing you more than a few hundred dollars. This system has worked for hundreds of people, and it sure and Hades can work for you. Interested? Then read on!

Step One: You Need Your Own Corporation

The was to own the dream car of your choice is to set up an automobile leasing corporation, which will serve both as a tax shelter, and as a vehicle (no pun intended) under which you can obtain a free car.

No matter what your line of work, or whether you are self-employed or work for another entity, you can gain great benefits from having your own corporation.

First, owning your own corporation is like owning your own business, except you can distance yourself from certain liabilities and responsibilities — including a lot of taxes. Another thing you can avoid with a corporation are Social Security taxes, and a few other kinds of taxes.

When you own your own corporation, you will have much greater leverage in seeking and getting credit. You can also raise money from non-credit sources by selling stock in your corporation to private individuals. Also, when you own your own corporation, you have a far greater range of repayment options to your creditors. including issuing common stock, preferred stock and dividends.

If your corporation flops, you are protected from personal bankruptcy, and you can deduct up to $25,000 on your personal tax return. That's like having the best of both worlds!

DIFFERENT STATES, DIFFERENT LAWS

Each state has different guidelines for incorporation, so check with your state's Secretary of State office and request information they have about incorporating.

You do not have to incorporate within the state you are living. That's good because some states make it more difficult to incorporate than others. For example, some states require a minimum of $1,000 of capital before you can form a corporation. Some states will demand that you have an entire board of directors, including president, vice-president, secretary, treasurer, and more.

You can find out everything you need to know from the either the state's department of commerce of the office of the Secretary of State.

We recommend that you form your corporation in the state of Nevada. The reasons are simple; they have very few restrictions or limitations, and you will get some 16 percent more in tax breaks than you will in any other state in the Union. You do not have to be a citizen of Nevada to incorporate there, you don't even have to go there. You do not have to spell out the exact business activities of your corporation, and you can assign any value you wish to your stock.

There are other reasons to form your corporation in Nevada, but suffice it to say, you'll get the best overall deal. For complete details on how to form a Nevada corporation, call the state's Secretary of State office and request a packet of information on incorporation guidelines.

Or you can dial the Secretary of the State of Nevada's Document-on-demand Service toll free: 1-800-583-9486. Call this number and they will FAX you back all the documentation you need immediately.

To call the Secretary of State's Corporation's Office directly and talk to a live person, dial: 702-687-5105.

NAMING YOUR CORPORATION

Give your corporation and impressive sounding name, such as The Global Leasing Corporation, or World Class Capital Corporation. You must be sure, however, that no other entity already has the name you choose. Cross checking your name against the State of Nevada's data base is no problem, however, and the state will do this for you for a small fee.

CONTACT THE CAR DEALER

With your new corporation in place, it's time to contact car dealerships, and tell them that you going to purchase 5 to 10 new cars from them every year for the next five to 10 years.

Tell them that you are the President and CEO of the Global Leasing Corporation, and that you have a list of high-income clients (we'll get to that in a minute) to whom you will be leasing automobiles. Inform the dealer that you will need a demonstration vehicle complete with dealer car tags so that you can show the car to your clients. If the dealer agrees, he will provide you with a demonstration vehicle that has, most often, 5,000 miles or less on it. After that amount of miles, the dealer will most likely sell the vehicle as used and replace it with a new one — unless you lease it first.

Here you are already in a new luxury car — yours to use as you please for free — absolutely and totally free — even your insurance is paid for by the car dealer. You have the use of this car because your leasing corporation is going to sell 10 cars for your parent auto dealer.

Here's how you are going to move out those 10 cars:

GET A CLIENT LIST

As we said, you will need a strong list of high-income people, most likely doctors, lawyers, business owners, major corporate executives, and such — and you will be contacting each of them with this proposal:

Tell them that you can put them behind the wheel of the luxury car of their choice FREE OF CHARGE by taking advantage of existing tax shelter laws afforded by your leasing corporation.

Tell your clients that there is no reason to buy a luxury car straight out even if they can afford it, because they can drive the same car for free by working through your leasing corporation.

Set up a personal meeting with each interested client. At the meeting, be ready to give all the details of how you intend to get your client their free car.

And this is how you will make it happen:

Tell each prospect that they will be one of 10 — and the only 10 — who will be allowed to participate in this incredible free car leasing plan.

Each of the 10 people will invest $5,000, in return for which he or she will receive corporate stock. All 10 investors get an equal share in the Global Leasing Corporation.

By the way, it is important that you sign no more than 10 participants of this program, since that will preserve your status as a Sub-Chapter 5 corporation. Consult with an attorney to to make sure you are following all legal guidelines, and to ensure you are doing things correctly.

Now, here's how the numbers play out:

1. Because of tax advantages available only to corporation such as the one you have formed, each participant will receive 20 percent additional depreciation on one car for the first year. Value: $3,000.

2. In addition to the above, they get the normal first year depreciation deduction on their car: Value: $2,500. (Based on an estimates 6 years of car use.)

Total for the above two is $5,500.

This amount will be a personal write-off for each stock holder. All automobile lease payments made to your corporation are 100 percent deductible.

3. The total business expenses for the corporation for one year are $14,000. One-tenth of this is $1,400, which is given to each stockholder. Value: $1,400.

4. Each share holder makes an annual payment of $11,400 to the corporation.

5.   Total of each stockholder's tax deduction, which you arrive at by adding the $5,500 depreciation to items 3 and 4 above: $18,300.

6.   You subtract 50 percent because each high-income stockholder will be in the 50 percent tax bracket. Fifty percent of $18,300 is $9,150.

Each stock holders personal cash expenditure then is $9,150. (You subtract item 6 from item 5.)

7. Now the good part. You subtract the estimated value of the automobile at the end of one year, at which time the stockholder may take the car back to the dealer and receive this value for the car. The stock holder may take the car with no down payment. Total estimated value to subtract is $9,150.

This leaves the stockholder with a big fat "0" for his total cost of a year's leasing of an automobile.

HOW DO YOU BUY THE CARS?

You use the $50,000 is stockholder money to make a down payment on 10 cars. Your corporation can finance the balance of the total cost through a local bank. Yearly payments are made with the yearly stockholder investment, which they pay eagerly because of the money it saved them in tax write-offs.

That's it! That the outline of a plan that works. This is an absolutely do-able plan that has benefits that go well beyond your free luxury automobile.   Those benefits include the dozens of contacts you will make with high-income individuals, and their banker friends, their venture capital friends, and their tax-shelter hungry friends.

Once you start your first successful auto leasing corporation, you can start a second — and that means possibly a second luxury car for you to use. Now both you and your spouse can cruise the town in style.

17 FIVE SOURCES OF PRIVATE CREDIT-- AND FIVE YOU AVOID

In this section I want to talk about easy sources of money and credit that may be available to you right now — sources of easy you may not know about, but may be right at your fingertips.

1. Unclaimed Property

You've heard about it often — they say you might have money being held for you in a trust somewhere, left to you by a rich uncle or cousin you never knew about. There could be a million bucks stashed away in your name right now, if only you knew enough to claim it!

Are these kind of stories real? Does this really happen? Well, the answer is certainly yes! More often than you might think, money gets lost. People die, move to a different country, change jobs without knowing their old company had an annuity plan ... and many times this money just languishes somewhere until the owner — or the owner's next of kin come along to claim it.

It has been estimated that as much as $7 billion in unclaimed money is sitting in treasury vaults right now, just waiting to be claimed.

Furthermore, all local and state governments are required by law to provide an unclaimed property name listing. How do you find them? Contact your state Department of Commerce office and ask for a listing of unclaimed property and unclaimed estate listings.

Unclaimed assets can be among the following categories:

Demand Deposits

Trust Deposits

Unclaimed Wages

Policyholder Dividends

Shareholder Stocks

Saving & Interest

Money Orders

Cashier's Checks

Safety Deposit Box Contents

Traveler's Checks

Accounts Payable

Life Insurance Payments

Insurance Premium Returns

Liquidated Assets

Wages

Certified Checks

To find the office of unclaimed property in your state, simply call your state Department of Commerce and ask for the unclaimed property division.

To take just one example, I picked a state at random — Minnesota — called their Department of Commerce, and received this press release back:

COMMERCE DEPARTMENT ANNOUNCES OVER $5 MILLION IN UNCLAIMED PROPERTY

Commissioner David B. Gruenes today announced that the Dept. of Commerce is seeking thousands of Minnesotans who are the rightful owners of abandoned savings accounts, misplaced payroll checks, forgotten stocks and other unclaimed items.

Approximately 18,000 persons and businesses who own $5,344,000 in unclaimed funds were reported to the Dept. of Commerce by financial institutions across the state in the past year. in addition. the Department received 662 safe deposit boxes and

5605 stock holdings from financial institutions unable to find the owners of the property.

The release goes on to say that since state began returning unclaimed property in 1969, some $153 million has been collected and $68 million returned to rightful owners!

This example from just one state shows the explosive potential of unclaimed property — and you may be one of those people for whom money is just waiting to be picked up with your signature.

I urge you to call you state's Department of Commerce now to possibly claim what is rightfully yours!

2. People Who Give Money Away

It's as simple as this: some people have so much money, they just give it away to people who ask for it. I'll warn you right away that chances are small that you will be able to get this kind of money — on the other hand, it will cost you no more than the time it takes to write a brief letter and the price of a postage stamp. You have a far better chances of getting an award from one of the following that you do of winning the lottery.

The following is a list of people who give money away. What you have to do is write a brief letter, explaining your need and what you will use the money for.

David Bendah

"Monthly Donations"

6150 Mission Gorge Rd., Suite 222

San Diego, CA 92120

Comments" Will give money to just about anybody who makes a good case for needing it.

Annie Renssalaer

Sherman $ Sterling

53 Wall Street

New York, NY 10005

Comments: Gives money primarily to women who want to better themselves, or women in demonstrable need.

Alfred DuPont

P.O. Box 1380

Jacksonville, FL 32201

Charles D. Gilfillian

555 First National Bank

St. Paul, MN

Comments: Money to residents of Minnesota who are "distressed."

The De Hirsch Fund

386 Park Ave. S.

New York, NY 100016

Comments: Give money to Jewish people.

Frank L. & Laura Smock

116 E. Berry St.,

Fort Wayne, IN 46802

Comments: free money to people of Presbyterian faith.

Otto Sussman

Sulivan & Cromwell

48 Wall St., 19th Floor

New York, NY 10005

Comments: Free money to people in New York, New Jersey, Pennsylvanis and Oklahoma.

Charles M. Cox

Boston Safe Deposit and Trust Co.

One Boston Place

Boston, MA 02106

Comments: Free money to residents of Boston.

Robert A. Welch

2010 Bank of Southwest Bldg.,

Houston, TX 77002

Comments: Free money for research projects.

Mary Lynn Richardson

P.O. Box 20124

Greensboro, NC 27420

Comments: Free money to those who can show need or distress.

Joseph Collins

One Chase Manhattan PLaza

New York, NY 10005

Comments: Give money to people who want to attend medical school.

Virginia Scatena

Bank of America

Trust Dept.

P.O. Box 37121

San Francisco, CA 94137

Comments: Money to retired school teachers who are sick or in dire financial need.

Bernard Daily

P.O. Box 351

Lakeview, OR 97630

Comments: Gives primarily to students in Oregon.

Edward Wagner & George Hosser

C/O Amoskeag Natl. Bank and Trust Co.

P.O. Box 150

Manchester, NH 03106

Comments: Gives to people in the Manchester area.

In addition to the above individual, there are many corporate, associational and foundation sources of money for a variety of needs — from out and out charity, to grant money to start up a new business. The following are just a few of the best you should try:

* American Music Center

* AT&T Foundation

* American Cancer Society

* Annenberg/CPB Projects

* Apple Computer

* Arthritis Foundation

* Benton Foundation

* Billfish Foundation

* Cable Television Laboratories

* Carnegie Corporation of New York
* Corporation for Public Broadcasting
* The Eurasia Foundation
* Fields Pond Foundation
* Freedom Forum
* Gas Research Institute
* J. Paul Getty Trust
* Global Fund for Women
* John Simon Guggenheim Memorial
* International Foundation for Science
* Elton John AIDS Foundation
* Robert Wood Johnson Foundation
* George Lucas Educational Foundation
* John D. and Cathrine T. MacArthur Foundation
* Mitsubishi Electric America Foundation
* The Karl E. Mundt Foundation
* Nieman Foundation for Journalism
* The North Atlantic Treaty Organization (NATO)
* Pauline Oliveros Foundation Inc.
* Rotary Foundation
* The SEGA foundation
* Sierra Club Foundation
* Alfred P. Sloan Foundation
* Society for the Psychological Study of Social Issues
* Sun Microsystems Foundation, Inc.
* W.E. Upjohn Institute
* The Whitaker Foundation
* The Winston Foundation for World Peace

* Robert Wood Johnson Foundation

3. Computers Can Sniff Out Credit For You

More and more, your computer is your connection to just about everything you need in life. Today, you can order a pizza over the internet. If you can order a double pepperoni with anchovies, why can't you find a loan through your computer screen? Why not indeed!

There are companies, such as Datamerge, Incorporated in Denver, Colorado, that will find investors and other alternative money sources for you through massive computer system searches, and they'll do it for you for a small fee, often less than $150.

The search is worldwide and you can find anywhere from from $5,000 to $15 million.

HOW IT WORKS

Datamerge uses a directory to mail information such as an explanation of your business idea and an estimation of costs, to tens of thousands of financiers.

If a financier is interested, their response is sent to Datamerge, which in turn responds to you through your computer via e-mail. You can then respond directly to the financier.

Contact Datamerge by phone at: 303-320-5840

4. Another Great Source of Funds

A Partners for Growth business start-up grant program has been formed by AT&T Capital Corp. and the American Institute of Certified Public Accountants (AICPA). It is being operated on a trial basis in Houston and Philadelphia. The purpose is to help socially responsible businesses of less than two years old.

Being socially responsible entails addressing community needs by participating in activities that help people with dis abilities, neighborhood revitalization, figuring solutions of fighting poverty and creating new jobs for poor people.

In each of the cities, three to four companies will be chosen to divide $50,000, which will be spent on furniture, rent, office space and other business related costs. The AICPA will also follow-up as monitoring consultants.

Grant application can be obtained by calling: (800) 235-4288.

5. Seek out Joint Government-Private Sources

In many states, government and private groups are joining together to give people who want to start small businesses have greater access to capital

For example, in Birmingham, Alabama, The Birmingham Community Development Corp. Inc., managed by Gilchrist & Co. Inc., is offering loans to socially or economically disadvantaged businesses.

The money is drawn from an $8 million allocation contributed by local banks and the city. The loan can be used for short-term gap or receivables financing, start-up and working capital, asset acquisition or credit enhancement. Loans range from $5,000 to $150,000, with the city guaranteeing up to 75%.

In 16 states, AR, CA, CO, CT, DE, IN MA, MI, MN, NH, OK, OR, UT, VT, WI, WV including New York City, there are loan programs set up using a portfolio insurance structure eliminating the need for government approval and establishing a reserve fund to cover losses.

In Hawaii small businesses can get loans up to $50,000 through a pilot program operated by the state and local banks.

The Hawaii Small Business Loan Program is made up of a $3 million fund established by commercial banks.

For information on other programs contact your municipal, county and state economic development departments.

6. Check Your Own Non-liquid Assets — How $100 can Get you $10,000

The greatest thinker of this century was Albert Einstein. He once said: "Sometimes, it takes a genius to see the obvious."

That statement is true of people who are scrambling for credit. What they don't realize is that they may have a great source of money right under their own noses.

For example, you may have heard of the famous (and now perhaps infamous) talk show host Jenny Jones. The Canadian-born Jones was struggling to get into show business in the U.S.A., but was finding that road a tough one. Then one day an agent told her that it might help if she were a bit more ... well, shall we say, chesty.

Jones decided she needed breast implant surgery, and needed $5,000 to get the job done. The problem was that she didn't have $5,000, and no bank would give it to her for what at the time was considered a risky and needless operation.

Jones, undaunted, decided to have a garage sale. To her surprise, Jones has enough "junk" laying around to gain the 5 G's she needed. She got her breasts enlarged, and went on to make it big in the talk-show-host arena.

The moral of the story is not that you need bigger boobs to make big money, although sometimes it probably helps. The point is that you may be sitting on a pile of cash without knowing it. Have you looked in your garage or attic lately? You should do so, and bring a pen and notepad with you. Make a complete inventory of everything you own. Hundreds of people have tried this, and many of those hundreds are amazed at all the stuff they have — stuff which can be converted into quick cash.

Now, what if you have never been a pack rat, and what if, after doing a thorough inventory, you find that you have perhaps no more than a hundred bucks worth of stuff you can sell?

Well, what you lack in hard cash, you can make up for in cunning and intelligence. If you take in just $100 after your garage or rummage sale, that money can be doubled as a source of credit. You do so by applying for a secured credit card, which will pay you from 150 percent to 200 percent of the amount you put up front.

Invest your $100 in a secured credit card, and you end up with $200 in credit.

Now that you have $200 to spend, I recommend you use the card several times, buying only small items, of $10 or $20, and then paying the expenditures back in full.

After several weeks of this activity, you will have built up a favorable credit rating with your card company, at which point, you can request an increase in your credit limit.

Before long, your $100 credit card can be expanded to a $10,000 credit limit. Thus, $100 can quickly become $10,000.

Furthermore, even if you put your $100 into a savings account, the fact that you have a savings account gets you a lot of extra points on your credit application. The same goes if you start an annuity or buy a CD. The bank will not ask how much money you have in your savings account, or how large your CD note is — they will just assume that you have enough extra money to be investing in savings — and thus your credit rating will sore.

Here I have demonstrated just a few ways that easy cash is available to you at this very moment. With just a bit of creative thinking, I have no doubt in my mind that you can come up with a many more on your own. Good Luck!

NOW ... THE FIVE CREDIT SOURCES YOU MUST AVOID!

It's an unfortunate fact that some of the easiest sources of credit are also the most harmful and destructive. I recommend that you absolutely avoid the following five source of so-called "easy money."

1. Illegal sources of money.

You have heard about this in the movies and on TV — loan sharks whom roam the streets of large cities, borrowing money to hard-up individuals, or people who are simply dumb enough to get involved with unsavory characters.

So-called loan sharks are usually associated with organized crime. They will borrow you money easily — but then will demand outrageous rates of interest, from 100 to 5,000 percent - and larger! And if you fail to pay them back in full? Yes, they actually will break your legs, even kill you. Does this kind of thing really happen? You bet it does! it Happens every day! Don't let it happen to you!

Most people get involved with loan sharks because of gambling debts, need for drugs, or for some other extremely bad decision they have made.

Yes, sometimes people need money for innocent purposes — for medical needs, or to help a person in trouble. But borrowing money from illegal sources or street criminals is a fast way to a suite in the bottom of a river with a pair of concrete overshoes wrapped around your ankles.

2. High Interest Credit Cards

Any credit card that starts edging its interest rate above 18 percent is nothing but ridiculous greed. You should avoid these high-rate, legal, yet rip-off credit card companies at all costs. You can always get a better rate, especially because there is so much competition these days among card companies. Simply shop around and get the lowest rate card you can find.

3. Rent-to-Own

Renting to own is one of the easiest sources of credit you can find. Rent-to-own stores advertise loudly that you can enter their store and walk out just minutes later with the high-ticket toy of your dreams — anything from a big-screen TV to a killer stereo system — without so much as a credit check.

The problem is, rent-to-own stores charge absolutely astronomical rates of interest. By the time you pay for your item, you will have shelled out 100%, 200% sometimes even as much as %500 percent more that the original sticker price of that item.

This is a lousy deal, to say the least. Do not deal with rent-to-own stores — they are getting extremely rich on the desire for instant gratification among millions of people. Don't be one of them.

4. Pawn Shops

I find pawn shop owners to be disgustingly greedy pigs. You can bring in a super-nice piece of stereo equipment, and they might give you 1/50th of what it is worth. Pawn shop owners are cranky, mean, greedy people who know you are desperate — otherwise you would not be pawning your own belongings. Believe me, pawn shop owners are totally committed to taking advantage of your misfortune, and most often will. When you are desperate, you'll take a thumping. Most often, there is no need to. Today, with the vast and easy availability of so many credit sources (read the rest of this book!) you should almost never need the services of a filthy pawn shop.

5. Mail-Order Credit Companies.

You have most likely seen their ads in a variety of magazines — some kind of firm seeming to offer you any kind of money you need on your signature alone.

But I recommend you never contact these organizations, again, because they most often barely legal loan sharks who know that you are desperate for money. They will take advantage of your situation, and before you know it, you have signed a huge contract full of fine print, which basically says that you own these people everything except the blood in your veins in exchange for the money they lend to you.

Many of these unscrupulous mail-order sources of money seek to get their claws into you for life — they will get rights to garnish your wages from now and into forever, take your tax refunds, claim right to any money you may inherit — and just about any other source of income you may ever have for the rest of your life.

You will sign away all of these right in cleverly written contracts that no sensible person will be able to read and understand.

If you want to borrow money, stick with high-profile credit card banks, or other well-recognized sources of capital. If you are thinking of dealing with a firm you have never heard of, call your state Attorney General office and check to see if these guys are a reputable firm. Other ways to check on the validity of a loan maker is the Better Business Bureau, your local Chamber of Commerce or other such entities.

18 HOW TO GET A LOWER INTEREST RATE

If you are going to borrow money, you might as well borrow with the lowest interest rate as possible. Why would you want to pay hundreds — and often thousands — of dollars in interest if you don't have to?

Yet, that's what thousands of people do every day. Like sheep being herded by a pack of wolves (bankers) they simply accept whatever terms are placed before them. Borrowers most often sign the papers at the first bank they try, never even thinking to shop around for a better deal, or asking for a lower rate,

In this section, I am going to talk about several common things you can do to get a lower interest rate on money you borrow, and several "little known" tips and tricks which I am sure you have never heard of before. So let's get started.

SHOP AROUND

I've already mentioned the most obvious way to get a lower interest rate, and that's shopping around. No, not all banks are created equal, not all banks have exactly the same interest rates, and banks are not the only source of credit. Before you take out any kind of loan, check with several banks before you accept an interest rate.

Second, check out nonbank sources of credit, such as credit unions, government agencies, venture capital firms — even with your rich uncle for better terms.

There are two Federal laws which help you compare costs, and you should know about them:

1. TRUTH IN LENDING

This law requires creditors to give you certain basic information about the cost of buying on credit or taking out a loan. These "disclosures" can help you shop around for the best deal.

2. CONSUMER LEASING

This can help you compare the cost and terms of one lease with another and with the cost and terms of buying for cash or on credit.

Two Terms You Must Know: Finance Charge and Annual Percentage Rate

By remembering the above two terms, you can compare credit prices from different sources, and always get a lower interest rate.

Under Truth the in Lending Law, the creditor must tell you — in writing and before you sign any agreement — the finance charge and the annual percentage rate.

The finance charge is the total dollar amount you pay to use credit. It includes interest costs, and other costs, such as service charges and some credit—related insurance premiums.

If you borrow $500, for example, the interest for a year might cost you $50. But if their were also a $25 service charge, you end up paying $75. Such an additional fee is common — and is truly bogus. Do you know what it costs a bank to process a small loan of $1,000 or less? About one dollar — yet many slap a $25 processing fee, simply because they can. I suggest you remind your banker that such fees are excessive, and often, they will wave the processing fee. or greatly reduce it.

The annual percentage rate (APR)is the percentage cost (or relative cost) of credit on a yearly basis. This is your key to comparing costs, regardless of the amount of credit or how long you have to repay it:

Again, suppose you borrow $500 for one year and pay a finance charge of $50. If you can keep the entire $500 for the whole year and then pay back $550 at the end of the year, you are paying an APR of about 10 percent. But, if you repay the $500 and finance charge (a total of $550) in twelve equal monthly installments, you don't really get to use $500 for the whole year. In fact, you get to use less and less of that $500 each month. In this case, the $50 charge for credit amounts to an APR of 18 percent.

All creditors—banks, stores, car dealers, credit card companies, finance companies-must state the cost of their credit in terms of the finance charge and the APR. Federal law does not set interest rates or other credit charges. But it does require their disclosure so that you can compare credit costs. The law says these two pieces of information must be shown to you before you sign a credit contract or before you use a credit card.

A COMPARISON

Even when you understand the terms a creditor is offering, it's easy to underestimate the difference in dollars that different terms can make. Suppose you're buying a $7,500 car. You put $1,500 down, and need to borrow $6,000.

If you were looking for lower monthly payments, you could get them by paying the loan off over a longer period of time. However, you would have to pay more in total costs, and more processing fees. Therefore, choose the shortest pay-off time you can live with and save a bundle on interest other phony-baloney fees banks love to charge.

Other terms—such as the size of the down payment—will also make a difference. Be sure to look at all the terms before you make your choice.

COST OF OPEN-END CREDIT

Open-end credit includes bank and department store credit cards, gasoline company cards, home equity lines, and check-overdraft accounts that let you write checks for more than your actual balance with the bank. Open-end credit can be used again and again, generally until you reach a certain prearranged borrowing limit. Truth in Lending requires that open-end creditors tell you the terms of the credit plan so that you can shop and compare the costs involved.

When you're shopping for an open-end plan, the APR you're told represents only the periodic rate that you will be charged—figured on a yearly basis. (For instance, a creditor that charges 1% percent interest each month would quote you an APR of 18 percent.) Annual membership fees, transaction charges, and points, for example, are listed separately; they are not included in the APR. Keep this in mind and compare all the costs involved in the plans, not just the APR.

Creditors must tell you when finance charges begin on your account, so you know how much time you have to pay your bill before a finance charge is added. Creditors may give you a 25-day grace period, for example, to pay your balance in full before making you pay a finance charge.

Creditors also must tell you the method they use to figure the balance on which you pay a finance charge; the interest rate they charge is applied to this balance to come up with the finance charge. Creditors use a number of different methods to arrive at the balance. Study them carefully; they can significantly affect your finance charge.

Some creditors, for instance, take the amount you owed at the beginning of the billing cycle, and subtract any payments you made during that cycle. Purchases are not counted. This is called the adjusted balance method.

Another is the previous balance method. Creditors simply use the amount owed at the beginning of the billing cycle to come up with the finance charge.

Under one of the most common methods-the average daily balance method—creditors add your balances for each day in the billing cycle and then divide that total by the number of days in the cycle. Payments made during the cycle are subtracted in arriving at the daily amounts, and, depending on the plan, new purchases may or may not be included. Under another method—the two-cycle average daily balance method—creditors use the average daily balances for two billing cycles to compute your finance charge. Again, payments will be taken into account in figuring the balances, but new purchases may or may not be included.

Be aware that the amount of the finance charge may vary considerably depending on the method used, even for the same pattern of purchases and payments.

If you receive a credit card offer or an application, the creditor must give you information about the APR and other important terms of the plan at that time. Likewise, with a home equity plan, information must be given to you with an application.

Truth in Lending does not set the rates or tell the creditor how to calculate finance charges—it only requires that the creditor tell you the method that it uses. You should ask for an explanation of any terms you don't understand.

GETTING INTEREST TO WORK FOR YOU

THE MAGIC OF COMPOUND INTEREST

Now let's talk about a way that you can pile up enormous sums of cash without doing a lick of work. You do it through the magic of compound interest.

Compound interest is the interest paid daily, weekly, monthly, quarterly or annually on interest bearing accounts of all kinds, from ordinary passbook savings to CDs and retirement plan vehicles.

The thing about compound interest is that it makes your money grow exponentially. For example, if you put $3,000 into a annuity which accumulates compound interest of, say 10 percent, you will have earned $300 by the end of the first year.

But the next year, the interest, because it is compound, accrues on the larger sum -- the $3,300 -- and at the end of year two, you will have $3,630. At the end of year three, you will have $3,993. At the end of year four, you will have $4,392.

In just 10 years -- and even if you don't put another dime into your fund -- you will have $7,778!

But the first 10 years is the rate of slowest growth. That's because the 10 percent annual interest accumulation is multiplying on the smaller amounts. As each year goes by, the principal on which interest is accrued increases by an cumulative of all previous years.

In just a few short years, you will have hundreds of thousands of dollars -- $100,000, $200,000, $300,000 thousand dollars and more!

All of this money build while you do absolutely no work!

Now let's go a step further -- if you start with $3,000, and manage to keep adding, say, just $100 a month to your principal sum, you will easily become a millionaire long before it is time for you to retire at the easy age of 62 -- the year in which life begins! The more money you invest, the faster you become a millionaire -- with the magic on compound interest, you can easily retire in just 20 years.

Therefore, I urge you, I beg you to start a retirement fund of some type TODAY! -- whether it be a 401K Plan, an Annuity, a Life Insurance Fund, or whatever -- as long as your fund build compound interest, you'll be getting incredibly richer with each passing year!

FILE VARIATION

Now I want to warn you about something called file variation. File variation can work both in your favor, but often against your ability to be granted credit.

File variation simply refers to differences in information as it appears on your different credit files, or credit application forms.

For example, if you sign your name "John Smith" on one credit application form and "John J. Smith" on another, you have created file variation. The two names above may or may not be the same person -- a credit source may not know.

John Smith may have a superb credit rating, while John J. Smith may have a lot of black marks against him. Some people try to create whole new, and clean credit records for themselves through subtle file variation methods. By starting over with a new or different looking name, you can work off an entirely new and clean slate -- and there is nothing dishonest about any of it as long as your variation does not constitute a falsehood. If your middle initial actually happens to be "J" you have not produced false information -- you have simply varied your file.

There are many ways to create file variation. You can list different incomes on different forms. You can vary your assets from one form to another. Oftentimes, the reason for the variation is purely innocent -- perhaps you changed jobs and have a whole different income and address from the last time you filled out a credit application form.

Another aspect of file variation is your signature. To ensure good credit, make sure you sign your name the same way every time. Many people actually vary the way they sign their name from one instance to the next. For example, a man by the name of Kenneth Smith may sometime sign his name simply as "Ken" Smith -- and this unwittingly creates file variation.

Many credit sources check a number of your credit records as they appear in different credit bureaus. If the lender finds a considerable amount of file variation, they may get suspicious, assume you have been "doctoring" your credit record, and turn you down flat.

The moral of the story is -- file variation can work to your advantage, but can also trip you up. Vary your file with care and use your common sense.

GLOSSARY OF CREDIT AND OTHER FINANCIAL TERMS

ACCRUED INTEREST-Interest on a loan that accumulates and is to be paid in installments at a later time (usually when the principal becomes due) rather than being paid from the time the loan is made. Accrued interest may be compounded or simple.

ADJUSTED GROSS INCOME (AGI)-Taxable income after all allowable deductions are made, such as IRA deductions, moving expenses, self-employment taxes and health insurance, Keogh retirement plans, and alimony paid.

AMORTIZATION- The reduction of loan debt through your monthly payments of principle.

ASSET PROTECTION ALLOWANCE- A sum subtracted from a family's total assets when determining the "expected family contribution" to college costs. This provides a safety net for families, and the allowance increases with the age of the parents.

ASSETS- The amount a family has in savings and investments. This includes savings and checking accounts; a business; a farm or other real estate; and stocks, bonds, and trust funds. Cars are not considered assets, nor are such possessions as stamp collections or jewelry. The net value of the principal home is counted as an asset by some colleges in determining their own awards but is not included in the calculation for eligibility for federal funds.

BASE YEAR- The twelve-month period ending on December 31 preceding the year in which a student will enroll in college. For example, applicants seeking aid for 1996-1997 will use 1995 as the base year.

BILLING SERVICER - A company that manages the billing and collection of loans for lenders.

BORROWER- Any "legal entity" — a person or group—that obtains funds from a lender for a particular period of time. A borrower signs a "promissory note" as evidence of indebtedness.

BUSINESS/FARM SUPPLEMENT- An additional financial aid form

required by some colleges for parents and students who own a business or farm. This form is processed by the College Scholarship Service as a supplement to the Financial Aid

CAPITALIZING INTEREST- A process where a lender adds any unpaid interest to the principal of the loan, thereby increasing the balance due and the monthly payment. Unlike many lenders, Citibank capitalizes only once upon repayment, and that means significant savings for you.

CAMPUS-BASED FINANCIAL AID PROGRAMS- Three major aid programs are funded by the federal government but the disposition of the funds is handled by colleges' financial aid offices: the Federal Supplemental Educational Opportunity Grant, the Federal Perkins Loan, and Federal Work-Study (FWS).

COLLATERAL- Something of value pledged as security for a loan. Banks do not require collateral for all loans.

COMMERCIAL BANK- An institution whose primary function is making loans to businesses.

COMPOUNDED INTEREST- Interest that is periodically added to a principal sum, resulting in a new principal balance which then triggers a new interest assessment.

CONSOLIDATION- Combining your loans and transferring them all to one lender. When you consolidate your loans, a new loan is originated with new terms.

COSIGNER- A second creditworthy party who signs a promissory note with a borrower who does not have collateral or good credit history. The second party guarantees that the loan will be repaid if the borrower fails to make payments.

CREDIT BUREAU- An agency that compiles and distributes credit and personal information to creditors. This information may include payment habits, number of credit accounts, balance of accounts, and length and place of employment. Note: You have the right to examine your credit file and to explain or correct information. There is usually a fee for this, but there is no charge if you have been denied credit because of information in a particular credit bureau's file.

DEFAULT- Failure to pay your loan back according to the terms disclosed oN your promissory note. You are in default on an FFEL Program Loan if your payments are more than 180 days past due or if you fail to comply with other terms of the loan. When this occurs, any of the following may happen: The default will be reported to national credit bureaus, recorded on your permanent credit record, and can significantly and adversely affect your credit history; You may be subject to legal action by the holder of the loan; Your wages may be garnisheed; You may be unable to get additional federal or state financial aid, including student loans.

DEFERRED INTEREST- Interest payments that are delayed while a borrower is not gainfully employed, as, for example, when the borrower is a student. This benefit is generally characteristic of federal and state guaranteed student loans.

DEPENDENT STUDENT- A student claimed as a dependent member of household for federal income tax purposes.

DISBURSEMENT NOTIFICATION - After the loan is approved, a letter goes out acknowledging approval and stating loan disbursement schedules, loan amount, and any fees (origination or guarantee). It marks the successful completion of the application process.

DISCRETIONARY INCOME- Income that is available to a person or family after all financial obligations, including taxes, have been accounted for.

EFT (ELECTRONIC FUNDS TRANSFER)- The fastest and easiest way to receive a student loan disbursement. Once the loan application is approved (and the school participates in this program), the funds are wired directly to the school. A paper check is not sent.

ELIGIBLE NONCITIZEN- A financial aid applicant who is not a U.S. citizen but is eligible to receive federal Title IV aid because he or she is a permanent resident, noncitizen national, or a resident of the Trust Territory of the Pacific Islands or Micronesia.

ENTRANCE INTERVIEW- Required counseling session at which a college administrator, usually a financial aid officer, must inform student borrowers about their rights and responsibilities.

EXIT INTERVIEW- A counseling session conducted when the student is leaving college at which the student's loan obligation and responsibilities are reviewed.

EXPECTED FAMILY CONTRIBUTION (EFC) or PARENTAL CONTRIBUTION- A figure determined by a congressionally mandated formula which indicates how much of a family's resources should be considered "available" for college expenses. Factors such as taxable and nontaxable income and the value of family assets are taken into account to determine a family's financial strength. Allowances for maintaining a family and future financial needs are then taken into consideration before determining how much a family should be able to put toward the cost of college.

FAFSA (Free Application for Federal Student Aid)- The official application students must use to apply for federal aid.

FEDERAL DIRECT LOAN- A group of federal loan programs for which the lender is the federal government. Included in these programs are government-subsidized loans for students and unsubsidized loans for both students and parents.

FEDERAL EDUCATION LOAN PROGRAMS- A group of federal loan programs for which the lender is a bank, savings and loan, credit union, or other private organization. Included in these programs are government-subsidized loans for students and unsubsidized loans for both students and parents.

FEDERAL FAMILY EDUCATION LOAN (FFEL) PROGRAM- These are funds that students and parents can borrow to help pay for college expenses. The program includes the Federal Stafford Loans (subsidized and unsubsidized) and the Federal PLUS Loan. Eligibility for the Federal Stafford Loans is based on need and the cost to attend college. Eligibility for the Federal PLUS Loan is based on the cost to attend college and requires a credit-check.

FEDERAL METHODOLOGY- A standard method of calculating how

much a family should be expected to contribute toward college costs. All the federal funds are awarded based on this need analysis formula.

FEDERAL PELL GRANT- Federal grant awarded to undergraduate students based on need.

FEDERAL PERKINS LOAN- A 5% loan funded by the government but awarded by colleges to both undergraduate and graduate students.

FEDERAL PLUS LOAN- A nonsubsidized loan program for parents of undergraduate students under the Federal Education Loan Program umbrella.

FEDERAL STAFFORD LOAN- A Federal Education Loan Program for students. Stafford Loans can be either government-subsidized, in which case the government pays any interest while the borrower is attending college, or unsubsidized, in which case interest begins to accrue when the loan is made.

FEDERAL STATE STUDENT INCENTIVE GRANT- Awards made as part of a state grant program utilizing both federal funds and state monies.

FEDERAL SUPPLEMENTAL EDUCATIONAL OPPORTUNITY GRANT (FSEOG)- A federal grant awarded by colleges to the most needy undergraduate students as determined by the federal need analysis formula.

FEDERAL WORK-STUDY PROGRAM- A federal, need-based financial aid program through which eligible students can earn a portion of their college expenses. Work-study awards are made by colleges, but a portion of the funding comes from the federal government. Several states also have work-study programs that are similar to the federal program.

FINANCIAL AID AWARD LETTER- Written notification to an applicant from a college that details how much and which types of financial aid are being offered if the applicant enrolls.

FINANCIAL AID PACKAGE- The total amount of financial aid a student receives for a year of study.

FINANCIAL AID PROFILE- A financial aid application developed by the College Scholarship Service that many colleges use to determine aid given from their own institutional funds.

FINANCIAL AID TRANSCRIPT- A record of any financial aid a student has received at a given institution. To be eligible for federal financial aid programs, students must submit such a transcript from all previously attended postsecondary institutions.

FINANCIAL NEED-The difference between a college's cost of attendance and a family's ability to pay (Expected Family Contribution) as calculated by the need analysis methodology.

FIXED INTEREST- A rate of interest that is set at the time a loan is negotiated and that remains constant over the life of the loan.

FORBEARANCE - A special arrangement granted by your lender in the event you encounter financial hardship, and you are not eligible for any other deferments. If you meet the requirements of forbearance, the terms of the loan might change so that principal payments can be postponed, the repayment terms can be lengthened, or smaller payments can be made for a specified period of time.

FREE APPLICATION FOR FEDERAL STUDENT AID (FAFSA): - The form required by the federal government to apply for financial aid. Additional forms may be required for campus-based aid.

GIFT AID- Grant and scholarship money given as financial aid that does not have to be repaid.

GRACE PERIOD- The length of time allowed by program specification when borrowers are no longer in school but do not have to begin repaying their student loans. Some loan programs have no grace period; others may not require repayment to begin for several months.

GROSS INCOME- A family's or individual's total income before deductions.

GUARANTEE AGENCY- The organization that administers the Federal Education Loan Programs in each state and insures lenders against losses due to a borrower's default, death, disability, or bankruptcy. The federal government sets loan limits and interest rate, but each state is free to set its own additional limits within the federal guidelines.

GUARANTEE FEE- An insurance fee, usually paid by the borrower, that the guarantee agency charges a lender. The fee for a Federal Stafford or PLUS Loan is 1%.

IMMIGRATION AND NATURALIZATION SERVICE (INS)- The federal agency responsible for administering immigration procedures and assigning citizenship status.

INTEREST - The price paid (or fee charged) to borrow money. The interest is computed as a percentage of the principal amount owed.

INTEREST SUBSIDY- Interest payments made by the federal government to the lender of a Subsidized Federal Stafford or Direct Loan while the borrower is enrolled at least half-time or is in a grace period.

INTERNAL REVENUE SERVICE (IRS)- The federal agency responsible for collecting income taxes. Student aid applications are often verified by their family's IRS forms.

LENDER- One who provides money on the condition that the money be returned, usually with an interest charge.

LOAN DISCLOSURE STATEMENT- A document that shows the amount of a loan; where, when, and what repayments must be made; the interest rate; and the cost of borrowing that loan.

LOAN SERVICER- The company that provides customer service on your loan for any type of activity that occurs on your account from the time you receive your first check disbursement until your final payment is made. This includes questions on loan status, deferment/forbearance, payments, address changes, school transfers and more. Your loan servicer may not be the same as your lender.

MERIT-BASED AID- Any form of financial aid awarded on the basis of personal achievement or individual characteristics without reference to financial need.

MINIMUM WAGE- Section 6 of the Fair Labor Standards Act of 1938 - currently set at 4.25 per hour.

MULTIPLE DISBURSEMENTS- When a loan is paid out in more than one check or electronic transaction. Multiple disbursements occur when loan proceeds are needed for more than one term during an academic year.

NEED ANALYSIS- The method of calculating a family's expected level of financial contribution toward college costs, resulting in an estimate of the amount of financial assistance a student will "need."

OFFICE OF STUDENT FINANCIAL ASSISTANCE (OSFA)- The U.S. Department of Education that has the responsibility for administering federal student financial aid programs and for developing aid policies and procedures.

ORIGINATION FEE- A processing fee charged to a borrower by a lender to make a loan. This fee, like the guarantee or insurance fee, is usually subtracted from the amount of a loan.

OVERAWARD- A situation that occurs when a student's family contribution plus any financial aid awarded exceeds the cost of attendance at a given college. Overawards result most often when a student's enrollment status changes or when additional resources (such as a private scholarship) become available to a student.

PLUS LOAN PRE-SCREENING- For potential parent borrowers who are concerned with their credit history to get a better idea of their eligibility for a Federal PLUS loan. For those parents the pre-screening process can save time during the loan application process.

POVERTY LINE - The poverty guidelines for 1996 as published by the Department of Health and Human Services are currently set at

$10,360 per year for all states and Washington DC,and ($12,940) for Alaska and ($11,920) for Hawaii.

PRIME RATE- The fluctuating interest rate that banks charge to their best business customers. Many commercial loans have interest rates that fluctuate based on the prime rate.

PRINCIPAL- The amount you owe. It's also the amount on which interest is charged.

PROFESSIONAL JUDGMENT- The legal authority of financial aid administrators to change a calculated Expected Family Contribution or any of the elements used in the calculation based on additional information or individual circumstances that would lead to a more accurate assessment of a family's financial condition.

PROMISSORY NOTE- A contract that legally binds a lender and a borrower. The note details all the terms and conditions of a loan, including the amount, the interest rate, and repayment obligations.

REPAYMENT SCHEDULE- A plan that sets forth for the loan recipient the amount due in each payment period, the number of payments required to pay back the loan in full, and the due date of each payment.

SATISFACTORY ACADEMIC PROGRESS- As determined by each college for its own students, the level of academic achievement expected of a student in order to continue to receive financial aid.

SECONDARY MARKET- Institutions that buy loans from lenders, usually at a discount. This practice provides more capital for lenders to make additional loans. If a loan is sold, the secondary market is responsible for managing anD servicing it. The sale of a loan does not affect the borrower since the terms of the loan remain the same.

SELF-HELP EXPECTATION- The principle that students have an obligation to help pay for a portion of their own education. The expected amount of self-help iS usually included in the analysis of a student's resources.

SELF-HELP AID- Funds from jobs and from loan programs, such as the Federal Perkins Loan, Federal Stafford and Direct Loans, and Federal Work-Study Program.

SIMPLE INTEREST -Interest computed only on the original amount of a loan.

SIMPLIFIED NEEDS TEST- A formula used in the Federal Methodology for families whose Adjusted Gross Income (AGI) is less than $50,000 and who file either the 1040A or 1040EZ IRS forms. In this formula, a family's assets are not included.

STATEMENT OF EDUCATIONAL PURPOSE- A separate form, or a statement on the FAFSA, that all students must sign in order to receive federal student aid. By signing you agree that:
   1. You are to use your student aid only for education-relateD expenses.
   2. You have complied with Selective Service requirements by registering with the Selective Service or indicating the reason why you are not required to register.

STUDENT AID REPORT (SAR)- An official document that colleges create for each student applying for federal aid.

SUBSIDIZED LOAN- A loan for which the borrower is not responsible for all of the interest payments. For Subsidized Federal Stafford and/or Direct Loans, the government pays interest to the lender on behalf of the borrower while the student is in college and during approved grace periods.

TREASURY BILL - Short-term U.S. government debt obligations. Treasury Bills are backed by the full faith of the U.S. government. The T-Bill rate is established weekly at an auction. The interest rates on the Citibank Assist Loans are tied to the T-Bill. This loan has a variable interest rate which changes every 91 days or quarterly.

UNMET NEED- When the combination of a student's financial aid package and the family contribution does not cover the costs of attending a particular college, the gap is called the Unmet Need.

UNSUBSIDIZED- You are responsible for paying all the interest that accrues on an unsubsidized loan. Interest can either be paid while you are in school, or it can be postponed while in school until graduation or withdrawal, at which time it will be capitalized.

VARIABLE INTEREST- The rate of interest that changes during the life of a loan on a regular basis and is generally tied to an index. Some student and parent loan programs have variable interest rates that change annually based on the one-year Treasury Bill rate.

VERIFICATION- A process by which a financial aid office substantiates the data that a financial aid applicant has reported on a financial aid application. Additional information from the student, a spouse, and the parents is used to confirm previously submitted data.

INVESTMENT RELATED TERMS

BRIDGE OR SWING LOANS- Short term loan made in anticipation of longer term financing or equity Investment on which a prior letter of intent has been issued.

DEBT OFFERING- A debt instrument offer by a firm and purchased by private investors. Normally carries warrants for future stock purchases at fixed prices.

DIVESTITURE- The outright sale of company assets, such as ownership sale to employees, sale of large blocks of stock or orderly liquidation.

EQUITY PARTICIPATION- Offer of an ownership position to induce the investment, can take the form of convertible note that has an option to convert from debt instrument to equity.

INITIAL PUBLIC OFFERING- A Corporation's first offering of stock to the public. Listed here are funding sources that assist you through the detailed process of an IPO.

MARKET MAKER EXCHANGE (NASDAQ)- A broker dealer who stands ready to maintain firm bid and offer prices of publicly traded stock. Called a "specialist" on the exchange (NASDAQ).

MARKET MAKER OVER THE COUNTER- A broker dealer who

stands ready to maintain firm bid and offer prices of publicly traded stock. Called a market maker in the pink sheets (OTC).

MERGER AND ACQUISITION - The combination of two companies by the process of joining or sale. If one company survives it is a merger, if both survive it is an acquisition.

MEZZANINE FUNDING- Company's progress makes positioning for an Initial Public Offering viable. Venture funds are used to support the IPO.

PREFERRED STOCK OFFERING- The offering for sale of non-voting, preferred dividend payment stock to investors. Leaves full control of the corporation with original owners.

PRIVATE PLACEMENT- The stock investment purchase by an "angel" or institution. No Securities and Exchange Commission registration is required.

RECAPITALIZATION- Exchange of corporate bonds for stock. Typically occurs in bankruptcy or turnaround, where preferred stock (equity) is exchanged for bonds (debt).

SECONDARY PUBLIC OFFERING- A Corporation's second offering of stock to the public.

TURN AROUNDS- Investors who speculate that poorly performing companies are about to turn the corner and show profits.

UNDERWRITINGS- Broker dealers who assume the risk of buying the IPO stock offering and then reselling those same shares to the public at a profit.

REAL ESTATE RELATED TERMS

ACQUISITION & DEVELOPMENT - Loan for raw land infrastructure development (streets, utilities, etc.)

ADJUSTABLE COMMERCIAL MORTGAGE- Interest moves up or down with a specific index (Prime, T-Bills, etc. Construction /Mini-Perm Building(s) construction with 3 to 5 year loan, usually on income property.

CONSTRUCTION WITH TAKEOUT PACKAGE- Building(s) Construction with pre-arranged takeout loan in place.

FIXED RATE COMMERCIAL MORTGAGE- Interest Rate remains constant throughout the term.

FORWARD COMMITMENT - Pledge to provide a loan at a future date.

INTERIM LOAN- A short term (2 yrs or less), bridge or project type loan.

JOINT VENTURE- A financial partner in the development of real estate.

MORTGAGE NOTE BUYERS- Individuals or companies that buy existing commercial mortgages.

NON-CONSTRUCTION MINI-PERM- A three to five year loan, usually on income property.

PARTICIPATING CONSTRUCTION WITH TAKEOUT- The lender receives a kicker for profits above a preset level.

PARTICIPATING MORTGAGE- The lender receives a kicker for gross income above a preset level.

PERMANENT WITH ACCRUAL- A Loan where interest is accounted for but not paid for some period.

REAL ESTATE PURCHASE- Lending for the purchase of commercial real estate.

SECOND MORTGAGE (COMMERCIAL)- A loan secured by equity behind that of the first lien.

SECURITIZATION/SYNDICATION- The bundling of mortgage notes for sale on the secondary market.

STANDBY- A loan commitment not expected to be used (a safety net for trouble).

WRAPAROUND- A lender that makes a second mortgage and assumes the first mortgage.

COMMERCIAL LENDING RELATED TERMS
ACCOUNTS RECEIVABLE- Accounts receivable serve as collateral for short term working capital loans. Also called factoring.

ASSET BASED- Seeking to convert a particular asset into working capital. Giving a security in an asset(s) in exchange for cash.

BANKRUPTCY/REORGANIZATION- Financing to reorganize in company in a turnaround. Typically secured by assets; equipment, inventory, A/R, PO's, etc.

EQUITY PARTICIPATION- Offer of an ownership position to induce the loan or can be a note that has an option to convert from debt to equity.

EXPANSION FINANCING- Growth has outpaced existing business. Loan for existing demand. Key here is existing demand, not projected.

FRANCHISE FINANCING- Specialized financing reserved for the franchisees of recognized, typically nationally known, franchises.

IMPORT AND EXPORT- Loans to promote the shipping or receiving of products or materials. Based on existing market, demand or orders.

INVENTORY LOAN- A loan typically made as part of a relationship where the lender will also provide retail financing for the product.

LETTERS OF CREDIT- A guarantee of payment for the customer's draft, substituting the lender's credit and eliminated the seller's risk.

PURCHASE ORDER ADVANCES- Loans on the written order to purchase goods at a stipulated price with an agreed to delivery date. Credit rating of orderer is key.

REVOLVING TERM LOAN- Contract between lender and borrower to extend a pre-arranged amount of credit. Based upon existing inventory, A/R and PO's.

EQUIPMENT RELATED TERMS
FINANCING- Making of a loan using the equipment as collateral. Good operating history, credit rating, debt ratios are the keys here.

LEASING- Contract for a fixed period of time in exchange for payments, usually in the form of rent for equipment. Typically lower credit requirements.

SALE AND LEASEBACK- Sale of an asset for cash, with a contract to lease the asset back from the funding source purchasing the asset. Sales tax an issue here.

VENTURE CAPITAL TERMS
STARTUP FUNDING- Use this for earliest stage of business, starting from scratch, etc. In this case, you will get your money based on your business plan. The more detailed and credible your business plan, the better.

FIRST ROUND FUNDING- This is money for growth in a business you already have. Funding is often in the form of a loan or convertible bond.

SECOND ROUND FUNDING- Money for an established company where a future buyout, merger or acquisition by another company is a possibility.

LATER STAGE FUNDING- For an established company where money is needed to support major expansion or new product development.

EQUITY LOAN- This is a situation in which you offer the venture capitalist an ownership position to induce the loan. Also, is can be a loan that has an option to convert from debt to equity.

MEZZANINE FUNDING- This means your company has made enough progress to sell stock to the public and venture capital is needed to support his effort.

SPECIAL BONUS SECTION

#1

THE CREDIT GAME

Credit is just a game, like a lot of other life activities. When we win we pay as little for credit as possible, and when we lose we may not get any credit, or we may pay more than the market rate for our credit. We never want to lose.

To give you some guidelines of winning the credit game I am going to present you with many topics, and the first that I wish to give you is the first reader to the game itself. If you just relax and think of credit as a game, rather than as a vital function of life, you won't be upset when someone tries to pull a fast one on you in a credit purchase, and you won't feel that you are cheating someone else when you find ways of shifting your credit costs from expensive credit agencies to cheap ones. Accept credit as a game, and all that you have to do is learn the rules and the game plan and you can increase the number of times you win. Only when you win this game you get to keep real money.

HOW TO USE OTHER PEOPLES MONEY TO BECOME RICH

The name of the game in credit is getting the use of other peoples money, and if you can become rich doing it all the better. Now, as you look around at Donald Trump and Ross Perot, and any of those other big money people you would think that they would just have banks full of their money. As it turns out they don't. What they do have is a lot of property and investments with a little bit of their money, and a lot of other peoples money. Furthermore, the amount they pay these other people when they cash out is only a small part of the profits they get, and they keep the rest.

People will give you their money much more easily if you guarantee that they will get it back with a small profit, called interest. And this gives you the introduction you need to talking to people with money. It is the people with money who give credit, and who can give you the credit to become rich.

PEOPLE WITH MONEY

Let's take a little closer look at who these people are with money. After all, they are the ones you are going to have to deal with, or compete against, at some time in the future.

People with money are always anxious to make more, and that is also why they give credit to those who look like they can make money too. In giving credit, or making investments they take risks. They are generally pretty good at coming up with business ideas, or at recognizing good ideas of others who come to them for investment funds. They have confidence that there are opportunities for making money. Finally, they know how to get other peoples money, credit, when they need it to get an investment started. Is it something to do with these qualities that ends up making money? Perhaps, but that is what we will try to find out by looking at people without money.

PEOPLE WITHOUT MONEY

Now that I have brought up the question of people without money, of whom you may well be one, how is it possible to go from being without money to having money? Perhaps the clue lies in looking at the money-less for a few lines.

People without money are also ambitious, and they may even be more ambitious than the ones who have made money. Will they take business risks? The problem is that they take business risks without enough money to get their projects working properly. In fact the business ideas of those without money are just as good as those of the ones with money. After all, all of our business ideas come from the same experiences.

But do they know that good opportunities for making money exist? This they do know, they just do not know how to get a toe into the opportunity to make money for themselves.

Which brings us to the real difference between these two groups, people without money don't know how to get other people's money to get started, and people with money do know how.

To see the truth in this just consider yourself. You want to make money, you know there are good opportunities, you have good ideas, you are willing to take risks, but you don't have the money to get started. The reason you don't have the money to get started is because you don't know how to approach other people for the use of their money. Let's answer the question: How do you get started in using other people's money for your investments and businesses?

HOW TO GET STARTED IN USING OTHER PEOPLE'S MONEY

To use other people's money you first need to have a little money of your own. While you can do it with as little as $100, you would be better off beginning with $1,000. Your purpose is to establish a credit rating with this $1000, and to end up with most of this money in the end as well.

If you deposit the $1,000 in a saving account in a bank you can then make an insured loan against your deposit. Even if you have never borrowed money before banks will loan you money against savings they hold since they can always take the savings to pay off the loan. This gets you a credit rating with one bank, and if you repeat this with 4 more banks you will have a perfect credit record with 5 banks total. This is pretty good, but you also need the use of a credit card and some credit accounts.

In the last bank instead of taking a loan ask for an insured credit card with a $1,000 limit. Next go to some of the stores that offer instant credit, and many do. If they check your credit they will find you listed on 4 banks, and you will get your credit. To have an active credit account with these stores you still need to use the credit accounts. Charge items at each store, but do not use them, they are to be returned in a few days so that you can show credit payments to the stores. Buy items like appliances in boxes, not clothing that could be a problem. After you have made payments for a few months to the banks, and used your credit card a couple of times, and used your store charge accounts a few times, you will have a triple-A credit rating, making you eligible for the use of other people's money for your own investment needs.

AN ALTERNATIVE METHOD OF GETTING CREDIT

The method that I am thinking of does not require you to have any cash, and will start you out with a minimum balance of $1,000. At least that is what I believe they are offering these

Now most credit card issuers get their offer lists off of the mailing lists they buy from other credit card companies. However, they all recognize that people are leaving and entering their credit years all of the time. They leave because of retirement or death, and they enter just because children become men and women.

The best source of these new adults, and especially the ones most likely to have an income that is most secure, is to find the most educated part of the population. These people generally spend a few years in college, and credit card companies figure that if they show up at the colleges and offer cards to anyone who will sign up they will capture most of these people for their companies. That is why each year at the colleges you will see Bank of America, and other credit card issuers, with little tables offering to give any student who signs up with them a free bottle of soda. All that you have to do to qualify for one of these cards is to enroll in a college, and pretty much any college will do. If you are a college student and want a credit card you can have whether or not you have a job, or any credit record whatsoever.

BORROW $50,000 IN JUST 72 HOURS

Raising large amounts of money in a hurry may not be as difficult as you might think. Regardless of your present financial situation — little or no credit, or even bad credit — there are ways that you can borrow the money you need in as little as 72 hours. What's more, you can borrow this money as unsecured loans. That means no collateral, no co-signers, and no credit check. You can have "cash in hand" on your signature alone. And you can use the cash to pay off pressing debts, make new purchases, save, or invest. In some cases, you can even take up to 40 years to pay the money back!

The creative financing techniques described in this report have been used successfully by hundreds of people to borrow $50,000 and more. Depending on your financial need and credit status you can use these techniques to get "quick cash" through credit card loans and bank overdraft protection.

If you have credit problems, there are government loan programs designed to help you get the money you need. With careful planning and preparation, these techniques could enable you to raise enough cash to take care of all your financial needs.

CREDIT CARD LOANS

Credit card issuers offer "open-end" or "revolving" credit which can provide card holders with a predetermined line of borrowing power. As a card holder you can use this borrowing power either to make purchases or to obtain a cash advance. In either case, you can pay back the money as quickly or as slowly as you want. You'll receive a bill each month which specifies the balance due, the interest being charged, and the minimum payment. In order to stay current, you'll need to remit at least the minimum payment each month.

Ordinarily the best way to use a credit card is to pay off the balance due each month. You not only avoid paying interest but you also avoid the risk of running up unmanageable credit-card debt. As a rule, limiting the number and dollar amount of your cash advances is also advisable. There are, however, exceptions to every rule. If you've carefully thought out how you plan to pay back the money, credit card loans can be an excellent source of $500 to $50,000 and more in quick cash.

Most everyone has credit cards. Millions of Americans carry as many as 20 to 30 cards. The credit limits on those cards range anywhere from $500 for first-time card-holders to $5000 or more for people with established creditworthiness. Such cards can be used as sources for unsecured loans to raise the cash you need. For example, suppose you have 10 credit cards with pre-approved credit limits averaging $5,000 each. That means you have up to $50,000 in unsecured credit you can tap whenever you need quick cash. By taking advantage of such pre-approved cash advances, you can have the cash you need in 72 hours or less.

So, how can you get 10 or more credit cards? The answer to that question may be in your mailbox. Credit card issuers are constantly looking to sign up new customers. The competition for business is fierce with many lenders offering low rates and other enticements. They flood the mail with applications for credit cards with pre-approved cash advances. In fact, insider estimates are that almost 60% of new credit card accounts are obtained through direct mail. Instead of discarding those applications as junk mail, look them over carefully. Apply for the cards which offer the lowest interest rates and no or low fees for cash advances. If your credit is in good shape, you should have no trouble obtaining several such cards. If you are married, you and your spouse may be able to apply separately for cards with pre-approved cash advances. If you own a small business, you also can apply for cards in the name of the business.

Once you obtain several cards with pre-approved cash advances, you can begin borrowing the money you need. You can borrow any amount up to your credit limit with no questions asked. No collateral, credit checks, or co-signers are required. The loans were approved as soon as you received the credit cards.

While you can pay back your credit card loans slowly by making minimum monthly payments, it's best to pay off the loans as quickly as possible. By doing that you can keep the interest from piling up, reducing the overall cost of the loans. Also, paying off your loans in timely fashion will strengthen your creditworthiness. In that event, many lenders will automatically increase your credit line, providing you with even more potential borrowing power.

OVERDRAFT PROTECTION

Another relatively easy-to-use technique to raise "quick cash" involves using overdraft protection as a line of readily accessible credit. For many people, overdraft protection is just that — protection. It provides for the transfer of money into their checking accounts whenever their account balances are overdrawn. Other people have discovered, through wise planning and careful preparation, that overdraft protection also can provide a quick source of cash for investments, purchases or other purposes.

In order to get the most borrowing power out of overdraft protection, you'll need to set up accounts at several banks. Here's an example of how this creative financing technique might work: Open checking accounts in at least five banks in your area. Apply for overdraft protection with a $5,000 credit line at each bank. Some banks may turn you down, especially if they know you already have similar accounts in other banks. For that reason, it's important that you be able to convince each bank that you are not overextended. Don't be discouraged if a bank does turn down your application for overdraft protection, or gives you a credit line lower than you requested. Stay with the bank for several months and then reapply. If you maintain your credit in good standing, and can show the bank that you are not overextended, your application will most likely be accepted.

If each bank approves your application for overdraft protection, you will then automatically have a credit line of $25,000. Since each account has a credit line of $5,000, you can write five checks for $25,000 or just one check on one account for $500. All that will be required is your signature and the money will be yours in whatever amount you choose, up to $25,000 in 24 hours or less. Obviously, your borrowing power with overdraft protection depends on the number of accounts you open and the amount of your credit lines at each bank. Overdraft protection credit lines can range anywhere from $500 to $20,000 and more depending on your account and the policy of the bank.

Using overdraft protection as a line of credit can provide you with a steady source of "quick cash", but it also can get you into trouble. Many people are guilty of overdraft abuse. These people are constantly tapping this line of credit to make monthly bill payments. The problem with that is that overdraft protection is expensive. Most banks charge a very high interest rate of 15% to 20% for overdraft credit. Borrowing on a regular basis can lead to deeper and deeper debt. In order to avoid such an eventuality, you should use your overdraft credit line only when necessary and only when you are certain you can repay the loan in a timely manner.

GET CREDIT CARD WITH NO CREDIT OR BAD CREDIT.

Here's good news for people who want a Mastercard or Visa and who have little or no credit or have bad credit history. You can apply to one of the following banks and get a credit card by depositing a certain amount of money in your own interest bearing savings account.

American Pacific Bank, 10300 SW Greenburg Road,
Portland, OR 97223.
Phone: 800/879-8757
Minimum income required: $1,000 per month.

American Savings Bank,
1600 Kapiolani Blvd, Suite 205, Honolulu, HI 96814.
Phone: 808/946-9502

California Security Bank
1694 Tully Road, San Jose, CA 95122.
Minimum income required: None
Phone: 408/270-1500

Dreyfus Thrift
Post Office Box 6003
Garden City, NY 11530
Phone 800-7-CREDIT
Min. income 1,000 monthly

Signet Bank
11013 W Broad Street
Richmond, VA 23261
Phone: 800-333-7116
Min. income: none

GET CREDIT CARDS WITHOUT HAVING A CREDIT CHECK

There are many banks across the country which offer MasterCard and VISA with no credit check. These cards are available to people who have little or no established credit or who have bad credit history. The only requirement for getting these cards is that you pledge to deposit a specified amount of money in your own interest bearing savings account. The required deposit may be as low as $250 at some banks. You may also be required to meet a certain minimum income requirement. You can apply to any of the banks listed below (with minimum income requirements shown, if applicable), and get a MasterCard or VISA by depositing an amount of money which falls within the bank's required deposit range.

Bank One, Lafayette, NA
P.O. Box 450, Lafayette, IN 47902
Phone: (800) 395-2556
Minimum income required: None

Central National Bank of Mantoon
Broadway & Charleston at 14th Street
Mantoon, IL 61938
Phone: (800) 876-9119
Minimum income required: N/A

First Consumers National Bank
Lincoln Center Tower, 10260
SW   Greenburg Road, Suite 600
Portland, OR 97223
Phone: (800) 876-3262
Minimum income required: 12,000 per year

First National Bank in Brookings
P.O. Box 784
Brookings, SD 57006-0784
Phone: (605) 692-2680
Minimum income required: $700 per month

Key Federal Savings Bank
P.O. Box 6057
Havre de Grace, MD 21078
Phone: (800) 228-2230
Minimum income required: $165 per week

YOUR MONTHLY BUDGET

Income   _____

Gross monthly income   _____

Net monthly income   _____

Spouse's monthly income   _____

Spouse's taxes withheld   _____

Spouse's net income   _____

Total family income   _____

Expenses

Rent or mortgage payments _____

Home insurance _____

Property taxes _____

Utilities _____

Car payment _____

Food _____

Car Insurance _____

Health Insurance _____

Entertainment _____

Clothing _____

Other transportation expenses _____

Credit card payments _____

Total monthly expenses _____

Monthly Savings _____

YOUR PERSONAL INFO SHEET

NAME _____

ADDRESS_____

CITY_____ST_____ZIP_____

PHONE_____

BANK ACCOUNTS

Checking act at _____

Account No_____

Savings act at _____

Account No_____

CREDIT CARDS

Mastercard/Visa _____

Mastercard/Visa _____

Mastercard/Visa _____

Mastercard/Visa _____

Mastercard/Visa _____

DEPARTMENT STORE CREDIT CARDS

#1 _____

#2 _____

#3 _____

#4 _____

#5 _____

INSURANCE INFO

Life Insurance Policy No._____

Term insurance no. _____

Auto insurance no. _____

ACTION TO TAKE TO HAVE MORE SAVINGS

Cut expenses_____
_____
_____
_____
_____

Earn more money by_____
_____
_____
_____
_____

SPECIAL BONUS SECTION

#2

HOW TO BUY A CAR
FOR THE LOWEST POSSIBLE PRICE

Introduction

Buying a car is one of the most risky things you will ever do, even though you will probably do it every 3 or 4 years. When you go to a car dealer you are an amateur trying to beat a bunch of professionals to get a good deal. When you buy from a dealer you are working with people who spend part of every day practicing how to sell you a car, and you have probably not spent more than a few days planning how you are going to go about buying the car you want.

When you are dealing with professional salesmen you should know that they are mainly people who sell things, and not people who know about cars, and especially not people who know about what you need in a car. Because these are people who are generally better than you at buying and selling cars the more you can find out about the cars and what they are really worth the better off you are going to be, and the better the price you are going to end up with. If you do not know what you are doing the salesmen will sell you the car they want at the price they want to sell it to you. You will not be either happy or satisfied with your purchase.

What they know can hurt you,

so don't tell the salesman what you know

If you are reading this little book to get some ideas on how to save money in buying a car, the biggest mistake you can make initially is to tell a salesman that you have been reading up on how to save money in buying a car. Never tell salesman what you know, or what you are doing to get ready to buy. While you are going to want to have check-off sheets for all of the cars you consider (detailed below), you don't want to let any of the salesman know that you have them. Salesmen, particularly at dealerships, have sales strategies that they will use to get you to buy cars at their price, and they aren't going to tell you what they are. You need to be just as good at not giving away your own strategy. In fact if they think you are coming in to buy and that you are a hard sell, they will just re-double their efforts, they won't suddenly come down to your price. The advice is to keep all of your preparations to yourself since your knowledge is your power, just as their sales techniques are their power. Most car salesman know very little about the cars they sell, but you should know as much as you possibly can about the car you want to buy.

How Sellers Will Try to Get the Most Money Out of You
When You Go to Buy a Car

The hook they use to drag you in: When you go to a car dealer, and means either a new car dealer or a used car dealer, is a highly efficient organization. In the first place you will probably see a line of cars facing the street with price stickers on their windows. These cars will look shiny and clean, and will be priced several thousand dollars lower than you had been expected to pay, no matter what you are looking for. Based on this view from the street, let us suppose that you have decided to enter the dealership and look into buying a car.

The salesman and his tricks: The first person to approach you on a dealer's lot will be the car salesman. The salesman may be a man or a woman, although most of them seem to be men. They may also be young or old, but most are in their thirties or forties, with the older ones becoming managers if they have been in the business for a long time. Younger car salesmen may have a hard time getting the trust of the older buyers who buy most of the new cars, and so you don't find many people in their early 20's out selling cars and doing real well. In any case the salesman will approach you smiling, and if they are any good they will spend ten minutes talking about your family and what you are looking for in a car. They will do this to get your confidence, and they will not bring up the unpleasant subjects of what you would like to buy and what you can afford, at least not at first. The salesman will eventually ask you what you are looking to buy and how much you want to spend. At this point it doesn't matter what research you have done, every car that you like will cost more than you originally said you wanted to spend. Car dealers know that people want to have a safety net when they buy a car, and it is the job of the sales agents to get as much of that safety net into their pockets as they can when you buy one of their cars.

But let us say that you have found a car you think you will be happy with, and, at the urging of the salesman, you go with him into his office to make an offer. At this point you may not even think that you are serious about buying the car, but you can bet that they salesman is serious about selling it to you. Once in the sales office the salesman will offer you some coffee, or water, or soda, and ask you what you would like to pay for the car (they always ask you what you want to pay, but they don't really care). The salesman will offer a slight discount, and will then become very concerned that what you want to pay is so much lower than what he has said he can sell the car for. When you reach a final price that needs a compromise, another player will come into the sales process. Of part of the bargaining process the salesman will have found out what you do for a living, checked out you credit with an agency, and offered you financing.

The manager who will try to finish off the sale: The manager is the one who closes the sale. He is usually not the manager of the lot, but only a promoted salesman who specializes in getting you to sign the papers to buy the car. Closers have worked their way up from salesman, and several salesman will be working for the closer on the lot. Initially, when the salesman first goes to see the closer you will not meet him. If you agree to a deal quickly, at their price, you have very little to do with the closer. But if you are stubborn, and try to stick to the price that you want to pay, based on the promises of the salesman, the closer will soon show up. He will tell you how much they want to sell you the wonderful car, and why they can't sell it to you at the low price you what to pay. If you do not stick absolutely to your offer, and you do not agree immediately to their price, you will enter the next stage of negotiations, and by this point you are almost gone.

The bargain, or what you have bought: The bargain is your agreement to buy the car at a price they are willing to sell it at. If the closer and the salesman are good the price agreed will be closer to what they want to sell it at than it will be to the price that you wanted to buy it at. If you are a hot prospect, and do not get up a walk out a some point, the sales people will keep you sitting in their offices all day, or until you give in. At any rate the deal will have been made.

After the sale, and can you live with it: Once the bargain is made the agency will do its best to get you to drive off the lot immediately. It doesn't matter how far you drive, but once you have taken the car off of their lot you have taken possession of it, and they no longer have to give you your money back even if you change your mind 5 minutes later. Ordinarily most people who buy a car by going through this process don't really realize how much they have payed, or if the car they have proudly taken possession of really fits their needs. It may take to two or three months before they really think it over.

However, through planning, and knowing what you are doing you can take command when you are out to buy a car buying. After all, you wouldn't be interested in reading this unless you expected to buy a car at some time, and by taking the care to plan ahead you can become the professional, and you can keep the profit in your own pocket rather than giving it to a car dealership.

Planning Ahead Can Save You Money

Before you go out shopping for a car the best way that you can protect yourself is by planning ahead. Planning ahead means deciding exactly what kind of car or vehicle you want to buy, what you can afford to pay, and how much the car should cost. By no means let a dealer decide what you can afford to drive in a car. Whatever they decide it will be more than you had originally decided upon for yourself.

While what you can afford may mean how much money you have to buy the car, for most of us it means how much we have for a down payment, and how much we can afford in payments each month. A major mistake that most people make is not taking into consideration the cost of insurance and upkeep on the car that you are going to go out and buy. Insurance can cost you any where from

$500 a year to $5000 or more. Very few people will buy a car if they know it will cost them $5000 a year to insure. Just look at the average payment s involved in buying cars. Except for luxury cars, most of them will not cost more than $200 to $300 a month. For that, which is less than $4000 a year, you can drive any new car which costs less than $5,000 to buy.   While that only gives you a choice of a couple of hundred new cars each year, it is certainly a lot better than giving that money to an insurance company.

In any case, unless you are looking for a high performance car or a luxury car, no new car should cost you more than $2000 a year to insure.   Of course insuring teenagers or others with poor driving records will cost a lot more, and in their case it doesn't matter what kind of car they are driving.

Choosing the car you want before you go shopping: Although you might not think it if you aren't in the market to buy a car at this time, actually choosing a car to buy is a difficult task. In spite of this difficulty though you have to make a choice before you look for anything to buy. Making your own decision as to what to buy is the only assurance that you have that you will get something that will reasonably satisfy your needs. If you don't make the decision in advance you can also be pretty certain that someone will eventually sell you a car they want to get rid of, and that you probably don't want.

To begin the process of choosing a car take a look at your motivation for buying a car at this time. Do you want it to carry you back and forth to work, or for your family, or because you need it in the job you are doing? Do you perhaps want a new car at this time because you want some luxury, and you figure you can afford it. Whatever might be the reason, if you aren't completely sure what you want begin by making a list of your needs and wants.

Make a list of your wants and needs in your next car: Begin the process of choosing a car to buy with a list of those things you want in a car, those you need, and those you don't want. Take a sheet of notebook paper, divide it into three columns, label the columns needs, wants, and not wanted, and begin listing everything you can think of in each of the columns.

Once you have made your lists you need a way to compare them to find out which ones are most important to you. Number the items in each column, beginning from one, and continuing to the end of the column. This is called rank ordering. Now compare the number ones, and start a new list with the most important of these three. Continue doing these comparisons until you have fifteen or twenty items on this fourth list. This is the list that will help you decide on your new car. You can discard the three column list since all of the other items on it are less important than those on your final list.

Compare cars you see to keep from being confused: Start going through the cars you like, or think you like, and compare each one with the items on your list. Chances are very good that those which have the most items, or qualities that match your list will make you the most satisfied if you buy them. It might not seem that way sitting in your home looking at a list and comparing it with the glowing descriptions of cars that the ads consist of, but it will be very important a year or two later when you are living with your choice, and you can't go out and buy another car to fix something you hate in the one you bought.

Going After Exactly What You Want

Now that you know exactly what you want most in your new car, that is what kind and make of car, and how you want it outfitted, you are ready to enter the buying market. To begin you want to find out as much about the value of your car as you can. If possible you want to know exactly what dealers pay for their cars, what there markups are, and what the bottom line is on their retail sales.

Finding the right price: If you are interested in buying a used car you can begin to find out about price by looking in the blue book for cars. Blue books are not hard to find as they are carried in most libraries. Whatever a dealer pays for his cars, he usually prices them by the blue book. If the car sells well in the area that you live it will be listed at high blue book, if it is a slow seller it will be priced at low blue book, and most cars will be priced somewhere in the middle. This way if you ever ask a car dealer why he is charging a certain amount for a car on his lot he will simply point to the blue book to show you how fair his prices are. The flaw in this is that his blue book listing also includes all of his overhead and profit. His actual cost was only a fraction of the blue book price he wants to charge you. This raises the immediate question of how can you bring the advantage to yourself, and cut out as much of the dealer profit as you can. The more of that profit you can cut out, the lower your price will be.

If you contact the number below you will get the dealer prices for the new cars they sell. This will allow you to make your choice with confidence, but you are going to have to know the make and model you want before you place your order. This is not a free service, so make up your mind about what you are interested in before you send in your money. Contact:

New Car Consumer Report Services

Box 8005

Novi, Michigan 483-76

Include make and model of cars, and $11 for 1 report, $20 for 2 reports, $27 for 3 reports, and add $3 more for each report over 3 that you wish to receive.

Where the dealer gets his cars: Dealers get their cars from a few basic sources, at least most of their cars. New cars always come from the manufacturers. However, dealers can't just go out and buy all of the cars of one type that they think they can sell. They have to buy a mix of cars, according to the types of cars that the manufacturer produces. This may include a few luxury cars, a lot of middle price models, and a few low cost models to be used for advertising. Since one of the main sources of car sales for manufacturers and dealers are businesses, many of the cars that come to dealers are for fleet sales. These fleet sale cars come with a basic set of items, and in fewer colors. But since they are all assembled at the factory in large numbers their average price is much lower than the same types of cars you will get if you custom order a car set to your own needs.

These cars also have different profit margins built in according to such things as luxury packages, sport outfitting, and a hundred other variables than manufacturers can put on them. In general the more rare the model and its packages the more you will pay for it, and the higher the profit of the dealer.

Dealer pricing: Dealers aren't entirely free to price cars anyway that they want to, but they will often bend the price guidelines to get the most value out of hot models, and to move the models that nobody is buying at the time. If you want to buy a car that everybody seems to want you will not save much money no matter what you do, and you might even have to pay a premium. On the other hand if you just want a car that will run from a certain manufacturer you can buy one of the models that no one else wants and easily save ten or twenty percent off of the list price. If you buy one of these non-sellers don't expect the dealer to do you many other favors since he is already taking bottom dollar on the sale. But suppose that you want a new car, and you want something other than the worst selling car on the lot. There is still something you can do that will save you money and get you the car at the same time.

Buy a new car at fleet sale prices to save the most money: To buy at fleet prices;

(1) Call a dealership that has the type of car you are looking for;

(2) Don't talk to anyone except the fleet sales manager about buying a car;

(3) Tell him what you want and ask for his fleet sale price. All new car dealers has a fleet sales department, and sell many of their cars through fleet sales. You cannot get all options through fleet sales, but they are all good cars.

(4) If the price and options offered are satisfactory to you, go down to the dealership and complete the deal. This saves you the entire salesman's commission, and will get you the lowest price a dealership will give you.

When to buy to get the best price: This comes up in every discussion of buying a new car. Many people believe that the best time to buy is when the new car lines are coming out. That used to be in th Fall, around October or November. However, these days new models are also brought out a mid year, and even occasionally at odd months. Just face the facts, new cars will be brought out at any time that one manufacturer thinks it will give them an advantage in sales.

On the other hand new cars are still tied to years, and no amount of timing will make a car dated in a previous year as desirable to sell as one dated in the current year, or in the next year coming. For this reason you can always save money on a car if you buy a last year's model. Normally this means in the months of January through March, though sometimes even later. These cars will be deeply discounted since all that they are doing for a dealer is depreciating. On the other hand the later in the year it is the less likely you will be able to find the car you want as a last year's model. An additional problem in buying year old models is that dealers will cannot customize them the way you may want. If you don't like the color, or you want a different engine or interior, you are out of luck. Since the production lines are closed on that model you have to take it as is, or not at all.

The third bit of timing may be just a popular myth, but may also be worth looking into. In general dealers measure their sales in monthly volumes. This is done for the manufacturers, and salesmen are paid on a monthly basis. For these reasons, so the story goes, if you go to a dealer in the last 5 or 10 days of the month they will give you a better deal than earlier in the month. This may or may not be true, but if you are serious about buying a car, and fleet sales aren't satisfying your needs, then timing your purchase to the time of month may be worth looking into.

Are advertised sales worth your trouble?: When you are looking for the cheapest method to buy a car you can't ignore the advertised sales. A short time ago a friend of mine bought a Dodge Torus at an advertised same, essentially a loss leader, and saved $1500 on the sticker price. While not every sale will give you this good of a deal, they are worth keeping an eye on. If you watch the sales weekly you will soon be able to spot those that really offer something worthwhile, and those that are offering a single car with the rest of the cars at a high enough price to make up the loss on the advertised ones. These good sales may the result of planning, a short term poor market, or just an attempt to get as many people in the door of the dealership as possible over a few weeks. The best sales are not going to go one for months, and you are going to have to go after them aggressively if you want to get the savings they promise. In any case I once heard a sale advertised on the radio, when manufacturers were offering rebates, for a car with a $1000 discount, a $1000 manufacturer rebate, and a $1000 dealer rebate. I have never heard of anything else as good as that since, and that particular sale only lasted a week.

Besides advertising in the local papers and other news sources, you need to drive by the lots you are interested in. And do it on a regular basis. For a purchase as large as a car represents you can never know the dealer you are going to work with as well as you should. While this only works if you have some idea of the dealer you want to buy through, it is always a good idea to learn as much about those you are giving money to as possible.

Where to get low priced used cars: Of course many dealers also sell used cars, and many used cars are also sold by individuals. You should not assume that all new car dealers who sell used cars get them as trade-ins for new car purchases. While some used cars come in that way, for many dealers there will be a better business in selling the used cars than the new cars. You can pretty well assume that all dealers get most or all of their used cars through the used car auctions. These auctions are held twice a well in most cities, and hundreds of cars are sold very cheaply. While it might cost a dealer more cash than if he had taken your car in on trade, it also gives him a lot more used cars to put on the lot.

However, just because you are not a dealer it does not mean that you automatically shut out of the used car auctions. Many of these auction lots collect cars on the days between the auctions, and will sell them to the public at a set price in the low Bluebook range. This may not be as low as the auction price, but you can do the buying yourself, and still save money over the dealer lots for the same cars.

But there is still another option. There are individuals in ever community who have dealer licenses, which are needed to go to the auctions, but who don't have car lots. These people are for sale. This is in the sense that if you hire them for a couple of hundred dollars they will go to the auction for you and buy the car at the auction price. This is perfectly legal although the regular dealer lot used car people don't like it.   With no overhead these auction dealer/buyers can simply take their contract money and turn the car over to you. For their trouble they have made a profit and you have saved some more overhead.

Are private used car sales worth the trouble?: Another excellent source of used cars are private party sales. Ultimately all used cars come from individuals. The only advantage in going to a dealer is that they will have many used cars on their lot while a private party will have only one used car, or at the most two or three. But in spite of the problem of going to see a lot of individual used cars, there are many advantages to dealing with private parties rather than car dealers. For one thing individuals are not usually as good at selling you something you don't want as a car salesman will be. When you start talking to a neighbor, or other local person, about a car they want to sell in most cases they aren't going to know any more about cars than you do.

Another point in favor of dealing with individuals is that they won't be able to hide problems with the car as well as used car dealers. If something is seriously wrong with the car your chance of finding out about it are much greater with a private party than with the used car dealer. Private parties also like to brag about what they have had replaced in the car, even if it's an engine, and to point out where they have had body work done. All this gives the buyer a great advantage.

Bargaining is another practice that private parties do less well than car dealers. With a car dealer bargaining involves trade-ins, financing, and a credit rating. With a private party you usually have to pay cash, but bargaining is just offering a price and then coming to some mutual agreement in regard to what you want to pay. Of course private parties are not going to offer you financing, but they may do something no dealer would do. You may be able to trade a private party something like season tickets to a ball game for a down payment on a car, or even for its total value. A private party can accept any kind of a trade you many wish to make, and many of them are so anxious to get rid of the car they are selling that they will both come down in price, and accept part of the payment in trade.

With a private party never be afraid to make a low first offer on a car, but if you really want the car then offer as much as you can and you with your opening offer and you might beat out the next person to come by and look over the car. Good cars at low prices are going to go rapidly. It is up to you just how much to offer, and in the end to determine if the sales price is really something you want to pay.

Why buy freight damaged cars?: While you may not have much enthusiasm for buying a damaged car, buying one this way will at least let you know the nature of the damage as well as save you a lot of money. You will also have a very large selection if you go for freight damaged cars. Because cars must be lifted on and off the ships they are transported in, and can have various accidents while aboard ship many of them arrive on our shores in less than perfect condition.

You may still ask why you should even consider buying a freight damaged car? One very good answer is that you may have already done so more than once and never even known it. When these cars arrive they belong to the dealers who have contracted for them. If the dealers decide to accept the damaged cars instead of disposing of them they will have them repaired and put them on their lots. If you go to a lot and buy one of these cars there is also a very good chance that the dealer will never inform you that it was damaged during transport and has been repaired. Once these cars are in the general circulation you may easily have purchased one as a used car through either a dealer or private party and never even known about it. Any time you look at the big bargains on a new car dealers lot look over the cars very closely for signs of repair, and ask the dealer if the car has ever had repairs. By law they are supposed to tell you.

But supposing that you will accept one of these cars willingly you need to know where to go and what to do to save the most money. The best sources are found around points of entry for cars that are shipped into your area. Inevitably many of the freight damaged cars end up in lots around these shipping points waiting to either be repaired and sold or scrapped. You will need to visit the lots yourself and either chose from the ones that have already been repaired or find someone to do the job for you. There are always freelance mechanics in these areas who will fix the cars for minimal charges. If you go this route, and this is the cheapest source of freight damaged cars, you should save at least 1/3 to 2/3 of the price at a dealers. You are still going to have to shop though, and many of the cars you see will be older used cars at very cheap prices. If you know a mechanic then pay him for an afternoon and get his opinion on the cars you are seeing.

What are freight damaged cars lots?: While you may not have noticed these lots in the past, there are car dealers who specialize in repairing and selling freight damaged cars. They are usually rather proud of it because they sell at prices much lower than new or used car dealers who claim that their cars have never been damaged. Furthermore these dealers will give you a great deal of information about the nature of the damages they have repaired, and how good they think the cars should be. They also deal in an area where desirable cars go very fast so you usually won't have to fight off aggressive salesmen. Just to find out what is going on look up one of these dealers in your area and see what he has to offer. It might be well worth your time and trouble.

Which Car is Best for the Money? Where You Can Read It

While there are several magazines that can help you compare cars, one of the best is Consumer Reports. Consumer Reports comes out every month, and always includes a section on road tests for cars. The real treasure though is their annual buying guide. The buying guide has a big section on new and used cars, and will tell you which cars break down most often, and which are better than the others. The only problem with Consumer Reports is that it might not include the particular cars and options that you are looking for.

If you want to get some information on new cars your best bet is the monthly Consumer Reports, although many other car magazines might cover the cars you are interested in. To look at the monthly road tests go to the library and look on the cover, or in the table of contents. If you see a car that interests you, look it up. The type of information you will get will be: (1) The type of car (large family sedans, sports cars, and like that); (2) The price level (this will go from a high price to a low price, and will depend on the options you put on it); (3) The models tested (such as Chrysler LHS, Pontiac Bonneville SSEi, or Ford Crown Victoria LX); and (4) The best alternatives (which are cars they haven't tested but which they think are just as good).

Following a written description of how they tested the cars and what they through of them there is a page that has ratings and recommendations. The ratings give information on acceleration, fuel economy, braking, weight and size, interior room, and engine and gearing. These are listed side by side so you can just look across the columns and pick out the things you like best. Above this test data is a section on test judgments which gives how well or how poorly Consumer's digest feels the cars performed.   These test judgments are given with little circles which can be clear, red or black, and may be partially filled in. The more red they have in them the better they are felt to be, and the more black the poorer. I would never advise you to buy a car with a lot of black circles. I've had 1 or 2 of those cars and they really do have the problems that Consumer Reports say they do.

If you are looking for a used car it is time to go to the yearly buying guide. Get the most current one that you can, they all have a very large section on used cars. For instance, the 1994 Buying Guide has a section on Autos that begins on page 140 and continues to page 226. The sections in this chapter include recommended 1993 cars. ratings of 1993 cars, how to buy a new car, and ends up with trouble indexes and owner satisfaction. There is even a section on good and bad bets in used cars. You get the same types of information here that you get in the monthly tests, except that the cars are used, and the information goes back to 1987 for some cars and models. If you are still trying to make up your mind, but need some more information find of a copy of the Buying Guide in the library or buy one. If you spend a few hours looking over all of the comparisons in detail you will gain more information than you can even use, but at least it should help to steer you away from bad buys and toward some good used cars.

It is best to make use of the Consumer's Digest after you have made some decisions as to what your needs are in a car. If you really need a four wheel drive vehicle it doesn't make much difference if they all rank poorly in some area. You still need one and your problem is to find the best one for the money you can afford to pay. So after you have decided what kind of the car you need, and what accessories you really need or want to have, look through the Consumer's Digest for ratings.

I have done on both ends and I know that their ratings are pretty accurate. I once purchased a car that had a poor repair record for brakes. As it turned out the brakes on that car needed a total overhaul every 25,000 miles. I had not believed the ratings because the car was nice to drive otherwise, and I thought they might be wrong. On the other hand when I have purchased a car which has high ratings I have also found it to live up to its record. This guide can even be helpful if you are buying a new car and the Digest hasn't done a rating on it. In that case look at the history of the make and model of car you are interested in buying. While this may not give you as much of an assurance as actually comparing the car to others you might be considering, it is still a pretty good predictor of how dependable the car should be.

There are a few shortcomings in using the Consumer's Digest. For one they may not have compared the type and model of car you are looking for at all. In that case you need to go to some other publication for advice. They also may include categories that you have no interest in, and ignore ones you have a need to know. Pricing can also be a big problem. Prices are for various packages, and for certain parts of the country. The area you are in might be a lot higher or lower than the information you get in the magazine. This makes the area of pricing one of the weakest so far as the help you are going to get here. To get the best price for your area compare everything you can find to compare. Even drive to another state if you have to in order to save some money on your purchase.

How to Compare Cars

Since comparing cars is not as easy as it sounds, and since you have to be able to compare cars as closely as possible in order to make the best deal for you, we have here a handy checklist of things to check to see what a car will really cost you to own. The cost of a car is not just in what you pay for it when you buy it. It also includes how much you are going to have to pay for maintenance, repairs, licensing, and insurance. The more accessories that you have on a car the more it is going to cost you to keep them in good working order. But if leather seats or air conditioning is important to you than you have to take their costs for each car you look at into consideration before you make a decision. If you use the categories and items listed below as a guide you should be able to have a pretty good ball park figure of what a car will cost you, both when you buy it as well as when you drive it.

Does who's selling make a difference?: It makes a difference whether it's a private party or a car dealer. A car dealer will be able to get you financing as well as hide problems in the car, but the private party will be able to give you a lower price. You can also deal with the private party more easily, as well as walk away from them if you don't like what they are offering.

In either case you need to build up some information if you want to really keep track of what you are doing. Nobody, either dealer or private party, is going to give you a car for less then they think they can sell it for to someone else. The only insurance you have that you are getting the best price possible is knowing as much or more than the person, or dealer, selling the car.

Begin by getting the dealer's name, address, city, state, and phone number, as well as any warranties he says he is giving you.

Do the same for the private party sellers, but remember that the best private party sales will go rapidly. In any case give yourself at least 10 to 20 comparisons before you make your deal. You probably won't need even that many, but if you do you won't go wrong in your judgement as to who you should buy from.

Get the model, make, and serial number of the car if you can. This isn't so important with private parties, but with dealers it can make all the difference between buying a car they say they have on sale and one which is the same except for the serial number, but which costs a lot more money.. Include the color and desirability of the car to you as well. Before you go and look at cars make a list of the cars you like and rank them beginning at one for the one you like best and going to at least 5 or 10 for those you like least. One of the lower ranking cars had better have something special to offer you or you will never be happy with it.

Next get a list of everything that is on the car. You need to know if it has air conditioning, power steering, AM/FM radio, a special engine and transmission, and anything else that may influence the price. Anything extra that is on the car can make the price go up or down, depending upon whether it is something you want or not when you buy it. If there is a window sticker listing all of the extras that the car includes than make sure that you note what they are as well.

Price, and all that it includes must be the next item. Price can be what you have to pay for it to a private party, but to a dealer it includes such things as dealer prep, taxes, license fees, transfer fees, and whatever else the dealer puts on it. Some of these costs are not part of private party sales, and you need to know which ones. If a dealer won't give you this information unless he is writing up an offer on a car for you, then walk out on him. Make the dealers do the work. They are getting the profit, not you.

Add it all up and find out what it will cost you a month, and over a year as well. Since you don't pay for insurance each month, and maintenance is only two to four times a year, you need to add these into the cost figures. Some major tuneups may cost you $200, and others can cost $1000. Similarly insurance e can vary from $500 a year to $5000 or more depending upon the car and your driving record.

Finally get an idea of the total cost to you to get the car out the door. If you have to put up a large down payment you may need

$5000 up front. But if everything is included in the financing then you may need as little as $500 to $1000, which is just enough to cover taxes and licensing fees.

Timing Your Car Buying

While watching when the dealers are likely to have the lowest prices is important to getting the lowest cost in buying a car, so is shopping for a car before you are in desperate need of one. The more desperate you are the more likely you are to buy a car just to keep from being of foot. This is largely a problem for most of us. We tend to look at our cars, and if they are running reasonably well we want to keep them even if they are old and have high mileage. Ideally we should shop for cars a year before we expect to be in desperate need of one.

This is a hard call to make, but it may be a good place to use the Consumer's Digest or some other car evaluation magazine. Look at the history of the car and model you have, and do a little research as to what the costs are to repair the types of breakdowns your car will probably have. When the costs get over $200 or $300 a month, you can probably buy a new car. When you get a new car you not only get rid of the costs of repairs every month, you also save all of the time that you have to spend taking your car back and forth to the mechanics.

But if you cannot buy a new car, and many of us can't, then start looking for a good used car a year before you figure that you will really need to buy one. In fact try to keep two or three good used cars in mind as you go around. In regard to new cars, watch for special deals. Over the course of a year there are always a few dealers who run special sales that will give you a lot of car for your money.

Mistakes to Avoid

Don't trust a salesman because a friend got a good deal from him: It is always a great temptation, and a bad idea to trust a salesman because someone you know was able to get the deal they wanted from them. Of course your friend may feel that the salesman will give everyone who comes in with them a great deal, but all they will normally get is the usual sales pitch. The salesman will say he is your friend, and if he is any good you will think you have gotten a good deal from him. However, no salesman who is any good at all is going to let you get away with the idea that you have overpaid on your car. Chances are quite good that your friend did no better than average, but that the salesman is better than average and that he was really the one who came out ahead. My advice is to trust no salesman to give you a break on price if he can avoid it. This goes for all of their except ones who are your friends or relatives, and even for them I would be careful.

Don't shop alone: Shopping alone sets you up for full manipulation by car salesman. While you may think this applies mainly to women, it is just as true for men. If you go to a dealer alone you will be a sheep in a lion's den. In fact when you go to a dealership give your companion the task of intervening for you at set times. That is after an hour or two have them insist that you go for something to eat, or that you have an appointment that can't be broken. As long as the companion isn't directly involved in the negotiation the salesman can't manipulate them. They should be non-committal regarding anything about the car you are in the process of purchasing. If possible have two companions go along. One to bring up questions that you might forget, and the other to play the bored friend who has to eat or leave after an hour or two. This will upset the salesman and may keep things moving faster than they would otherwise.

Don't be in a hurry: If you are in a hurry about buying a car you will never get your best price. Being in a hurry means that you go out and buy the first car you see that you think you like. The truth is that you can never know what the best car is for your money, whether new or used, until you look over at least 3 cars. Preferably you should look over more than 3. When you go to a dealer or a private party, never buy on your first impression. Gather all of the information regarding the age, condition, and packages the car has, and then compare it with other cars you have also looked over just as closely. You have to be strong when you are looking at a car that you really want and a car salesman is hanging over your shoulder.

Don't take possession until the car is in the shape you want: If you have ever bought a car, particularly one from a dealer, you will know how fast they want you to take possession of the car. They don't want you to say you will take it after they have fixed from problem. After all, you can back out of sale any time up to where you have driven it from the lot, and there is nothing the dealer can do to you. For private parties you don't have quite the same risk, but you still have to insist that any defects be fixed before you take the car. That is unless it is being sold as-is, and you are satisfied with the price on those grounds. I once went in to buy a car, and the car had mismatched from seat covers. The dealer promised to fix it right away, except that when I asked him to give me a time in writing all that I got was a brush off. This led me to the conclusion that this dealer would never have fixed anything. All that he wanted was to get my name of a contract and get me off of the lot with his car.

Don't let anyone know how badly you need a car: Next to telling anyone that you are in love with the car they are selling, this is one of the biggest mistakes you can make. If any seller thinks that you are in desperate need of a car they will not negotiate with you. If they think that they are the last chance you have of getting a car because you don't have much money, you have poor credit, or you need it for a job, they will sell you something they have on their lot. Dealers love this kind of buyer. If you tell a dealer that you can only afford a certain monthly payment, and you must have a car, you will get your monthly payment all right, but it will cost you thousands of dollars. It is best not to let anyone know exactly what your needs are when you are looking for a car. The less they know the better for you, and the more capable you are of buying a car the more likely the dealer is to come down on his price.

Never offer full price: This can also be a huge mistake. Dealers always expect to come down on their list prices, and private parties almost always expect to come down as well. Dealers list their cars at the high end of the Blue Book values no matter how good or bad they are. If you start dealing with them they have plenty of space to maneuver. Make your first offer 30% or 40% under the list price. While dealers won't usually come down quite that much they are likely to give you a quick 5-10% discount. After the initial discount you are going to have to negotiate very conservatively to get the dealer down a few percent more. If you offer full price on your first bid you will get the car, and you will also end up paying a lot more than you should.

Financing Your Car Purchase

While you don't always realize it when you are buying a car, how you go about paying for it can make a lot of difference in what you actually end up paying. The cheapest way to purchase a car is to pay cash, but most of the time you can't do that because cars cost too much. Still, it makes a great deal of difference if you pay 5% for your financing or if you pay 15% for it. Dealers will always promise to get you cheap financing, and they have arrangements with lending institutions so that they can set up virtually anyone with financing over an hour's time. My advice to you is don't do it if you have any other choice. Car dealers want to arrange your financing so that you have one less excuse for not buying their car, not to do you any favor.

If you can't pay cash, then at least get your own financing, and get it from someone you know and trust. Most banks and savings and loans finance car purchases. If you are going to go look for a car that needs financing talk to your lenders before you start out. You will be glad you did this, and it puts you in charge when you are talking to the car dealer. If you have gotten your own financing set up, then keep your personal business to yourself. You don't have to tell the dealer where you work, how much you make, or let them run a credit check on you. So long as you are not financing your car through the dealer buying a car is no different than going to the store and buying a loaf of bread. It will also keep the dealer from selling your personal information to agencies selling things you don't want.

The amount you are going to finance comes from the total of the sales price for the car, plus other expenses such as sales taxes, title fee, and licensing, and minus the down payment:

Cash price	$15,000
Title fee	$15
License	$375
Other charges	$1,500
Total sales price	$16,890
Less down payment	$2,390
Amount financed	$14,500

What a finance contract will include:

Annual percentage rate	10%
Amount financed	$14,500
Finance charge	$ 2,900
Total payment	$17,400
Number of payments	48
Amount of payment	$362.50 / month

How long a loan should you have?: While you have to keep the loan payments low enough to make them easy to pay, also keep the loan as short as possible to minimize the amount of financing you pay. Because of the cost of cars these days there are car loans that run five or six years. Unfortunately the average length of time people keep cars is only about 4 years. As a result you end up paying more money out every year for your cars, and you aren't getting much for it in return. Keep the length of loan for your car no longer than the amount of time you expect to own the car. If possible keep it shorter. Because of the nature of cars as they get older the require more repairs and maintenance, and by 4 or 5 years the upkeep on your car may be as high as the car payments themselves.

Is leasing cheaper than buying?: There is another way to buy cars which is between buying and renting. Leasing cars lets you have some of the benefits of both, as well as some of the disadvantages. When you lease a car you take on all of the responsibilities of ownership, but only for a limited time and at a lower price than if you were really buying. Leases run for 3 or 4 years, and they are very hard to break. A lease is a contract which you are liable for. To get out of a lease you have to find someone else to take it over for you.

Of course the savings you will get on the monthly payments as well as on the down payment may be enough to sell you on it. On the other hand you could have a penalty if you are a high mileage driver, and if you want to buy the car at the end of the lease you will have a residual amount to pay that will be around 1/2 the original sales price of the car. While it may not seem like it, the residual is probably more than you would pay for a similar used car after 3 or 4 years.

Dealers love leases and are always advertising them. Leases allow dealers to make a steady cash flow, and in the end give them more profit than outright sales. This should be a warning to the public that for many people leases are not such a good deal. Leases only make sense if you are a low mileage driver with a steady income, or you have a business that requires cars. Leased cars are always late models since they are new cars to begin with, and are only kept on a lease for 3 or 4 years. For businesses that go bankrupt a lease is just another creditor, while cars that are owned are assets that someone else can seize to pay debts. In addition it is easy to adds to the fleet, or to cut down its size according to what your business is doing. Most leases are to business, although dealers would be happy if more private parties got them too since it would help their profit margins.

Will a trade-in help you on your loan?: If you already own a car, should you use it as a trade-in, or should you sell it yourself or do something else with it? These are all separate questions, and each requires a separate answer. But since some of the answers don't have anything to do with getting the lowest cost to you when you buy a car, I will stick to just a few.

First, should you trade in your car. While your experience may be different, this is what I ran into when I went to trade in a car. The car I wanted to buy at the time cost around $7,000, and the car I was driving was not worth over $1500. Because dealers always start off by offering to sell you their cars below the sticker price I expected a price quote of $6,000, and an offer of $1500 for the trade-in value of my car. What happened though was completely unexpected. The dealer took one look at my car and offered me $2500 for it as a trade-in. I took a moment to think about it and saw that I would be paying an extra $80 in sales taxes if I accepted the offer, and made a counter offer. First I asked if he would give me the $1000 off on the sticker price, and the $1500 on my trade in as I expected. He refused and said that he didn't discount his sticker prices when there was a trade-in. Since he was now taking all of the advantage for himself, and I was getting stuck with extra sales taxes, I told him I would take $100 for the car if he would discount his car by $2400. This would save me $200 in sales taxes, and as far as I could see wouldn't cost him anything. He refused and I walked out.

From this adventure I conclude that dealers get large profits from used car sales, and it help s their taxes and profit margins. I would never try to use a trade-in again since I don't trust dealers in this area.

My advice is that you sell your car yourself, and take whatever discount you can get from the dealer. This will give you cash to use as a down payment, and you can still deal with the dealer to at least save some sales taxes. Take every advantage you can get if you want the lowest cost for a car possible.

Find an Alternative Mechanic

Unless you have a very unusual car, find yourself an alternative mechanic to the dealership's to do your tuneups and repairs. I have used an alternative mechanic for years and save from 1/2 to 2/3 of the price on all of my automotive work. The shop I go to is owned by a man who was trained by a dealership, and who supervises the other mechanics in his shop. I have watched some of his work and it is all very professional. All repairs he has made have worked out well, and I can even get in for a quick oil change and lube job without an appointment. Not only do I save money by using this mechanic, but once my car broke down 4 miles away from their shop and the mechanics drove out to the car and fixed it on the street for the same price they would have charged had I been able to bring it in. How many times have you heard of a dealership mechanic doing this. These mechanics will also use salvaged parts, such as windows, if I authorize it. So far as I have been able to see these mechanics have never cheated me in any way, or done a poor job on my car. I trust them as much as I would if my work were done by my dealer. Over a year I would estimate that I save $500, more or less, and this is just mainly on tuneups and minor repairs. While there are some jobs that the shop won't undertake, in over 100,000 miles of use I haven't had any trouble that they couldn't repair.

Which New Cars Will Cost You the Least

If you want to buy a new car, and you want to get the least costly car that will give you the best transportation, there are several standard packages you can look for. This is assuming that you are not sold on a particular make or model, but want the most dependable and best outfitted car you can get whatever the make or model. With this lack of limitation I am not going to look at American cars or foreign cars, but just at cars in the way they are marketed by all manufacturers.

Every manufacturer produces some bottom of the line cars. These carry a name such as "standard," and usually come with no accessories. But since these are the cars that get featured in the ads of dealerships sometimes they come outfitted with a radio and air conditioning, and even other packages that would cost a lot more if you were to add them on yourself. If one of these cars will give you the transportation you want go after them.

In terms of individual packages the lowest cost items are small engines, usually 3 or 4 cylinder, black wall tires, vinyl seats, hatchback models, manual transmissions, and the basic colors that are stocked on the lot. It may be surprising to consider, but manufacturers color code their models so that you can only get the more interesting colors in more expensive models.

Besides the basic packages, never upgrade any more than you absolutely have to. If you want a sports package then look at the basic model that comes with the sports package and not the "standard" to which you might add it. You will pay more for anything you add, but there will be dealers who will carry some sort of a minimal model with a package already installed.

Finally, do not make the deal until the car is on the lot and everything is as you want it. If you give your money and the dealer doesn't have what you want you may have to wait a long time before he gets around to it. Besides, it does not cost a dealer anything to get one of these cars on his lot since they are the easiest cars he has to sell. If you don't believe it just call a few   dealers at random and ask if they have basic models and packages on hand. Most will have either none at all, or only one or two. These cars sell very rapidly because a lot of people know they have the same quality as the more expensive models that dealers and manufacturers like most to sell since they make more profits on them.

Never Buy Today!!

"Today only" sales are designed for one thing only, and that is to get you to make a decision before you have the opportunity to think things over. It goes without saying that if you have a chance to think about the cost of something you want to buy, and you go out and compare prices, then you are going to change your mind at least some of the time. Well this is even more so with cars. Cars are not only a means of transportation, but they are also an expression of our personalities, a display of our wealth or lack of it, a show of our love for technology, of our indifference to the world and what it cares about, and even of what we think of ourselves in terms of everyone around us (that is whether we want to be noticed or ignored by our neighbors).

Car dealers grab onto these images of what we think of ourselves and our cars and try to sell us any car that raises any interest in us. In most cases this will not be the best car we can get for the price we want to pay. It will be whatever is sitting on the car lot without regard for anything else we might be considering. Salesmen and managers are trained to watch for anyone who shows an interest in a car, and then to engage that person so that he will feel an obligation to the salesman and dealership. They will smile at you, and help you admire the cars that you see. If you don't like a car the salesman will say something negative about it. If you do like it he will praise it, and don't look too closely for any criticisms of it, there won't be any. If you really seem to like a car a salesman is not going to point out the dents on the bumper and a scratch on the passenger's side. These will be up to you to discover, and you will hopefully not discover them until you have gotten into the negotiation phase of the sale. At least so far as the salesman is concerned.

The real pressure comes when you show any reluctance to make the deal today. If you don't want to buy the car on that particular day, you may have half of the dealership in the room with you telling you that you should. They do this because they know that if you go to the next dealership and tell them what you have been negotiating on they will do their best to beat it. If a dealership loses out on a sale of, say a $20,000 sale, they will also lose out on the $6.000 to $8.000 in profits that they will get from the sale. They have a lot more money to work with than they will let you know about. While a dealer will try to convince you that a 10% discount on a sticker price is a good deal for you, they can easily go to a 20% discount and still make a good profit on their car sales. You are going to have to hold out for the extra discount it you want it in your pocket instead of putting it into theirs.

Dealer Tricks to Avoid

Dealers are full of tricks to make you pay more money for your car than you should. They are salesmen first, and good citizens second. Never listen to a hard luck story by a dealer. The dealer is a businessman who is selling a product that has been marked up nearly 100%, and his accessories have been marked up even more than that. To get your best price you have to protect yourself from these dealer tricks or your will think you are getting a good deal when you are really just being cheated out of your money.

Don't be a tired buyer: Dealers love to get their buyers exhausted. A tired buyer is a buyer willing to sign a contract in order to get out of the dealership, and will often do so even if it costs him $1000. The game of tiring the buyer out begins when you enter the salesman's office. You talk for a few minutes, debate price, and the salesman will excuse himself to talk to his manager. He will be gone to 10 or 15 minutes and you go into negotiations again. If you begin to get stubborn about the price the periods alone will get longer and longer. Pretty soon you get tired out, sign what they want you to, take the car and leave. The have won and you have lost.

To counteract this strategy, if you want the car, is to excuse yourself after an hour in the office, if you don't have a deal. If you are trying to get the best price for yourself you won't have a deal in an hour anyway. If you leave, have a sandwich or a cup of coffee, the salesman will be the one getting nervous. If things drag on for another hour then leave for the day. If the dealer doesn't make some big moves to close the deal at that point then they aren't very anxious to close the deal. You leaving them will get action.

Don't take freebies from the dealer: Since dealers aren't in the business of selling cars so that they can give soda and coffee away, why do you think they do it? If you just consider the customs we have, when you accept something from some one it makes you obligated to spend time with them, and to listen to them with interest. The dealer will give you a 25 cent cup of coffee to sell you a $20,000 car. Avoid this gentle trap by buying your own drinks and snacks. If you refuse these little freebies you won't have the obligation to listen to the dealer if he isn't saying things you want to hear.

Don't be too trusting, and don't be bullied: While these may seem like two different strategies to get you to buy at a high price, they are really just two sides of the same coin. Dealers like to present themselves are friendly places to buy a car, and you will certainly meet someone who is friendly if you go there, but who it will be and what they will do is the question.

The game is played by having either the salesman or the manager be a trusting person, and the other be a bully. The bully will be authoritative and try to force you into a deal you know is bad for you. The nice one, either salesman or manager, will intervene and try to protect you from such a high price by giving you a few dollars off. However, if you believe either of them you will pay more than you should for the car you want to buy.

Protect yourself from both the nice dealer agent, and the bully, by having a plan and sticking to it. When you go to the dealership the first time get information only, and do not buy a car even if you really think it is the best deal you have seen. You will be surprised how many good deals don't look so good the morning after you have spent a hard night at a dealership. Gather your information and leave. If the dealer won't give you his best price for the car then walk out. It doesn't matter how nice or how mean they have been to you, whether you buy or walk out they will have forgotten all about you in a day or two anyway. Dealers are not your friends, and you should consider them no more than the salesman they are. They are just salesman who try to trick you into paying more for your car than you want to.

Dealer Add-ons to Avoid

Dealer Preparation: If you have ever bought a car from a dealer you will see a dealer preparation charge on your contract. Typically this adds $50 to $100 to your bill, and you are never told exactly what it is for. Dealer preparation is basically cleaning up the car after it has been shipped across the county to the dealership. Since dealers have to clean there cars anyway you shouldn't be charged for it when you buy the car. If you look into exactly what it is you will find some low level employee out in the back of the lot washing the cars and scraping off the dealer stickers. He may have an hour's work to get the job done, and he will earn no more than $10 for it. My advice is to discount the sales price of the car by whatever amount in entered into dealer prep.

Extended service plans: With an extended service plan you are betting that your car will break down after the warranty runs out, but before you are ready to get rid of the car. With a used car you usually get a 30 to 90 days warranty. With a new car you get a year or 20,000 miles, whichever comes first. Of course there are variations on the warranties, but they all have limits, and the dealers have a good idea that the car you buy will not develop problems before the warranty runs out. However, to be sure that the car won't break down in the warranty period they give themselves a margin of error of at least 100%, and probably longer for many auto systems. By selling you an extended service plan there is still a very good chance that your car won't break down, and the plan can add up to a lot of money in the meantime. Rather than paying your dealer for an extended service plan put the difference into the bank and every year you don't use it for repairs take it out and go on vacation or something. For 9 out of 10 of you, you will save money.

Air conditioners and other add-ons: Any of this equipment that you have a dealer add on to your car you are going to pay a premium on. This includes not only air conditioners, but also radios, trim, sports packages, wire rims, and anything else you can imagine. To dealers this is one of the major profit areas that they exploit. Whatever it is that you might want you can get it cheaper outside from a specialist. Dealers these days charge $65 an hour for their services. They may not pay any of the people who work for them that much, but that is what you are going to have to pay them for any services they give you.

Rust proofing and undercoatings: This is another service that new car dealers offer as a great protection against rust for your car. While these coatings work, they are generally put on by the manufacturer, and the dealer has nothing to do with them. Not only are they put on when the car is manufactured, the only service a dealer will give you if you have them do it is to spray a little rust inhibitor around under your car. If you really need your coating replaced or added onto, you would do much better going to a specialist in any case. They will be quicker and cheaper, and do a better job than a dealer.

Businesses You Can Start with $500 or Less --and Make Money

How Can You Start a Business on $500 or Less?

If you are tired of working for someone else and being paid less than you're worth, and you're tired of the 9-to-5 grind of making a living, there is a better way. But like all better ways this one takes some work. In fact that is precisely what this little booklet is about, working, but working for yourself and not for someone else. Of course the greatest obstacle to starting your own business is finding something you can do that you can afford. Most of us can't come up with thousands of dollars to start a business, but most of us can come up with a few hundred. This charm of this booklet is that it will give you businesses you can start with less than $500. Some require a lot less money, and some are close to the $500 figure. In either case these are businesses that can be successful if you work at them. Every business takes time, and these businesses take more time than money. That is the usual trade-off in business, the harder you work the less money you need to be a success. Success in this sense is a business that will make money. While any business can fail, it is also true that any business can be a success as well. But of course you are interested in finding out about the businesses you can do for such little money. Read ahead for a proven list of businesses, and some of which can even be fun if you are interested in them.

While every business requires that you either have something to sell, or a skill to offer, it is not necessary that the objects you sell cost a great deal of money, or that they skills you offer require years of work to learn. A skill can simply be something that people would rather pay to have done than to do themselves, and the rule of buying and selling is to buy low and sell high. Many of the businesses offered here can begin as hobbies or collections that are turned into businesses. The object is not just to choose the business that will make the most money (after all, you can make money with any of these businesses), but to choose the one that best fits your personality and interests. If it is something that you like you will work harder at it and do a better job. If there is a secret to being a success in business, than this is it.

Skills and interests; Any business that you go into should be based upon your own skills and interests. If you can't think of a skills you have that you would like to turn into a business, then look to your interests. Interests are those things you like to do even if you aren't getting paid for doing them. What do you do in your spare time, or as a hobby, or what have you always wanted to do but never had the time for? If you are also have skills that match your interests, so much the better. In fact, if your skills are the same as your interests you have no reason not to go into business for yourself. Many people have skills that they sell to someone else for a weekly paycheck. If you do this, but you also enjoy what you are doing, then you have both your skills and your interests in one spot. Never give up an interest if you can make a business of it, and never give up a skill if it will allow you to do what you want. The real joy of having your own business is that you can decide what services or products to offer without anyone else telling you that you can't do it. This is something you always lose when you work for anyone else.

Many of the businesses discussed here will list skills needed to carry them out successfully. If you don't have the skills, and have no interest in them, then don't go into those businesses. Find something else. Because the start-up costs are so low (under $500) for all of the businesses discussed here, you can often take a chance and see if it will work out. Never give up on a business if you really want to do it, but always be willing to give up, even on one making money, if you hate it. What is the fun of a business if you can't stand what you are doing.

Competition; These are the other people who are selling the same goods and services that you are. You do not want to go into a business in which one company is in control of everything, and you don't want to go into one where there is a business on every street corner. Competition implies that there is a need for the business. Basically you want to find a group of people who are not being well served by the competition, and you can ether do something different, or better, or cheaper than everyone else. You also want to be ignored by the competition since they can always get rid of you by going after your business and running you out.

Professionalism; It is a great temptation as an independent businessman to run things just the way you want to and not even think about what anyone else wants. If you do that, no matter how good you are as a person, you will fail. What ever the business you are in you have to play the part. If you are a gardener, then you dress as a gardener and not in a suit. If you are coming to someone's house to repair their appliances, then come with a tool belt and overalls. Dress and act the way you think that people doing that job should act. If you are playing the part then people will believe that you are who you say you are. Its up to you, but the more professional you are in your business the easier it will be to get contracts and sell services and products.

Start-up costs; For every business there are start-up costs. Many businesses will require that you have a reference book, or supplies and tools. Often you will need to do some advertising, and you may need entry fees for a temporary sales location. Start-up costs will be limited to those things that are directly related to the business. They won't include your living expenses, such as meals, or travel. Some businesses will require transportation, and this will not be included either. If you need transportation for a business you are going to already have to have a vehicle, or else depend upon public transportation or walking. It will be up to you. On the other hand you may not be aware of some of the expenses needed to start a business. For instance, how about a business license? And do you always need one? And so forth. Start-up costs for these businesses will be kept to less than $500, so at least that part is easy enough to figure out.

Steps to take; Other than figuring out what you want to do, and getting the $500, this is a highly important section, and it is included in every business that is outlined. Now not every step can be given, that would take a chapter as long as this whole book for each business. You will get some of the necessary steps you need to know to get started. Once you have gone as far as you can with the information given here you will have to find more instruction, and references are given, or else talk to others who are already carrying out the business. Still, this is a start, and it will get you started.

How hard will you have to work? Being self-employed you can work as much or as little as you want. But being in a business in which you want to make money you need to plan to work harder, initially, than you would on a job for someone else. This means that many times you may be doing more than 8 hours a day, 5 days a week. Of course if this is an extra money job then you can cut back to whatever is comfortable for you. Also, the start-up hours and work load should lighten up after you get to know the business and start selling things. When you have learned how much your work is worth, and how much trouble it is to sell it, you can decide to work less or more, just according to how much you want to make. Start-up should usually be given at least a year, and can be longer for some jobs that don't go well right away. Give yourself time to learn the business before you start thinking that you are working too much for too little money. Things will get better.

Selling Antiques and Collectibles

If you thought it took a lot of money to get into the antiques and collectibles business you were wrong. All that it takes is a collection of antiques or collectible items that you can sell. Of course you have to be able to buy them at a low enough price to be able to sell them at a profit. The usual method by which people get into the antiques business is through being a collector themselves until they build up a sufficient collection to start selling it off. This also has the advantage that over time antiques tend to go up in value. The problem with antiques, if you like the idea of selling them, is that start-up costs are usually much greater than $500. So if you don't already have a collection of antiques you are interested in selling I advise you to go into the collectibles business. Walking into any antique store these days and you will usually see more collectibles than antiques anyway. After all, a collectible might be brand new while an antique has to be old. Legally antiques have to be at least 100 years old, but most people consider some objects as antiques when they are as little as 40 or 50 years old. Collectibles become antiques when they get older. In any case you need the steps to take to become an antiques and collectibles dealer, and how you can get started for under $500.

Start-up costs:

1. Inventory--Initial costs much be kept to under $300 to do this on a $500 budget. What can you get for $300? New baseball cards, books from $1 a bag library sales, furniture from thrift shops and garage sales, collectible postage stamps. The best source is one you have built up over a long time span as a collector.

2. Marketing location--Use a stall at an antiques mall at a cost of around $100 a month.

3. Business license--From $15 to $35 at your local government offices.

4. Advertising--Business cards or flyers only, cost $50.

5. Overhead--Do your own bookkeeping, and the mall will take care of the shop overhead with no additional cost to you.

Steps to take:

1. You must first find out what is selling in the area where you live. The only way to do this is to go to antique malls and swap meets and see what people are buying. This should also be something you continue to do after you have started your business.

2. Getting inventory is a necessity. If you have been a collector and want to sell off your own collections, you are ready to go ahead. If not, you need sources. You do not buy your inventory from other antique dealers, not at this point. Sources include garage sales, swap meets, sales of unclaimed freight that is auctioned off by the shipping companies each year, and retail stores.

3. You need to market your inventory at low cost to you, and a potential for retail sales to the public. Since advertising is expensive, use the route of renting space from an antiques mall. The trend for several years has been for older business buildings to be converted into a sort of cooperative antique super store. You can go to one of these in your area and rent space for around $100 a month.

4. A business license is often necessary. For this you need to go to the local departments of city government, fill out an application, pay a fee of around $15, and advertise the name of the business in a local paper for 3 days. For a start-up business such as yours it is most common to use your own name as the business name, and your social security number for tax purposes. Employ no permanent employees at this point to save money.

5. Set prices on your stock of at least twice what you have paid for them. This will be a 100% markup, and is common in this type of business. If your markup is much less than this you will have trouble making money at this point.

6. Set up your sales space by arranging things on the walls and tables of your sales areas. There is a problem with your best items. Everyone wants to have those in glass cases in most malls to prevent stealing. But glass cases are pretty expensive so go with items in the lower end of costs, or ones that you don't need cases for such as furniture.

7. A least once a month visit your sales space to renew and rearrange merchandise. Things that don't sell might be marked down, but don't be too anxious to do that. In any case if an object sits for more than 6 months without selling, in spite of mark downs, then take it out and store it for a while. Replace it with something else with better potential.

8. File your tax reports each 3 months to keep legal, and pay your sales taxes.

9. At the end of a year decide whether or not you should change the type of merchandise you are selling. If you have failed to sell much of your stock, you need to change your sales items. Also renew your sales license, this will also let you buy from other dealers at a discount, and save you money in getting more stock.

Swap Meet Seller

Being a swap meet seller is much like being a dealer in antiques and collectibles except that much of what you sell will probably be clothing and household goods. In fact you can sell pretty much anything as a swap meet seller. Some sellers at swap meets do so well that they make a living at it and never even have a store front business. When you sell at swap meets you get rid of almost all of your overhead. Even a small store is going to cost you more than $500 to get into, but a day of selling at a swap meet will only cost you $10 to $25. This leaves you a lot more money to use for merchandise, and selling merchandise is what is going to make you money, not paying a lot of money out to rent space.

Start-up costs: For your initial start-up costs I am going to assume you have no costs for the first set of merchandise that you are going to sell. The best of all is your own home discards. These are the things in your closets and garage that you do not use regularly, or do not use at all. Selling these items in the first sale should net you from $500 to $1000. After that you will have to find more things to sell. The best sources for additional items are garage sales. Auctions are also good sources of merchandise, but they will   cost too much money if your budget is limited to less than $500.   However, at garage sales you can get clothing items for 25 cents to 1 dollar, and at the least you should be able to mark these up three or four times at a swap meet and still get good sales. Other than things to sell, the only costs you will have is the $15 to $25 a day for rental space, and the gas to get your car to the meet.

Steps to take: A few simple steps will get you started.

1. Clean out your house and garage for anything you can do without that can be sold. Clothing and glassware are always good, buy anything else you have can be sold as well.

2. Price your goods. If you don't know what to charge go to some of the swapmeets in your area and see what things are selling for.

3. Choose a swap meet to set up your business. You want the swap meet with the most buyers, the lowest space rental fee, and closest to your home.

4. Choose a sales day.

5. The evening before sale day pack your car with sales items, and get at least $20 in change and $1 bills. Also have extra pricing tags and a notebook to keep track of your sales for any tax purposes. You will need card tables or blankets to place on the ground to put your items on. Have a folding chair for yourself, something for shade, and make certain to pack a lunch and bring plenty of cold drinks (but nothing alcoholic). Whatever your own feelings about drinking alcohol this is business and you need to be clear headed.

6. On sale day get up at 4 A.M. and drive to the swap meet by 6 A.M. Have a friend or family member go with you so you won't be tied to your sales spot for the whole day. Most swap meets start selling by 7 A.M. or 8 A.M., but by getting their early you can look over the other sales and maybe even pick up something additional to sell.

7. Set up everything you have at least 30 minutes before the meet opens. Most meets run to about 4 P.M. and even though most buyers are gone before then you should not plan on leaving until closing time (remember that this is a business).

8. One little trick used by a lot of sellers is to mark slow moving items down during the last hour. This often helps to boost sales and move hard to sell items.

9. To be successful you need to do this at least once a week so you will have to be aggressive about finding new merchandise to sell.

Gardener

Do you like to work outside? Do you like to set your own hours? And do you like to work as much or as little as you want as a businessman, or just to make money for a special purpose. Of course you need to be able to do yard work, but the way gardening works is that every job you do on a yard is a separate contract which can be charged for individually.   If you a lawn once a week, you might charge $50 a month. If you also weed the flower, that could be another $25 a month, if you trim trees it could be an extra $25, and so on for every individual job that you do. For a complete yard care contract you can easily get $100 from many homeowners. Actually doing the yard work is not the problem, its setting up your contract schedule and finding the customers. One thing in your favor though is that many people will contract with a new yard service every 2 or 3 years as their income levels change, or their families grow. Make no mistake, being a gardener can be a very profitable business that requires very little money to get started, if you start small.

Equipment can be a problem since it can be expensive, although if you start small you can use a lot of hand powered tools and small power tools and keep the costs low. If you get contracts that call for the bigger and more expensive equipment you can rent that by the day, and still keep your costs low. The trick is to find out how to market your labor as a gardener. Gardening is not a penny ante job, it can pay big money, and many of those gardeners you see around the better neighborhoods are buying their own homes and cars on what they are making.

Start-up costs: You will need tools and advertising to become a gardener. While $500 will not get you a full set of the best tools, it will buy a fairly decent set of basic gardening tools. Buy rakes, shovels, hand trowels, 100 feet of hose, hose nozzle, hoe, a rotary mower, hedge clippers, a 10 foot ladder, bow saw, measuring twin, hammer, screwdriver, and an electric weeding whip. Get as many of these as you can, they will all be necessary at some time. You must have a pickup truck or a car large enough to carry these things to become a gardener.

Steps to take:

1. Buy your tools.

2. Take an ad out in the local newspaper offering gardening services. You can also post it in nearby supermarkets. Here is a sample:

Gardening Services

Inexpensive and Professional Quality

For Prompt Services Call Bill at: (---) ----------

3. Do not just wait by the phone for calls. After you have taken out your ad visit your neighbors and tell them what you are doing. Those people who know you best may be the first ones who would like to hire you. This is a business that will take some time to build, but you can definitely support yourself and make a very good living out of being a gardener.

Freelance Writer

What do you need to be a freelance writer? Do you think you need a special talent, or something important to say, or perhaps that you have to know someone in the publishing business to break in? The answer is no to all of these. What you need is the ability to type and the willingness to write. Writing is mainly a job that takes time, and the more hours you spend at it the more you will get done. Of course learning to be a great writer takes many years, but writing for a living takes no more time than it does to write a letter. The joy of being a freelance writer is also its curse; while you can work any time of the day or night and no one makes you punch a clock, you only get paid for what you can write and sell. However, there are many sources of help, and the hardest working writers are the most successful.

The personality you need to be a freelance writer includes that you like to read. If you don't read, then don't try to write. But if you read regularly than you already know what the market is in what you are reading. If you read a lot of romance novels, then you can write one of those. I have a friend who makes an extra $10,000 a year writing one romance novel each year. You can do the same with mysteries, or science fiction stories, or children's stories, and so on and on. If you don't want anything that ambitious you can still write Hallmark type card sayings, or jokes for Reader's Digest. Basically you can write anything you like, and if you find a publisher who likes what you write you have a career and an business.

Start-up costs: Start-up costs can be limited to a few dollars. Obviously writers need something to write on, and because people are now going to word processors you can get an IBM Selectric typewriter, used, for under $200. These were once $1,000 machines and they will do for you to start on. Otherwise you need a ream of typing paper at $10, a copy of Writer's Marketplace from the library, 500 business envelopes for $5, and some mailing envelopes at $1 each, as needed.

Steps to take: Before you follow this path you much want to write.

1. Buy your supplies, as listed above.

2. From the Writer's Marketplace choose 10 publishers who publish what you would like to write.

3. Write to each of the publisher's and tell them what you would like to write. If none of the publishers write back, then go back to "2" and start over.

4. Of those who write back choose at least 3 and send them specific ideas.

5. If any of them say they would like to see your work, send it to them and see what they say. You must give them at least a month before writing or calling them to see how they liked your submission.

6. If none of your submissions were accepted, then go back to "2" and start over. While you are waiting you can also go back to "2" and try something else with some new publishers.

7. If a publisher wants to see your finished work, and offers

you a price, write it up and send it in. Make sure to include a self addressed, stamped, envelope or you may not get your work back if it is later rejected.

8. You will usually be paid for magazine pieces when work is published, although sometimes you will be paid when it is accepted. If you can sell a book you will generally be paid an advance when it is accepted, and you will later receive royalties according to how many copies are sold.

9. The best way to be a successful writer is to be very productive. Write everyday, and keep in touch with the publishers if you want to make this into a business you can live on.

Tax Preparer

Being a tax preparer mainly takes being good with numbers and very good with details. You are going to have to have training, and some states, such as California, require a license for a paid tax preparer. Also, even though tax preparers do most of their work between January and April of each year, there are actually tax returns that have to be prepared all year around. There are also a lot of very hard working tax preparers who do all of their work in those 4 months of the year, and then leave cheaply and simply for the other 8 months. How would you like 8 months of vacation each year? If you want more action you can turn tax preparation into a year around job just by running ads. Make no mistake about it, being a tax preparer is hard work, but it isn't work that requires a lot of capital to get into. But what interests should you have to be a good tax preparer? Basically you have to have some interest in the law because preparing taxes is a constant review of the laws dealing with taxes. There is of course a lot of help, and you can even get tax preparation programs for computers, but those are only practical if you already have the computer since you can't buy one for you new business and set if up for less than $500. But if you already have the computer, then getting the program for the computer and putting it to use does not cost very much at all.

Start-up costs: The prerequisite is that you be good with figures and with details. Otherwise, start-up costs are very low. To learn how to be a tax preparer begin with a good class in tax preparation.

This will cost you up to $300, and should take at least 8 weeks. Anything that is much less is not going to teach you enough about taxes or the forms to be vary useful to you. H&R Block runs programs every year, but so do other companies. You will need forms, but these cost nothing and can be obtained from any post office or library. Special forms are available from the IRS office (for Federal), or the Franchise Tax Board office (for state), somewhere in your area, and the cost is zero. Buy a dozen pencils at $1, a simple calculator at no more than $15, and advertise your services in the local paper at a cost of no more than $25 a week. To be really professional about this you should work for a company like Block for at least a year before you go out on your own.

Steps to take: The steps are simple but the work is hard.

1. Take the tax preparation class, beginning no later than October of the year before you want to begin.

2. Go to the library or post office and pick up copies of all of the forms they have available.

3. Buy you calculator and pencils. Run an ad for tax preparation, "I will come to your home or business," on a weekly basis, and with your phone number.

4. Doing a return: have a minimum fee charge set up for every return. People will like you to do the tax return, but not so happy about paying for it. For a Federal and state charge at least $25 for a short form, and $40 for a long form. Then add from $5 to $25 for every form that you have to add. You are going to have to decide how much to add for the forms since some are a lot easier than others. This is where a year with a tax preparation company would come in handy. Based on your interview time you should get at least $20 per hour.

5. Never complete the tax return in front of the client. Take it home to complete it and double check all numbers. But always collect your fees before leaving the interview. Also take the earnings statements from the tax payer. This makes you look more professional, lets you put them into the finished returns, and prevents the tax payers from going to another tax preparer later for less money.

6. After you finish the tax returns make copies for both you and the tax payer. If something unpleasant comes up, like they owe

more taxes, call them and let them know right away. This protects you. Double check anything that you aren't sure on. Don't be unpleasant is anyone   quits on you, there are a lot of people out there who want help on their taxes and the nicer you are the more likely you are to get referrals from past clients.

7.   Do everything on time, no matter what!   There are no excuses for taking money from a client for tax preparation and then costing them money by not getting their taxes done on time.

8. Repeat 1 through 7 each year for at least 10 years.

Book Sales

If you are a salesman who likes the thrill of the hunt book sales can be a lot of fun. I go to a lot of library book sales and I see the professionals at a lot of them. They always come in with boxes, and when they enter the sales they simply go in and sweep whole sections of books into their boxes. In fact one man I recognized came to a book sale in a pickup truck whose bed was already filled to the top with books from a sale he had gone to earlier that day.

But that's about where the sellers get their books, and you want to know how to get into it. To be in book sales you can either be a specialist, say sell only romance novels, or you can be a generalist and sell everything. The basic requirement to be a book seller are that you have a source of books and you have someone to sell them to. What kills most book stores is that they have too much overhead. Overhead is the money that you have to put into your business to sell your stock. What I will give you here are some ideas on how to have a business of selling books with little cost to you for overhead or stock. What you want it that most of the money that comes through your hands gets to stay in your pocket.

Start-up costs: Assuming that you don't already have a pile of paperback books you would like to get rid of, start up costs will be less than $50 for stock. To get into book sales you need books. The absolutely cheapest way to get books for sale is to go to the $1 a bag sales that they have at the end of library book sales. You can easily get 50 paperback books into a shopping bag, thereby costing you no more than two cents a book, and you can retail them for 50 cents a piece, or 3 for $1. In either case you want to be able to sell them quickly. At 50 books per $1 bag you should be able to get about

2,500 books for $50. Your other costs will be a selling space at a flea market, $25 per day, some old blankets to put the books on at $2 each, and a chair and sunshade for yourself, at $20 at the local thriftshop. This puts you into business for less than $100.

Steps to take: The prerequisite is that you like selling and retail sales.

1. Go out an buy the books. Library sales are often listed in the newspapers, or in the local library, and $1 a bag sales are usually included.

2. When you buy the books, go ahead and buy mysteries and romance novels. They are the most plentiful, and everyone reads them.

3. Price your new merchandise at 50 cents each, or 3 for $1. If prices go higher or lower than this in your area you can adjust as needed.

4. Pack your priced books, blankets, chair, and sunshade into your car the day before the flea market.

5. Get up at 5 A.M. the day of the flea market, go to it and set up your sales.

6. Sales will run from about 8 A.M. to 4 P.M., be there the whole time, this is a business and not a hobby.

7. Depending on what you have sold, go out and replace your stock. If only romance novels sold, then buy another 500 of those. If westerns or mysteries have sold, then build up your supplies of those. If prices at other dealers are higher or lower than yours, then raise or lower your price accordingly.

8. Repeat steps "1" through "7".

Photographer

Being a photographer is very much like being a freelance writer, except that you are taking pictures instead of writing. But since a good camera can cost a lot of money, you have to be able to get into the business for as little money as possible. Of course what can you take pictures of that people will buy. There are many ways to go with that, some of which can make a lot of money but aren't very interesting, and others that can be a lot of fun, but it is hard to make money. Also to keep costs down you aren't going to be setting up a darkroom as well. You are going to be the one who snaps the pictures, and I will give you some ideas of what you can do to make photography into a business.

To sell photographs the first thing you are going to have to have is the skill to take pictures. Now there are many kinds of pictures that can be sold. The type that most people are willing to pay for are pictures of themselves, and this is where I would suggest you go if you want your photography to be a business and not just a hobby. There are many places where you can take pictures, and where you don't need a lot of money to do it.

Start-up costs: To be a photographer you need some familiarity with taking pictures. If you were a high schools newspaper or year book photographer you have a basic understanding of photographic styles and abilities needed to do most of professional photography these days. Otherwise, what you are going to need is a camera. These days a lot of photographers use 35mm cameras with a fine grained color print film. Cost can be under $200 for a good used camera. Film will cost you no more than $10 a role to purchase and process 24 frames, and you need very little else. Alternatively you may buy a Polaroid type camera for $150 and film at $1 a shot. No further costs are necessary.

Steps to take: You have some photographic experience, and that is all that you need to begin.

1. Buy a camera and film. Have sufficient film with you at all times for 100 pictures.

2. What are you going to photograph? You can look at a copy of Photographer's Marketplace in the library for ideas, or you can simply choose something like rock concerts or major pet shows where people like to have pictures taken. Do not, at this time, try to sell your work to newspapers.

3. Go to the event of your choice and offer to take pictures for a minimum of $5, paid in advance. Deliver anything that you say you will even if you lose some money. If people can depend on you they will pay you when you have to increase your fees because you started out too low.

4. Deliver everything within less than 1 week, and adjust your

fees accordingly if you do not make enough.

5. You can repeat "2" through "5" is you need more guidance. You will need to attend at from 2 to 4 events each week to insure a profit at this business.

Dog Walker

Being a dog walker takes mainly finding people who are willing to pay to have their dogs walked. Not everyone will pay for this service, but people who own dogs know that they have to have their exercise. Dogs that do not get enough exercise get very unhealthy, just like we do when we don't get our exercise. The problem with dogs and exercise is that dogs needed to be walked every day, and for many people that is impossible. Even though someone might love their dog very much, it they are a busy and successful person they may just not have the time to take the dog for a walk each day. Luckily it is also just these people who have the money to pay for a dog walking service.

If you decide to take it up as a business here are a few hints on how to make it a success. First, always try to walk more than one dog at a time. If you are getting $5 an hour to walk someone's dog, then if you can take 5 dogs at a time you are suddenly making $25 an hour, and if you can do this for 4 hours a day and 5 days a week, you are suddenly making $500 a week. The trick is finding the dogs to walk, but you can offer your service in any affluent neighborhood where there aren't already a lot of dog walkers working.

Start-up costs: You need very little equipment to be a dog walker. Buy 5 good leads of various sizes for $50, obtain a business license in your name so that you can advertise in your community legally for $25, and begin running ads and posting your services in local supermarkets. Posting should cost you nothing, and you can keep advertising down to $25 a week.

Steps to take: You need know very little to be a dog walker, but you have to keep your commitments or you will lose all of your business.

1. Buy your dog leads.

2. Go to your local city hall and take out a business license.

3. Make up some cards offering your services and post them

in supermarkets.

4. Begin running ads in local papers. It is also a good idea to have an answering machine so you don't miss calls from potential clients. The more up-scale the neighborhood you plan to service the more work you should get.

5. Set your rate at say $5 per hour per dog. You should be able to handle 5 or 6 dogs at a time if they get along with each other.

6. Whenever you go to a clients home be clean, neat, and sober. The better you look and act the more likely people will be to trust you. Wealthy people are also used to paying other people to do tasks that are very simple, but for which they do not want to take their time.

7. Keep records and file quarterly tax returns. Use a tax preparation service if you can't do this yourself.

8. Get and keep the best reputation you can. A few recommendations from clients who like you can make the business take off in a big way.

Mr. Fixit

Everyone has appliances and things around the home that break down. While the tendency is to through them away, actually most of them can be fixed very cheaply, but people usually either don't know how or don't have the time to do it themselves. This is where you come in, and you can go two ways; you can either set up a little shop somewhere and have people bring their things to you, but this will likely cost you much more than $500 to set up and it may be 6 months or a year before you start making money. Or you can become a mobile Mr. Fixit. That is you can put the tools you are going to need in a car or van and go to people's homes. It is always a great temptation when you make a house call to charge extra money, but if you want to make this a successful business in a hurry, charge less.

If you can do the job in front of the homeowner and charge 10% less than they do at the shops you will soon be getting more business than you can handle. But how do you learn how to fix things, if you haven't already. There are many paths to the mysteries of fixing household appliances, but the main and most important one is that you like to work with your hands. If you have spent weekends and holidays puttering around your home and trying to fix things, and you enjoy it, you are already half-way to having a business.

Start-up costs: To be a general repairman you need to have tools to fix things. Sears has a toolbox set of basic tools (Craftsmen) that are guaranteed forever. A full set runs about $350. In addition you should have a basic set of carpentry tools, if you know some carpentry: saw, hammer, measuring tape, screwdrivers, and so on. Pay no more than $100 for carpentry tools. You also must have advertising so post your services at local supermarkets and run an ad at $25 a week in a newspaper local to the area you want to serve. Buy an answering machine for under $50.

Steps to take: You must have a good set of skills before you begin the process of making this into a business.

1. Buy the tools listed above, if you do not already have them.

2. Make up your advertising information. Supermarkets have forms that you must use, and you need to keep your newspaper advertising to around 10 words.

3. Set up the answering machine with the message that you are in the business of home repairs, and ask for names and phone numbers of those who call in when you are out.

4. Answer all calls promptly, and set up appointments for as soon as possible after being called, the following day if you can. Always be prepared to give estimates, and stick to them even if you lose a little money at first. If you don't know how much to charge for your services call some of the repair services in the Yellow Pages and ask how much they charge for particular jobs, then charge 1/4 less if possible.

Errand Service

Everyone has errands they must do to keep their lives in good order. The errands are not highly technical, in fact they require no particular skills most of the time. What they do require is time. Some of the errands that are constantly required are walking the dog, washing cloths, shopping either for our daily needs or when we are having a special party, yard work, picking up or dropping off people who are visiting. Errands are what fills up many of our days, and it is often our failure to keep up with our errands that is the difference to having a pleasant and comfortable life or one that is harried and too busy.

The start up for an errand service is really simple, just advertise in a local paper. While you must have reasonable rates, you are not going to work for free either. If you get people to really depend upon you there is a lot of money that can be made by being willing to work for others. You will also find that most of the things they ask you to do are things you do for yourself anyway.

Start-up costs: You need very little to start this business. Begin with a business license from your local government office, and take it out in your name--cost $25. Advertise in local papers at $25 a week, and in local supermarkets for free. That is all the start up costs you need. Buy the best maps you can get of the area you are going to service--cost $50 or less. You will also need a phone answering machine, and good ones can easily be purchased for under $50.

Steps to take: 1. Buy local city maps.

2. Go to your local city hall and take out a business license in your names listing your business as personal services.

3.   Get your advertising out to the markets and local newspapers.

4. Set up the answering machine with the message that you will do personal errands for home owners.

5.   Make up a price list to quote to people, or to read on request. It should give you at least $20 per hour for your services, including driving time, and have extra charges for heavy lifting or special difficulties.

6. Answer all call promptly. If you can get customers to commit to using you at a particular day and time on a regular basis, but be flexible. If you get too busy have someone in mind that you can call for extra help. Pay them half the rate you are getting, and you take care of the billing.

Genealogical Researcher

This is a very special service, and one that you shouldn't undertake unless you have some experience with genealogical research yourself. On the other hand it costs you very little to become a genealogical researcher. and their are fifty million Americans who are looking into their family genealogy at any one time. Because Americans are so mobile many of them live away from the areas where family records are kept, and these people often have to hire someone else to research their families since that is cheaper than doing it themselves.

But you have to know the territory. You must find out where the genealogical information is kept in your area. Often libraries will have a genealogical room, or historical records that include family names. The Mormon church maintains its own genealogical libraries, because tracing your families genealogy is very important to their church teachings, and access is free and open to anyone. You don't have to be a Mormon to use the Mormon church genealogical library.

What kind of information will you be finding for these people? Pretty much records of births, deaths, siblings, and spouses. Although families would like a lot more information about their families, most of the time there is nothing more than these names and dates. But what all people interested in genealogy want is the earliest records that they can get, and that is where American records break down. Most of the time our records stop back a couple of hundred years, and the rest of the information may be in Europe somewhere. But this is another opportunity for you. If you have traced a number of families back to their migration from Europe, and you want to take a trip you may get some of them to pay you to continue the research while you are over there. This will allow you to offset the cost of your trip as well as write it off on your income taxes.

Start-up costs: If you are not as familiar as you should be with genealogical research methods, enroll in a night school class to help you out. This should cost no more than $100. You other major costs are advertising in genealogical magazines. These are monthlys, and should cost no more than $25 each. Of course you should have 3 or 4 ads at a time until you get some customers. You will find these magazines in libraries if you look around. Get a post office box for incoming mail for the business, cost $15 a month.

Steps to take: 1. Get your advertising out. You can only get clients if you advertise.

2. Check your mail daily, and answer all letters the same day you get them.

3. Before actually doing any research get an advance, and set up the limits of exactly what is wanted. Remember that you get paid for your time, not just for your success.

4. Carry out the research by going to all genealogical libraries, and local records bureaus if necessary.

5. Keep in touch with every client at least once a month, and more often if possible. Any client you do not contact that often will probably lose interest in you.

Typist

Who does a typist work for? And where do you see typist services advertised? While typists can work for anyone, where you are most likely to see their services advertised is around colleges and writers' magazines. While all students are required to write as a part of their college education, many of them have never learned to type. The same is true for writers. And what do you need to be a typist? Actually you don't need to be able to type very well when you are in business for yourself, you just need to be able to get the work out.

If you apply for a typing position at a business they will have you take a typing test. To pass it you have to be able to type 50 words per minute with 5 or fewer mistakes. However, when you go into business for yourself you set your own standards. If you can only type 20 words per minute, and that is about average for someone who has just learned to type, that is still not too bad. The problem comes when you are typing on a typewriter. Hardly anyone types on a typewriter anymore, not with all of the word processors and computers around these days. If you are limited to a typewriter you can still type term papers for students, but it will take longer and be more work. But there is a way to solve that problem and still keep in the price range of $500, you can buy an older model computer or word processor for under $300, and do your typing on it.

How much money can you make? At $2 a page, and 20 words per minute, you should easily get through two pages an hour. While that is only $4 an hour, you will get faster, and at 50 words a minute you can make $10 an hour. If you are doing this every day you will not stay at 20 pages an hour, and your earning will go up. Just look at your beginning pay as being paid to learn.

Start-up costs: The most important cost is the typewriter or word processor, cost should be no more than $300. Buy a ream of good typing paper at $6, and advertise in local college papers. College students are often poor typists, but are nevertheless required to write constantly. Advertising should be under $25 a week. Get an answering machine and list your business on the message.

Steps to take: 1. Buy your typewriter or word processor, and paper.

2. Contact local colleges and advertise your services in as many as you want.

3. Set up your typing rates: $2 to $3 a page for regular typing, and at least $5 a page for tables.

4. Set up an answering machine with your services listed.

5. Follow up all inquiries within 24 hours.

6. When you get a job work like crazy. Make sure you know the deadlines of the person requesting the work, and charge extra for anything that someone puts a rush on. An extra 10% to 25% would be fair.

Tutor

Tutors are always needed. Volunteer tutors are always needed to teach reading, and English. But tutors are also paid, and they can teach anything. In fact many of the skills you have can be used to tutor. You don't have to have a college degree to be a tutor, although it helps, but you do have to have some special skills if you want people to pay to be tutored. Tutors are always needed to teach math skills, even basic math, and you can get paid for tutoring in reading or English. Computer skills are very marketable, but just offering to teach typing can be an avenue to tutoring. Depending on your skills you can sign up with a business that places tutors, but then you will lose part of your earnings. Do it yourself, and when you advertise your services you don't have to tell anyone your credentials.

What can you expect to make as a tutor? The more or less standard rate is $10 an hour, but if you do your tutoring to groups it will drop to $5 an hour per student. That will still end up giving you a lot more than $10 an hour in the end anyway.

Besides the things already mentioned people hire tutors to teach music (piano for instance), or even how to exercise (you have all heard of the personal trainers that a lot of rich people hire). If you have any special skills, training, or hobbies you can turn them into an opportunity to be a tutor. And depending upon who you are tutoring you can have a successful business at it.

Start-up costs: Mainly you need advertising in order to go into business as a tutor. Take out ads in local newspapers, and local college newspapers if you have a college degree. Keep your costs to $25 a week, and purchase an answering machine to take care of calls when you are away from your phone. Acceptable answering machines can be purchased for under $50.

Steps to take: Assuming that you have a skill to tutor, the steps to take to become a tutor are very simple.

1. Decide on your rate per hour. Most tutors can charge $10 an hour without any   problem, but you have to do a lot of hours to make any money. As an alternative to individual tutoring offer to tutor groups of no more than 5 or 10 students for $5 an hour. People feel that they are getting a bargain, and you will make a lot more money for your time.

2. Advertise. Go to your local paper and advertise your services as a tutor in math, computers, English, history, or whatever. Do the same thing at the local colleges and high schools if you have the skills to offer.

3. Buy and set up your answering machine with a message such as: "Hello, this is Joe _____ math tutoring, please leave your name and phone number and I shall get back to you promptly." And do get back to any callers you have on the same day if possible. If they really want a tutor and you don't follow up, they will hire someone else.

4. When you call back stress how good you are in your subject. Don't lie, but don't be reluctant to brag a little at this time.

5. When you go to a client's home dress professionally, even if it is only for one hour with one student.

6. Collect fees as you do the work. If you tutor for an hour, then collect a check. If you tutor a group get a check before the

session starts.

7. Always sound positive, and always do your best. You may get more work through word-of-mouth than you will get from your advertising.

Herbal Sales

Most herbs are used in cooking. Herbs are used in very small amounts because not very much of them is needed to flavor a dish of food. Furthermore, you don't need a very big space to grow herbs. If you can get a 10x10 foot plot to grow in, you can grow enough herbs to have a business. You also need to do your own drying, packaging and marketing. But once you have done the manufacture you can sell your herbs in country markets anywhere in the country. Herbs in the supermarket are ridiculously expensive. By doing the who job yourself you can easily sell your herbs for 1/2 the price of the supermarkets, and still make money.

A typical label for your herbs should look something like this:

Name of herb:

Quantity:

Expiration date:

Cost:

You need the name because no one will buy it unless they know what it is. You need the quantity for the same reason. The expiration date is useful because the public will think it is fresher if the expiration date is there, and it will help you because you shouldn't keep an herb more than maybe 3 months without replacing it. The cost is just another necessity.

Start-up costs: Start-up costs can vary greatly. If you have to set up a greenhouse to grow them in you can easily use all of your money, and more for materials. For this reason I would suggest sticking to outdoor, warm weather, growing and indoor plans. Your $500 can go for growing, and you have to keep it below this. Seeds will cost you no more than $1 a packet, and soil, water, and fertilizer no more than a few cents a day.

Steps to take: 1. Set up your growing area, and do it a cheaply as possible.

2. Buy seeds, and get a selection.

3. Plant and tend your crops. A few hundred square feet of growing area can produce a large amount of herbs if taken well care of.

4. Harvest and dry your crops as they mature. If you aren't sure when to harvest the herbs, go to the market and see what theirs look like.

5. Package your dried herbs in 1 once bags, clearly labeled and priced. You can easily charge 50 cents or more per once of dried herbs, but look at the supermarket and at least cut their prices in half.

6. Market your herbs, which will be in small supply initially, in the local farmer's markets, flea markets and swap meets. Don't try to supply supermarkets unless you have a large production of herbs and can meet their needs as required.

7. Take a sufficient amount out of your sales to reseed and care for your crops.

8. Repeat 1 through 7 as often as necessary.

Hand Bookbinding

Bookbinding is not a business for everyone, but only for those who like to put a high quality of skill into their work. Furthermore, you won't have a very broad cliental as a bookbinder. But what you will have is the opportunity to work with wonderful materials such as rare and valuable books, to do a quality job that you can put all of your effort into, and that you will be paid nicely for.

Now who uses book binders? The libraries re-bind books all of the time, so any library can be a customer. Of course libraries these days don't have much money and you may not get much work from them. On the other hand the collectors of rare books have lots of money and have books re-bound all of the time in order to save them. But to go to these people you also have to have skill before they are going to hire you.

To get the skill you are going to have to train. Some night schools and colleges offer courses in book binding, and this is a good place to start to get the basics. Then you are going to have to practice to a sufficient degree that you will have some examples of your work to display at rare book fares. If you can offer a high quality product at a price in line with your competition you will get work.

Start-up costs: Class costs will be at least $100, and you should figure on at least an additional $100 for supplies. The only way to find out exactly what is required is by taking a class and reading books on hand bookbinding. Business cards are a necessity, at about $50, and rare book show fees at $5 each. You can hand out your cards and talk to dealers and collectors without additional fees at this point.

Steps to take: 1. Take one or more classes in hand bookbinding, and read whatever books are available in the library.

2. Attend 3 or 4 rare book fairs to look at the books, and to look over the bookbinders who are there. This will give you an idea of the prices that can be charged, and the quality that is required.

3. Bind several books on your own until you have a selection of at least 5 to 10 that are of a quality equal to the book binders at the book fairs.

4. Have your business cards made up. Take Polaroids of your work to show off.

5. Attend more book fairs and hand out your cards. Also go to libraries and post your business cards. Librarians often meet people interested in having books re-bound.

6. When you get a client do the best job that you possible can. Always do this.

7. If you get a large order, such as a set of books to bind, get an advance of at least 25% of the costs to cover your materials.

8. Return re-bound books only when you are paid. Some people will walk out and leave you with the books. If they are worthwhile books you should be able to sell them yourself for costs, and even make a little extra for your trouble.

9. Keep practicing book binding to improve yourself, and don't take any very rare books (books worth over $500) to re-bind until you

have bound at least 100 books. Remember that you can also be sued if you ruin a valuable book.

10. Practice, practice, practice.

Janitorial Service

If offering janitorial services does not seem like a very glamourous job to you, at least it is a job that every business has to have. Every store front you see in your town has to clean up after itself every single day of the year. Now if the business is small enough the owner's will do the job. And if it is big enough they will hire full time janitors, but if they are in-between they will not have the time to do it themselves or the money to hire someone full time, and that is where you fit in.

What you have to do though, since you will be doing this on your own, and you need business, is to undercut the competition. If a large firm everyone has heard about will clean a small office for $100 a month, then you have to be willing to do it for $75. Cleaning an office of this size should take less than 30 minutes a day, and it may only be for 5 days a week, but you have to be able to steal potential business from the other competition in the area.

When you are starting a business like this you want to remain as invisible as you can to the competition while being as visible as possible to the people you want to hire you. Don't go on a big advertising campaign, since this will only alert your competition and eat up all of your money. Do the personal thing; have business cards and flyers made up and go to every business in your area, particularly the new ones, and talk to anyone who will talk to you personally. Explain exactly what you will do for them and how much it will cost and in a few months you should start getting contracts. As soon as you have established yourself, within less than a year, you can stop the business to business canvassing and just depend upon word-of-mouth to get new contracts. If you do this right within a couple of years you will be hiring other people to help you out with your business.

Start-up costs: You will need your own cleaning supplies. Figuring that most of your early jobs will be small companies or homes, you need to have supplies you can trust. Buy a good, maneuverable vacuum. While this could cost $200 or more, you can probably get a very serviceable vacuum for $20 at a thrift shop. Also buy a broom, mop, bucket, dust cloths, gloves, and cleaning chemicals. You may pay as much as $200 or $300 for these items. You will need to advertise your services in local papers at $25 a week. This is a constant expense you will have to keep paying until you have all of the clients you can service. Also buy some billing invoices. They will cost no more than $5. Also buy an answering machine at $50, for calls while you are out. With businesses you may be working late at night and sleeping during the day.

Steps to take: 1. Buy your supplies.

2. Take out advertising.

3. Set up your answering machine.

4. So far as possible schedule your services to match exactly what the clients want.

5. You rate can be as high as $20 per hour. Therefore, a small office that will take an hour per night to clean completely will be worth a $400 a month contract. Of course you can make deals if you want to, but get a contract for your services.

6. If you get too much work then hire someone else to work with you, and pay them 1/2 of the rate you collect.

7. For home contacts use the free bulletin boards at the supermarkets. There are a lot more homes than businesses, and they can pay just as well.

Balloon Sales

Now this doesn't even sound like a business, after all how can you have a business selling balloons? Actually balloon sales is one of the businesses that have sprung up in the 80s. Balloon people do a lot of children's' birthday parties, and they can do any other type of gathering where a lot of people get together. But since you will do a lot of birthday parties it is important to find out what you are expected to do in a balloon business. It is going to be more than just blowing up a bunch of balloons and delivering them to a party. If you can do some balloon animals, or have any other special tricks that will make it more interesting you will get a lot more business.

But the reason for going into balloon sales and not some other form of entertainment is that it is the public that decides whether or not to buy your services, not some executive sitting in a big chair with a bunch of accountants around them. It is these people who may call you occasionally, but they would never hire you for a permanent job. The balloon sales business can be very good, and all that you need is a car big enough to hold a bunch of inflated balloons, a tank of helium, and some advertising in the newspaper.

Start-up costs: You will need a large canister of helium, which you can rent from a welding supply house for under $50, and some advertising in order to go into the party balloon business. Since you will be advertising you will also need a city business license. And finally you will have to have a supply of balloons to sell. Besides the gas and regulator, advertising will cost you $25 a week in your local paper, a business license may cost you about $25, and the balloons could run another $25 for a first set. Incidentally, some companies also sell franchises for balloon businesses, but you won't get much for your money that you can't do on your own for free.

Steps to take: 1. Find a welding supply company and price a canister of helium with a regulator.

2. Contact some balloon party companies and get a list of their prices. Just tell them you are pricing balloons for a possible party. Then set your prices accordingly the same or a little lower than they do.

3. Buy the balloons and rent the helium, and spend a few dollars worth of balloons and gas to get used to using the equipment.

4. Advertise in a local paper, and post an ad for your services in local supermarkets.

5. When you are called always be willing to quote prices, but make the callers be as specific as possible about what they want you to do, and charge accordingly.

6. Be on time for every job. There is nothing worse that you can do than be too late for a party. You will lose business, and customers all at the same time.

7. To keep costs down only fill your helium tank and buy balloons as needed. Besides, the rubber in balloons will rot after a few months and you will lose money.

Carpet Cleaning

Every house and every apartment has carpets that sometimes need cleaning, and cleaning carpets is hard work. Of course the heavy duty equipment that most carpet cleaners use costs too much to keep your start-up costs under $500, and that is why you aren't going to start out buying it. This is one of those businesses where you are going to have to be a little smarter than the professionals in order to get started.

In the first place there is nothing mysterious about carpet cleaning. And if you still don't feel comfortable with the idea take a look at the carpet cleaning equipment in your local supermarket tomorrow. There are a few chemicals to use and a lot of work. Still, one good contract can give you enough money to live on for a week, and you will see why in just a minute.

One hint before you go on, if you are considering whether carpet cleaning might be a good business for you first go rent a supermarket system and clean your own carpets thoroughly. After you are done if you can still stand the idea of the work, then go ahead. This is not a business for those who are frail of body, or who don't want to work hard, and that is precisely why you can start a carpet cleaning business just about anywhere.

Start-up costs: You are going to need a carpet cleaning machine, but these can be rented for $25 a day from supermarkets as needed. Chemicals will cost you about another $15 a job. You will also need to advertise, and local papers and supermarkets will work best. Newspaper ads will cost about $25 a week, and supermarkets will let you put up a little ad for free. You will also need to have a vacuum cleaner. These cost around $100 new, or $20 used.

Steps to take: 1. Call carpet companies and find out how much they charge per square foot to clean carpets, and if there are extra charges for moving furniture. Set your rates accordingly about 1/4 less than the other companies if you can.

2. Advertise. Call the newspaper and list your services. Visit the supermarkets and put up notices telling what you do. Do not put your prices in your advertising unless other companies in the area are doing it too.

3. When you get a call go out and rent the equipment you need.

4. When you get to a job make an estimate before you begin. If the homeowner agrees then have them sign a contract. This way you can always sue them if they don't pay for some reason.

5. When you are done, and collect your money sign the contract paid and give a copy to the homeowner.

6. If you need help to move furniture, pay the person you hire 1/4 of your fees, and make them earn it. You do the cleaning, but have them help move equipment from room to room for you.

Childcare

It seems like everyone with children needs childcare, and there is never enough good childcare to go around that people can afford. If you are considering childcare for a business, then I should tell you right now that you will have a much better chance of a successful business if you are a woman. People are suspicious of men who care for small children, but women are looked on as having the ability to mother a child.

Things you need to know is that some states require childcare people to be licensed, and this means that the number of children you can take care of is limited as is the number of bathrooms and so on. Of course you want the best conditions possible to do your childcare business, but it can also get out of hand in a hurry if there are a lot of state restrictions you have to follow. A lot of people offer childcare services, but don't get licensed. I can't advise you to do this if it is required in your state, and this might limit the choices of some of you.

Basically, what you need to go into the childcare business is a home where you can do it. If you go to someone else's home they will have to file tax returns and pay social security taxes for you. If at all possible don't put your clients into this situation. If you have a home, your a woman, and you can take care of state requirements it is not at all impossible to earn from $300 to $500 per child, per month, for each child you can take care of.

Start-up costs: Start up costs are very low if you keep the number of children you intend to care for very small. If you have a fenced yard and a home the only start up costs you will need is advertising. And for childcare you can just post notices in the area in which you live. Everywhere that people live childcare is needed. If you live in an area that requires licensing your costs could be much higher and you may not be able to open a childcare center for under $500. Otherwise your costs will be ongoing. You will have to supply snack as well as supervision, and lunch as well. Costs for these will be no more than $3 per day per child.

Steps to take: 1. Decide on the rates you are going to charge. Rates are generally around $2 per hour   per child, although infants who require more care will warrant a higher rate.

2. Get your advertising out in the form of supermarket postings and posted signs in your neighborhood.

3. Tell anyone who calls what your rates are, what days you will do childcare, and whether or not you will take problem children.

4. Limit the number of children you care for. If you are alone and the children are small you should have no more than 5 or 6 children under your care. Of course you could also take a few late afternoon children for 2 or 3 hours to increase your daily earnings.

5. Collect your fees weekly.

6. Keep your home and yard clean and in good repair at all times. A trashy yard and dirty home will scare away clients.

Gold Panning

If you like the outdoors and dislike anyone looking over your shoulder while you work gold panning might be the ideal business for you. Can you really make money at it? Yet you can, if you are also willing to work hard. Every state in the country has areas where you can pan for gold, but you will have to do some research. The richest areas are in the west, and Alaska, but potential areas are everywhere. And at the value of gold these days is about $400 an ounce.

The most valuable form of gold is nuggets, but the easiest kind to find is gold dust. Most gold is in veins, and has to be dug out at great expense. Of course you don't have to have a gold mine to dig for gold. In fact you don't even have to research the sources of gold yourself in order to go gold panning. There are gold clubs where ever gold can be found. So for a fee of $50 a year you can join a club, have access to the claims that the club has in your area, and get instruction and help from other members. While most gold panners do it just for fun, if you go into any area where gold can be found you will find people who are looking for more than just a good time. Besides being a reasonably healthy lover of the outdoors you are also going to have to have your own transportation. At least you don't need a license to pan for gold, and if you find an area that proves rich, but someone has a claim on it, you can usually rent the use of the claim for a period of months or a year for a reasonable amount. Gold panning is fun even if it is hard work.

Start-up costs: Basic start-up costs would be a gold pan ($14), a shovel ($10), and read up on where to find gold in the local library. As a beginner a membership in a local gold panning club would also be very useful ($25). To get any real gold you will have have to have a sluice, which you can build for $25, or buy already built for $100. While other tools would help you get more gold they would also push your budget over $500.

Steps to take: 1. Buy the basic tools from a rock shop or gold supply store. Find these stores in the Yellow Pages.

2. At the store where you get your supplies inquire into gold panning clubs in your area.

3. Contact the gold club and join up. Get directions to local gold panning sites and go out and have a look around.

4. If you have never panned for gold before then go out with other club members as often as possible until you learn the ropes yourself.

5. All gold that you find should be put into small glass bottles with screw tops. Nuggets are the most valuable, but are also much more difficult to find. Flour gold, or gold dust, can be found in many locations.

6. Sell your gold when you get enough. Since gold sells for around $400 an once right now, if you can get as much as 1/4 once a day you can make a business out of it. Nuggets are worth at least twice as much per once as gold dust since they are popular for jewelry.

7. Work at this every day for 6 or 7 hours and you might make a living out of gold panning, even today. Work less often and for shorter hours and you will still have a good time in some beautiful places out of doors.

HOW TO GET A PART OF THE BILLIONS THAT THE GOVERNMENT IS HOLDING

Your $25 Billion Opportunity

If you can read English and speak on the phone, you are eligible to obtain a share of the $25 billion in spare change the federal government holds in reserve. All you have to do is find the owners of lost money. One out of every 10 Americans has either not claimed or lost his/her money in bank accounts, stocks, insurance premiums, etc. By informing people of such untapped cash reserves, you can obtain a major profit. Even though states are required by law to make lists of owners who have unclaimed property, most people are unaware of such lists.

Locating People

The only ingredients you need to contact individuals who own unclaimed property are a phone book, library references and a little patience. Included in the following pages is a simple outline of the processes you need to go through to find these people.

Getting Started

Your first step on the path to prosperity is to find the owners of unclaimed property and make a profit by telling them about their unfound riches.

Unclaimed money is property that a person leaves in an institution (bank, insurance company, business, government office or security company), which reported the money it receives to the state. If the unclaimed money is not picked up within a specified period of time (five to seven years in California), then it is handed over to the state treasury department.

Contacting the State Offices

Lists of unclaimed property are available in many public libraries. Estates of deceased persons also can be claimed if the rightful heirs to the property don't take possession of it within a specified number of years.

The Freedom of Information Act of 1966 will allow you to inspect any public document, including any lists of unclaimed property. If you visit your state's unclaimed property office, you won't be charged for any information you may obtain.

Below are the names, addresses and numbers of state offices of unclaimed property:

ALABAMA,
Unclaimed Property Division,
Revenue Department
206 Administration Building ,
 Montgomery, Alabama 36130,
(205) 261-3369

ALASKA
Unclaimed Property Division
Revenue Department
State Office Building, Pouch S A
Juneau, Alaska 99811
(907) 465-2322

ARIZONA
Unclaimed Property Division
Revenue Department
Capitol Building
1700 W. Washington Street
Phoenix, Arizona 85007
(602) 255-4425

ARKANSAS
Unclaimed Property Division
Finance & Administration Dept.
DFA Building
Little Rock, Arkansas 72203
(501) 371-1458

CALIFORNIA
Unclaimed Property Division
Controller Office
P.O. Box 1019, State Capitol Building
Sacramento, California 95804
(916) 322-4166

COLORADO
Unclaimed Property Division
Revenue Department
140 State Capitol
Denver, Colorado 80203
(303) 866-2441

CONNECTICUT
Unclaimed Property Division
Tax Department
20 Trinity Street
Hartford, Connecticut 06106
(203) 566-5516

DELAWARE
Treasury Department
Thomas Collins Building
Wilmington, Delaware 19801
(302) 376-4208

FLORIDA
Unclaimed Property Division
Revenue Department
1401 The Capitol
Tallahassee, Florida 32301
(904) 487-2583

GEORGIA
Unclaimed Property Division
Revenue Department
405 Trinity-Washington Building
270 Washington Street S.W.
Atlanta, Georgia 30334
(404) 656-4244

HAWAII
Unclaimed Property Division
Taxation Department
425 Queen Street
Honolulu, Hawaii 96813
(808) 548-7650

IDAHO
Dept. of Revenue and Taxation
State Tax Commission
P.O. Box 56
Boise, Idaho 83756
(208) 334-4516

ILLINOIS
Unclaimed Property Division
Revenue Department
11th & Ash Street
Springfield, Illinois 62708
(217) 782-5552

INDIANA
Unclaimed Property Division
Revenue Department
State Office Building #1022
Indianapolis, Indiana 46204
(317) 232-6348

IOWA
Unclaimed Property Division
Revenue Department
Hoover Building
10th Street
Des Moines, Iowa 50319
(515) 281-5540

KANSAS
Unclaimed Property Division
Revenue Department
State Office Building
535 Kansas Avenue
Box 737, P.O. Box 1517
Topeka, Kansas 66601
(913) 296-2031

KENTUCKY
Unclaimed Property Division
Treasury Department
Capitol Annex
Frankfort, Kentucky 40620
(502) 564-2100

LOUISIANA
Unclaimed Property Division
Revenue & Taxation Dept.
P.O. Box 201
300 N. Ardenwood Drive
Baton Rouge, Louisiana 70804
(504) 925-7424

MAINE
Unclaimed Property Division
Bureau of Taxation
State Office Building
Augusta, Maine 04333
(207) 289-2771

MARYLAND
Unclaimed Property Division
Controller of the Treasury
State Treasury Building
Baltimore, Maryland 21201
(301) 383-4984

MASSACHUSETTS
Unclaimed Property Division
Treasury Department
Lansing, Michigan 48922
(517) 373-0550

MINNESOTA
Unclaimed Property Division
Revenue Department
Centennial Office Building
St. Paul, Minnesota 55155
(612) 296-2568

MISSISSIPPI
Unclaimed Property Division
Tax Commission
102 Woolfolk Building
Jackson, Mississippi 39205
(601) 354-7117

MISSOURI
Unclaimed Property Division
Revenue Department
227 State Capitol
P.O. Box 210, Jefferson Building
Jefferson City, Missouri 65102
(314) 751-2096

MONTANA
Unclaimed Property Division
Revenue Department
Sam W. Mitchell Building
Helena, Montana 59620
(406) 444-2460

NEBRASKA
Unclaimed Property Division
Revenue Department
P.O. Box 94788
Lincoln, Nebraska 68509
(402) 471-2455

NEVADA
Unclaimed Property Division
Treasury Department
Capitol Building
Carson City, Nevada 89710
(702) 885-5200

NEW HAMPSHIRE
Unclaimed Property Division
Taxation Board
19 Pillsbury Street
Concord,New Hampshire 03301
(613) 271-2621

NEW JERSEY
Unclaimed Property Division
Division of Taxation
W. State & Willow Street
Trenton, New Jersey 08625
(609) 292-4827

NEW MEXICO
Unclaimed Property Division
Taxation & Revenue Dept.
Manuel Lujan Building
P.O. Box 30
Santa Fe, New Mex.87509-0630
(505) 988-2290

NEW YORK
Unclaimed Property Division
Tax & Finance Department
Campus Tax & Finance Bldg.
Albany, New York 12227
(518) 457-2902

NORTH CAROLINA
100 Albemarle Building
325 N. Salisbury Street
Raleigh, NC 27611
(919) 733-4440

NORTH DAKOTA
Unclaimed Property Division
Tax Department
Capitol Building
Bismark, North Dakota 58505
(701) 224-2806

OHIO
Unclaimed Property Division
Taxation Department
30 E. Broad Street
Columbus, Ohio 43215
(614) 466-4433

OKLAHOMA
Unclaimed Property Division
Tax Commission
2501 Lincoln Boulevard
Oklahoma City,Oklahoma73194
(405) 521-3237

OREGON
Unclaimed Property Division
Treasury Department
1445 State Street
State Capitol Building
Salem, Oregon 97310
(503) 378-3806

PENNSYLVANIA
Unclaimed Property Division
Revenue Department
Strawberry Square
Harrisburg, Pennsylvania 17127
(717) 787-6960

RHODE ISLAND
Unclaimed Property Division
Tax Department
289 Promenade Street
Providence, Rhode Island02908
(401) 277-2905

SOUTH CAROLINA
Unclaimed Property Division
Tax Commission
Calhoun Office Building
Columbia, South Carolina29214
(803) 758-2196

SOUTH DAKOTA
Unclaimed Property Division
Revenue Department
Kneip Building
Pierre, South Dakota 57501
(605) 773-3378

TENNESSEE
Unclaimed Property Division
Andrew Jackson Building
Nashville, Tennessee 37219
(615) 741-6499

TEXAS
Unclaimed Property Division
Revenue Department
111 E. 17th Street
Austin, Texas 78701
(512) 475-2086

UTAH
Unclaimed Property Division
Tax Commission
219 State Capitol
Salt Lake City, Utah 84114
(801) 533-7183

VERMONT
Unclaimed Property Division
Tax Department
109 State Street
Montpelier, Vermont 05602
(802) 828-2301

VIRGINIA
Unclaimed Property Division
State Treasurer's Office
P.O. Box 6-H
Richmond, Virginia 23207
(804) 225-2393

WASHINGTON
Unclaimed Property Division
Revenue Department
General Administration Building
Olympia, Washington 98504
(206) 754-2630

WEST VIRGINIA
Unclaimed Property Division
Tax Department
W. State Capitol Building
Charleston, West Virginia 25305
(304) 348-2281

WISCONSIN
Office of State Treasurer
Unclaimed Property Division
P.O. Box 2114
Madison, Wisconsin 53707
(608) 267-7977

WYOMING
Unclaimed Property Division
Revenue & Taxation Dept.
State Capitol Building
Cheyenne, Wyoming 82002
(307) 777-7408

Business Basics

Upon locating an individual with unclaimed property, you should contact him/her either by phone or by mail. Tell this person that you will send him/her a check for a designated amount if he/she signs the contract you are sending. When the person signs this contract, you can collect a share of the unclaimed money.

The average "finder's fee" is around 33.3 percent of the amount charged for locating someone's unclaimed money. This percentage is by no means the rule, and you can charge whatever rate you believe is fair.

Don't forget to write up a contract between you, the investigator and the unclaimed property owner (the claimant); include a separate charge for your services. Before anyone signs a contract, ask a lawyer to inspect the agreement to see if it meets all legal standards.

The Contract

The contract that your attorney will draw up states that the person will pay you either a percentage of the property you have retrieved for him/her, or a flat fee for your expenses, time and services. The following is an example of a contract between an investigator (you) and a person with unclaimed property (the claimant).

Investigator Agreement/Contract

Claimant_____

Address_____

Reported_____

Social Security Number_____

Type of Account _____

Stock_____

Amount_____

This agreement is entered into by and between

_____

hereinafter referred to as "Claimant," and

_____hereinaft
er referred to as "Investigator."

II   The Investigator, through his/her efforts, has located the Claimant, who will be entitled to the assets described above.

III   Investigator and Claimant do hereby agree that in consideration of Investigator's efforts in locating Claimant and assisting in the actual recovery of the assets described above to which the Claimant is entitled, claimant hereby assigns to the Investigator a set fee of $ _____

for expenses and services rendered, providing Claimant recovers described assets.

IV   Agreement Continued.

Investigator and Claimant agree that in the event the Claimant is not entitled to assets described above and such assets are not recovered, there is no obligation on either party to the other.

This agreement is void unless executed by both parties.

Investigator_____

Phone _____

Address_____

Date_____

Investigator's Signature_____

Claimant_____

Phone_____

Address_____

Date_____

Claimant's Signature_____

When the Contract Is Returned To You

After the contract is signed by the Claimant, send the contract as well as a copy of the person's drivers license or social security card to your state's unclaimed property office. Ask a representative from the state office to mail you the necessary forms to fill out. After you return these simple papers, the state will mail you a check.

Tracking Down The Address

There are several ways to locate the person who owns unclaimed property.

The Post Office

More often than not, the person you are looking for no longer resides at the address listed in the state's records. For a fee of $1, the post office will locate the current address of the person you are searching for. The postal service is likely to process your request faster if you send your letter by registered mail. Or, you can print "DO NOT FORWARD" and "ADDRESS CORRECTION REQUESTED" on the letter.

In some cases, you may have to get a street address from a P.O. Box number. To do this, go to your county clerk's office and fill out a subpoena form. Go to the post office and ask for the street address of the person so you can serve him/her a subpoena. You should be able to locate your street address this way.

Directories

Another way to find people with unclaimed property is through telephone books or city directories. If you can't find the person you are looking for in a current phone book, go to a public library and find older editions.

Don't be afraid to call people with similar surnames, for they may be relatives of the person you are looking for. Ask them if they know that person's current address.

Real Estate Plot Maps

You can look up the owner of every piece of land in the United States on a plot map. If you can't find these maps at your local library or any real-estate office, you can obtain one from your county assessor's office.

On the map you will see the name and address of the owner of the property. Contact the owner and coyly ask him if he or she knows the whereabouts of the person you are looking for.

You can verify the person's name, address and phone number with your state's Department of Motor Vehicles. They will tell you if they have the person's same address in their records. There is a DMV list of services provided in the following chapters.

Neighbors, Relatives & Friends

If you can't find someone using the aforementioned techniques, contact the neighbors by phone and ask them if they know the whereabouts of the person you are looking for. Use the following methods to contact neighbors and relatives:

1) Use telephone books to look up relatives or people with similar last names.

2) Use city directories to find neighbors and ex-neighbors.

3) Use plot maps to locate neighbors and their landlords.

Relatives and Friends

It is harder to drag out important information from relatives or friends than it is from neighbors. Not only do relatives and friends ask a lot of questions, they may not trust you if they can tell you are lying to them. Use your best judgement when trying to find a person with unclaimed property.

Drivers Licenses & Automobile Records

Drivers licenses are public records in every state except Arkansas, North Carolina, Pennsylvania and Wisconsin. You can find out a person's address, his/her driving record and if he/she has applied for a social security card in a particular state. In addition, the DMV will locate the person you are looking for and physically identify him/her.

Ask the DMV for a complete background of your subject's driving record, especially his/her full name, address, phone number and date of birth.

Data Research Inc. has a large data base that you can access through your computer to obtain drivers license information about a person. Here is where the company may be reached:

Data Research Inc.
3600 American River Drive, Suite 100
Sacramento, CA 95864
(800) 425-DATA
(916) 485-3282

Listed below are the state agencies that provide drivers license information.

ALABAMA
Drivers License Division
Certification Section
P.O. Box 1471
Montgomery, Alabama 36102
(205) 832-5100
Fee: $2.00

ALASKA
Department of Public Safety
Drivers License Section
Pouch N
Juneau, Alaska 99801
(907) 465-4396
Fee: $2.00

ARIZONA
Motor Vehicle Department
1801 W. Jefferson Street
Phoenix, Arizona 85007
(602) 255-7011
Fee: Record check -- $2.00

ARKANSAS
Office of Driver Services
Traffic Violation Report Unit
P.O. Box 1272
Little Rock, Arkansas 72203
(501) 371-1671
Fee: $5.00 Write for forms

CALIFORNIA
Department of Motor Vehicles
P.O. Box 11231
Sacramento, California 95813
(916) 445-4568
Fee: $0.75 Write for forms

COLORADO
Department of Revenue
Motor Vehicle Division
Master File Section
140 W. Sixth Avenue
Denver, Colorado 80204
(303) 892-3407
Fee: $1.25

CONNECTICUT
Department of Motor Vehicles
Copy Record Section
60 State Street
Wethersfield, Connecticut 06109
(203) 566-2638
Fee: $4.00

DELAWARE
Motor Vehicle Department
P.O. Box 698
Dover, Delaware 19901
(302) 736-4760
Fee: $2.00

DISTRICT OF COLUMBIA
Department of Transportation
Bureau of Motor Vehicles
301 C Street, N.W.
Washington, DC
(202) 727-6680
Fee: $0.75

FLORIDA
Drivers License Division
Department of Highway Safety
Kirkham Building
Tallahassee, Florida 32301
(904) 488-9145
Fee: $3.00 Write for forms

GEORGIA
Department of Public Safety
Drivers Service Section
Merit Rating
P.O. Box 1456
Atlanta, Georgia 30301
(404) 656-2339
Fee: $2.00

HAWAII
District of The First Circuit
Violations Bureau
842 Bethel Street
Honolulu, Hawaii 96813
(808) 548-5735
Fee: $1.00

IDAHO (WRONG ADDRESS)
Dept. of Law Enforcement
Violations Bureau
Honolulu, Hawaii 96813
(808) 548-5735
Fee: $1.00

ILLINOIS
Secretary of State
Drivers Services Department
Driver Analysis Section
2701 S. Dirksen Parkway
Springfield, Illinois 62723
(217) 782-3720
Fee: $2.00 Write for forms

INDIANA
Bureau of Motor Vehicles
Paid Mail Section
Room 416, State Office Building
Indianapolis, Indiana 46204
(317) 232-2798
Fee: $1.00

IOWA
Department of Transportation
Records Section
Lucas Building
Des Moines, Iowa 50319
(515) 281-5656
Fee: $1.00

KANSAS
Division of Vehicles
Driver Control Bureau
State Office Building
Frankfurt, Kentucky 40601
(502) 564-6800
Fee: $2.00

LOUISIANA
Department of Public Safety
Drivers License Division
O.D.R. Section, Box 1271
Baton Rouge, Louisiana 70821
(504) 925-6343
Fee: $2.00

MAINE
Secretary of State
Motor Vehicle Division
1 Child Street
Augusta, Maine 04333
(207) 289-2761
Fee: $3.00

MASSACHUSETTS
Registry of Motor Vehicles
Court Records Section
100 Nashua Street
Boston, Massachusetts 02114
(617) 727-3842   Fee: $3.00

MICHIGAN
Department of State
Bur: Driver & Vehicle Services
Commercial Look-Up Unit
7064 Crowner Drive
Lansing, Michigan 48918
(517) 322-1460
Fee: $5.00

MINNESOTA
Department of Public Safety
Drivers License Office
Room 108, State Highway Bldg.
St. Paul, Minnesota 55155
(612) 296-6911
Fee: $2.00 Write for forms

MISSISSIPPI
Mississippi Hwy. Safety Patrol
Drivers License Issuance Board
P.O. Box 958
Jackson, Mississippi 39205
(601) 987-1236
Fee: $3.50

MISSOURI
Bureau of Drivers License
Department of Revenue
P.O. Box 200
Jefferson City, Missouri 65101
(314) 751-4600
Fee: $1.00

MONTANA
Montana Highway Patrol
303 Roberts
Helena, Montana 59601
(406) 449-3000
Fee: $2.00

NEBRASKA
Department of Motor Vehicles
Drivers Record Section
P.O. Box 94789
Lincoln, Nebraska 68509
(402) 471-2281
Fee: $1.00

NEVADA
CBM of Nevada
Box 1964
Carson City, Nevada 89701
(702) 885-5360
Fee: $1.25

NEW HAMPSHIRE
Division of Motor Vehicles
Driver Record Research Unit
85 Loudon Road
Concord, New Hamp. 03301
(603) 271-2371
Fee: $5.00

NEW JERSEY
Division of Motor Vehicles
Bureau: Security Responsibility
25 S. Montgomery Street
Trenton, New Jersey 08666
(609) 292-7500
Fee: $5.00

NEW MEXICO
Transportation Department
Drivers Services Bureau
Manuel Lujan Sr. Building
Santa Fe, New Mexico 87503
(505) 827-7522
Fee: $1.10

NEW YORK
Department of Motor Vehicles
Public Service Bureau
Empire State Plaza
Albany, New York 12228
(518) 473-5595;
Fee: $2.00

NORTH CAROLINA
Traffic Records Section
Division of Motor Vehicles
Raleigh, North Carolina 27611
(919) 733-4241
Fee: $1.00 Write for forms

NORTH DAKOTA
Drivers License Division
Capitol Grounds
Bismarck, North Dakota 58505
(701) 224-2600
Fee: $2.00

OHIO
Bureau of Motor Vehicles
P.O. Box 16520
Columbus, Ohio 43216
(614) 863-7500
Fee: $1.00

OKLAHOMA
Driver Records Service
Department of Public Safety
P.O. Box 11415
Oklahoma City, Ok. 73136
(405) 424-4011
Fee: $3.00

OREGON
Motor Vehicles Division
1905 Lona Avenue
Salem, Oregon 97314
(503) 371-2200
Fee: $6.00

PENNSYLVANIA
Department of Transportation
Bureau of Accident Analysis
Operator Information Section
Room 212, Transportation and
Safety Bldg.
Harrisburg, Pennsylvania 17120
(717) 783-6605
Fee: $1.50 Write for required form

RHODE ISLAND
Registry of Motor Vehicles
Room 101G, State Office Building
Providence, Rhode Island 02903
(401) 277-2970
Fee: $1.50

SOUTH CAROLINA
Dept. of Highways and Public
Transportation
Driver Record Check Section,
Room 201
Columbia, South Carolina 29216
(605) 758-2125
Fee: $3.00 Write for forms

SOUTH DAKOTA
Department of Public Safety
Driver Improvement Program
118 W. Capitol
Pierce, South Dakota 57501
(605) 773-3191
Fee: $2.00 Write for forms

TENNESSEE
Department of Safety
Jackson Building
Nashville, Tennessee 37219
(615) 741-3954
Fee: $3.00

TEXAS
Department of Public Safety
License of Issuance & Driver
Records
P.O. Box 4087
Austin, Texas 78773
(512) 465-2000
Fee: $1.00 Write for forms

UTAH
Drivers License Division
314 State Office Building
Salt Lake City, Utah 84114
(801) 965-4400
Fee: $1.00

VERMONT
Agency of Transportation
Department of Motor Vehicles
Montpelier, Vermont 05602
(802) 828-2121
Fee: $3.00

VIRGINIA
Division of Motor Vehicles
Driver Licensing & Information
Department
P.O. Box 27412
Richmond, Virginia 23269
(804) 257-0538
Fee: $3.00

WASHINGTON
Division of Licensing
Department of Motor Vehicles
Olympia, Washington 98501
(206) 753-6969
Fee: $1.50

WEST VIRGINIA
Driver Improvement Division
Department of Motor Vehicles
1800 Washington Street, East
Charleston, West Virginia 25305
(304) 348-3900
Fee: $1.00

WISCONSIN
Department of Transportation
Driver Record File
P.O. Box 7918
Madison, Wisconsin 53707
(608) 266-2261
Fee: $1.00 Write for forms

WYOMING
Department of Revenue
2200 Carey Avenue
Cheyenne, Wyoming 82001
(307) 777-6516
Fee: $1.00

License Plates

Listed below are state agencies you can contact when trying to find the owner of a car with a particular license plate:

ALABAMA
Motor Vehicle & Licensing Div.
P.O. Box 104
3030 E. Boulevard
Montgomery, Alabama 36130
Fee: $0.25

ARKANSAS
Motor Vehicle Division
P.O. Box 1272
Little Rock, Arkansas 72203
Fee: $1.00

ALASKA
Division of Motor Vehicles
P.O. Box 960
Anchorage, Alaska 99510
Fee: $2.00

ARIZONA
Arizona Motor Vehicle Division
P.O. Box 2100
Phoenix, Arizona 85001
Fee: $1.00

CALIFORNIA
Department of Motor Vehicles
P.O. Box 11231
Sacramento, California 95813
Fee: $1.00

COLORADO
Department of Revenue
Motor Vehicle Master Files Sect
140 W 6th Avenue
Denver, Colorado 80204
Fee: $1.25

CONNECTICUT
Commissioner: Motor Vehicles
60 State Street
Wethersfield, Conn. 06109
Fee: $1.00

DELAWARE
Motor Vehicle Division
Registration Section
P.O. Box 698
Dover, Delaware 19901
Fee: $2.00

DISTRICT OF COLUMBIA
Bureau of Motor Vehicles
301 C Street, N.W.
Washington, DC 20001
Fee: $0.50

FLORIDA
Dept: Hwy Saf. & Motor Vehicle
Kirkman Building
Tallahassee, Florida 32301
Fee: $0.50

GEORGIA
Department of Revenue
Motor Vehicle Division
Trinity Washington Building
Atlanta, Georgia 30334
Fee: $0.50

HAWAII
Director of Finance
County of Hawaii
25 Apuni Street
Hilo, Hawaii 96720

Director of Finance
County of Kauai
Lihue, Hawaii 96766

Director of Finance
County of Maui
Wailuku, Maui 96793

Director of Finance
County of Honolulu
1455 S. Bertania
Honolulu, Hawaii 96814

IDAHO
Motor Vehicle Division
Dept. of Law Enforcement
P.O. Box 34
Boise, Idaho 83731
Fee: $1.50

ILLINOIS
Secretary of State
2701 S. Dirksen Parkway
Springfield, Illinois 62756
Fee: $2.00

INDIANA
Bur. of Motor Vehicles, Rm. 314
State Office Building
Indianapolis, Indiana 46204
Fee: $1.00

IOWA
Department of Transportation
Office of Vehicle Registration
Lucas Building
Des Moines, Iowa 50319
Fee: $1.00

KANSAS
Division of Vehicles
Department of Revenue
State Office Building
Topeka, Kansas 66626
Fee: $1.00

KENTUCKY
Department of Justice
Bureau of State Police
State Office Building
Frankfurt, Kentucky 40601
Fee: $1.00

LOUISIANA
Department of Public Safety
Vehicle Regulation Division
P.O. Box 66196
Baton Rouge, Louisiana 70896
Fee: $2.00

MAINE
Motor Vehicle Division
1 Child Street
Augusta, Maine 04333
Fee: $2.00

MARYLAND
Motor Vehicle Administration
6601 Richie Highway N.E.
Glen Burnie, Maryland 21062
Fee: $1.00

MASSACHUSETTS
Registry of Motor Vehicles
100 Nashua Street
Boston, Massachusetts 02114
Fee: $1.50

MICHIGAN
Department of State
Bur. of Driver & Vehicle Service
7064 Crowner Drive
Lansing, Michigan 48918
Fee: $4.00

MINNESOTA
Driver and Vehicle Services
Transportation Building
St. Paul, Minnesota 55155
Fee: $1.00

MISSISSIPPI
Motor Vehicle Controller
P.O. Box 1140
Jackson, Mississippi 39205
Fee: $1.00

MISSOURI
Department of Revenue
Vehicle & Drivers Licensing Bur.
Jefferson City, Missouri 65101
Fee: $1.00

MONTANA
Department of Justice
Registrars Bureau
Motor Vehicle Division
Deer Lodge, Montana 59722
Fee: $2.00

NEBRASKA
Administrator of Titles & Reg.
Department of Motor Vehicles
Capitol Building
Lincoln, Nebraska 68509
Fee: $1.00

NEVADA
Department of Motor Vehicles
555 Wright Way
Carson City, Nevada 89711
Fee: $1.50

NEW HAMPSHIRE
Motor Vehicles Division
85 Loudon Road
Concord, NH 03301
Fee: $3.50

NEW JERSEY
Division of Motor Vehicles
Bureau of Office Services
Certified Information Unit
25 South Montgomery Street
Trenton, New Jersey 08666
Fee: $5.00

NEW MEXICO
Motor Vehicle Division
Manuel Lujan Sr. Building
Santa Fe, New Mexico 87503
Fee: $1.10

NEW YORK
Motor Vehicle Department
Registration Records Section
Empire State Plaza
Albany, New York 12228
Fee: $2.00

NORTH CAROLINA
Division of Motor Vehicles
Motor Vehicle Building
1100 New Bern Avenue
Raleigh, North Carolina 27611
Fee: $0.50

NORTH DAKOTA
Motor Vehicle Department
State Office Building
9th and Boulevard
Bismarck, North Dakota 58505
Fee: $0.50 Write for forms

OHIO
Bureau of Motor Vehicles
Correspondence Sec MVVRRC
P.O. Box 16520
Columbus, Ohio 43216
Fee: $0.50

OKLAHOMA
Oklahoma Tax Commission
Motor Vehicle Division
2501 N. Lincoln Boulevard
Oklahoma City, OK 73194
Fee: $1.00

OREGON
Motor Vehicle Division
1905 Lana Avenue, N.E.
Salem, Oregon 97314
Fee: $1.00

PENNSYLVANIA
Department of Transportation
Motor Vehicle Bureau
Harrisburg, Pennsylvania 17122
Fee: $2.50

RHODE ISLAND
Registry of Motor Vehicles
State Office Building
Providence, RI 02903
Fee: $1.00

SOUTH CAROLINA
Dept. of Hwys. and Public Trans.
Motor Vehicle Division
P.O. Box 1498
Columbia, South Carolina 29216
Fee: $1.00

SOUTH DAKOTA
Department of Public Safety
Division of Motor Vehicles
118 West Capitol
Pierre, South Dakota 57501

TENNESSEE
Motor Vehicle Division
Information Unit
Jackson Building
Nashville, Tennessee 37242
Fee: $0.50

TEXAS
Dept. of Hwys. & Public Trans.
Motor Vehicle Division
40th and Jackson
Austin, Texas 78779
Fee: $0.25

UTAH
Motor Vehicle Department
1095 Motor Avenue
Salt Lake City, Utah 84116
Fee: $1.50

VERMONT
Department of Motor Vehicles
Montpelier, Vermont 05603
Fee: $1.50

VIRGINIA
Division of Motor Vehicles
Box 27412
Richmond, Virginia 23269
Fee: $3.00

WASHINGTON
Vehicle Records
Department of Licensing
P.O. Box 9909
Olympia, Washington 98504
Fee: $2.00

WEST VIRGINIA
Division of Motor Vehicles
1800 Washington Street E.
Charleston, West Virginia 25305
Fee: $0.25   Correspond on
business letterhead

WISCONSIN
Vehicle Files
Department of Transportation
P.O. Box 7909
Madison, Wisconsin 53707
Fee: $1.00

WYOMING
Motor Vehicle Division
2200 Carey Avenue
Cheyenne, Wyoming 82002
Fee: $1.00

Get the Government To Help You

A file at your county courthouse may have the information you need to find a particular person. Under your state's Freedom of Information Act, all information in the courtroom is supposed to be available to the public. If the clerk refuses to give the necessary information, keep bugging him/her until the file you demand is obtained.

You should never pass over the possibility that the person you are looking for may have passed away. If this is the case, the individual's address can be found at your county clerk's office if he/she last lived in that county.

Social Security Records

While records kept by the social security department can provide any possible information you want to know about a person, they are only available if you know someone who works there.

There is, however, one division within the social security department that will forward your letter to any person. They won't disclose the address of that person, but they will forward the letter. If you decide to do this, enclose your phone number and address so the person who wants to claim the money can contact you. When you write to the Social Security Administration, which is headquartered at Location Services, 6401 Security Blvd, Baltimore, Maryland 21235, include as much information as you know about the person and be brutally honest, if you can.

The prefix of an individual's social security number will tell you where such a person is from. If you have his/her social security number, you can try to use these prefixes to find out more information about him/her.

001-003 NEW HAMPSHIRE

004-007 MAINE

008-009 VERMONT

010-034 MASSACHUSETTS

035-039 RHODE ISLAND

040-049 CONNECTICUT

050-134 NEW YORK

135-158 NEW JERSEY

159-211 PENNSYLVANIA

212-220 MARYLAND

221-222 DELAWARE

223-231 VIRGINIA

232-236 WEST VIRGINIA

237-246 NORTH CAROLINA

247-251 SOUTH CAROLINA

252-260 GEORGIA

261-267 FLORIDA

268-302 OHIO

303-317 INDIANA

318-361 ILLINOIS

362-386 MICHIGAN

387-399 WISCONSIN

400-407 KENTUCKY

408-415 TENNESSEE

416-424 ALABAMA

425-428 MISSISSIPPI

429-432 ARKANSAS

433-439 LOUISIANA

440-448 OKLAHOMA

449-467 TEXAS

468-477 MINNESOTA

478-485 IOWA

486-500 MISSOURI

501-502 NORTH DAKOTA

503-504 SOUTH DAKOTA

505-508 NEBRASKA

509-515 KANSAS

516-517 MONTANA

518-519 IDAHO

520-WYOMING

521-524 COLORADO

525-NEW MEXICO

526-527 ARIZONA

528-529 UTAH

530-NEVADA

531-539 WASHINGTON

540-544 OREGON

545-573 CALIFORNIA

574 ALASKA

575-576 HAWAII

577-579 DISTRICT OF COLUMBIA

Military People

If a person you are looking for is in the service, send $2.85 plus the individual's full name and social security number to: World Wide Locator, Fort Benjamin Harrison, IN 46216. A letter will be sent to tell you where the person is stationed.

Other Methods of Locating People

It is easy to obtain information about an individual from a credit bureau if you own a business and are willing to pay its $50 a year fee. While you won't be able to get the exact address, once you know a person's general whereabouts finding him/her is relatively easy.

Credit Card Companies

You also can find a person's current address if you know what type of major credit card he/she has as well as his/her credit card number. If you are somehow able to obtain this hard-to-find information, it should not be difficult to track a person down.

The Salvation Army

Believe it or not, transients have been seen with thousands of dollars on their person. Contact the Salvation Army if you have substantial information to prove the individual is a transient. Below are the three major offices of the Salvation Army.

If you live in CT, DE, ME, MA, NH, NJ, NY, OH, PA, VT or RI, write: Salvation Army Missing Person's Service, 120 West 14th St., New York, NY 10010.

If you live in AK, AZ, CA, CO, HI, ID, MT, NY, NM, UT, WA or WY, write: Salvation Army Missing Person's Service, 30840 Hawthorne Blvd, Rancho Palos Verdes, CA 90274.

If you live in AL, AR, FL, GA, KY, LA, MD, MS, NC, OK, SC, TN, TX, VA, DC and WV, write: Salvation Army Missing Person's Service: 1424 N.E. Expressway, Atlanta, GA 30329.

The Money Could Be Yours

In the past, you may have lost money or have been an heir to someone who owns a large stockpile of unclaimed money. The following questions will help you to determine whether or not you are eligible to obtain this money. Have you ever:

1) Been married or divorced?
2) Changed jobs?
3) Changed your name?
4) Moved in the past 15 years?
5) Retired?
6) Owned a safe-deposit box?
7) Endured a death involving your immediate family or a close relative?
8) Purchased bonds, stocks or any type of a security measure?
9) Been employed at a city, state, county or federal government office?
10) Been employed at a railroad?
11) Been a member with any division of the U.S. armed forces?

Getting Your Money

If you answered yes to any of the preceding questions, read the following list to determine the procedure by which to claim your money.

1) Write down every relative you know who has died. You may be an heir to one of them if the deceased ancestor had few direct descendants.

2) Contact your state's unclaimed property or treasury office. Using the addresses provided in Chapter 2, give them your name, address, phone number and social security number.

3) Wait for your state office to contact you with your thousands of dollars in unclaimed money.

4) Locate the insurance policy of your deceased relative by writing: American Council of Life Insurance, 1850 K Street, N.W., Washington, DC 20006, and ask for a free policy search.

5) Find out if you or the deceased person ever worked for a city, county or state government and thus has been eligible for a pension.

Government Employee Retirement Pensions

Contact the following government offices if you would like to find out whether you or a relative has an unclaimed pension. Include the name and address of your place of government employment, as well as the dates you worked there, your social security number and birthdate.

ALABAMA
135 Union Street
Montgomery, Alabama 36130
(205) 832-4140

ALASKA
Department of Administration
Pouch C
Juneau, Alaska 99811
(907) 465-4460

ARIZONA
1777 W. Camelback Road
Phoenix, Arizona 85015
(602) 255-5131

ARKANSAS
One Capitol Mall
Little Rock, Arkansas 72201
(501) 371-1458

CALIFORNIA
1416 9th Street
Sacramento, California 95814
(916) 445-7629

COLORADO
1300 Logan Street
Denver, Colorado 80203
(303) 832-9550

CONNECTICUT
30 Trinity Street
Hartford, Connecticut 06115
(203) 566-2126

DELAWARE
Thomas Collins Building
Dover, Delaware 19901
(302) 736-4208

FLORIDA
Department of Administration
Cedars Executive Center
Building C
Tallahassee, Florida 32303
(904) 488-5541

GEORGIA
Two Northside 75
Atlanta, Georgia 30318
(404) 656-2960

HAWAII
Dept. of Budget & Finance
888 Mililani Street
Room 502
Honolulu, Hawaii 96813
(808) 548-7593

IDAHO
Office of the Governor
820 Washington Street
Boise, Idaho 83720
(208) 334-3365

ILLINOIS
2815 W. Washington Street
Box 4064
Springfield, Illinois 62708
(217) 753-0444

INDIANA
State Office Building
Room 800
Indianapolis, Indiana 46204
(317) 232-1606

IOWA
Public Employees Retirement Job
Service
1000 E. Grand Avenue
Des Moines, Iowa 50319
(515) 281-5800

KANSAS
400 First National Bank Tower
Topeka, Kansas 66603
(913) 296-3921

KENTUCKY
226 W. Second Street
Frankfort, Kentucky 40601
(502) 564-7986

LOUISIANA
Dept. of the Treasury
P.O. Box 44213
Baton Rouge, Louisiana 70804
(504) 342-5088

MAINE
State House: Station 46
Augusta, Maine 04333
(207) 289-3461

MARYLAND
Department of Personnel
301 W. Preston Street
Baltimore, Maryland 21201
(301) 383-2344

MASSACHUSETTS
Office of the Treasurer
One Ashburton Place
Boston, Massachusetts 02108
(617) 727-2950

MICHIGAN
Mason Building, 2nd Floor
P.O. Box 30026
Lansing, Michigan 48909
(517) 373-0001

MINNESOTA
529 Jackson Street
St. Paul, Minnesota 55101
(612) 296-2761

MISSISSIPPI
1704 Sillers Building
Jackson, Mississippi 39202
(601) 354-6191

MISSOURI
P.O. Box 209
Jefferson City, Missouri 65102
(314) 751-2342

MONTANA
Department of Administration
1712 9th Avenue
Helena, Montana 59620
(406) 449-3154

NEBRASKA
301 Centennial Mall S.
Lincoln, Nebraska 68509
(402) 471-2053

NEVADA
1100 E. William Street
Carson City, Nevada 89710
(702) 885-4200

NEW HAMPSHIRE
6 Loudon Road
Concord,New Hampshire 03301
(603) 271-3351

NEW JERSEY
Department of the Treasury
210 W. Front Street
Trenton, New Jersey 08625
(609) 292-3676

NEW MEXICO
Pera Building
Room 334
Box 2123
Santa Fe, New Mexico 87503
(505) 827-2517

NEW YORK
State Comptroller
A E Smith Building
Albany, New York 12244
(518) 474-2600

NORTH CAROLINA
State Treasurer
Albemarle Building
Raleigh, North Carolina 27611
(919) 733-6555

NORTH DAKOTA
316 N. Fifth Street
Bismarck, North Dakota 58505
(701) 224-2975

OHIO
277 E. Town Street
Columbus, Ohio 43215
(614) 466-2822

OKLAHOMA
Jim Thorpe Building
Room 580
Oklahoma City, OK 73105
(405) 521-2381

OREGON
1099 S W Columbia
Portland, Oregon 97207
(503) 229-6176

PENNSYLVANIA
Labor and Industry Building
Room 204
Harrisburg, Pennsylvania 17120
(717) 787-6780

RHODE ISLAND
Department of the Treasury
198 Dyer Street
Room 101
Providence, RI 02903
(401) 277-2203

SOUTH CAROLINA
Blatt Building
Box 11960
Columbia, SC 29211
(803) 758-8952

SOUTH DAKOTA
Department of Labor
Foss Building
Pierre, South Dakota 57501
(605) 773-3731

TENNESSEE
Department of Treasury
Andrew Jackson Building
13th Floor
Nashville, Tennessee 37219
(615) 741-7063

TEXAS
Box 13207
Capitol Station
Austin, Texas 78711
(512) 475-6431

UTAH
540 E. Second Street
Salt Lake City, Utah 84111
(801) 355-3884

VERMONT
State Administration Building
Montpelier, Vermont 05602
(802) 828-2305

VIRGINIA
Supp. Retirement System
11 N. Sixth Street
Richmond, Virginia 23219
(804) 786-3831

WASHINGTON
1025 E. Union Street
Olympia, Washington 98504
(206) 753-5290

WEST VIRGINIA
Capitol Complex 5
Room 148
Charleston, WV 25305
(304) 348-2031

WISCONSIN
Employee Trust Funds
201 E. Washington Avenue
Room 151
Madison, Wisconsin 53702
(608) 266-3285

WYOMING
Retirement System Board
Barrett Building
Cheyenne, Wyoming 82001
(307) 777-7691

AMERICAN SAMOA
Dept. of Manpower Resources
Utulei
Pago Pago,Amer.Samoa 96799
633-5456 (* no area code)

GUAM
Retirement Fund; Box 3 C
Agana, Guam 97910
(671) 472-6627

M. MARINA ISLANDS
Retirement Building Fund
Box 222, CHRB
Saipan, CM 96950;
Overseas 9310

PUERTO RICO
Division of Retired Personnel
Minillas Station; Box 42003
Santurce, Puerto Rico 00940
(809) 724-5550

How to Prevent Your Money from Being Lost

If you are worried that your assets will, at some point, be lost, abandoned or taken away from you, it is recommended that you take the following precautions:

Insurance policies

* Notify your attorney and family of all your insurance policies.

* Inform the beneficiaries of your policy that they are beneficiaries.

* Maintain a record of your policies and policy numbers and keep them in a safe place.

Safe-Deposit Boxes

* Tell your family, attorney and accountant the location of your safe-deposit box.

* Pay the rental for the box when it is due.

Bank accounts

* Make sure you keep track of all accounts opened for your child by you, a friend or a relative.

* Make a deposit or withdrawal from your savings account at least once a year.

* Note the maturity date of all certificates of deposit, so you can claim them when due.

Stocks, Bonds, Interest, Dividends

* Record all stocks and bonds that you own.

* Note on a calendar(s) the maturation date of all bonds.

* Vote your "proxy card" on issues facing stockbrokers, if you can.

* Verify your holdings for errors if you change brokers.

If you don't do anything else, be sure you notify everyone you do financial business with if you move, change your name or job, switch banks, retire or don't receive your mail.

DISCOUNTED VALUABLE BOOKS

The following books are offered to our preferred customers at a special price.

BOOK   PRICE

1. Health Secrets $26.95 *POSTPAID*
2. Money Tips $26.95 *POSTPAID*
3. The Guidebook of Insiders Tips $14.95 *POSTPAID*
4. Proven Health Tips Encyclopedia $17.95 *POSTPAID*
5. Foods That Heal $19.95 *POSTPAID*
6. Healing & Prevention Secrets $26.95 *POSTPAID*
7. Most Valuable Book Ever Published $14.95 *POSTPAID*
8. Book of Home Remedies (hard cover) $28.95 *POSTPAID*
9. Book of Blood Pressure & Cholesterol $28.95 *POSTPAID*
10. Good Time Money Book $26.95 *POSTPAID*
11. How To Have It All Money Book $26.95 *POSTPAID*
12. Over 50 Advantage Newsletter $34.00 1 year subs.

Please send this entire page or write down the names of the books and mail it along with your payment

NAME OF BOOK_____PRICE_____
NAME OF BOOK_____PRICE_____
NAME OF BOOK_____PRICE_____
NAME OF BOOK_____PRICE_____
NAME OF BOOK_____PRICE_____

TOTAL ENCLOSED$_____

SHIP TO:

Name_____
Address_____
City_____ST_____Zip_____

MAIL TO: American Publishing
Book Distribution Center
P.O. Box 15196
Montclair, CA 91763-9945

BUSINESS BOOKS & REPORTS

[ ] **Book #601 How To Slash Your Property Taxes and Save Hundreds of Dollars.**Complete manual with instructions forms and step by step plan that can reduce your property taxes. $24.95

[ ] **Book #609 The Book of Wholesale Bargains & Free Things.** Insiders sources for wholesale buying. Guaranteed to save you money or return it for a full refund. $23.95

[ ] **Book #604 The Book of Real Estate Profits.** Insiders guide for making money in real estate. Complete full size manual with more than 300 pages of instructions for beginners to start building wealth ...starting on a shoestring budget (Money back guarantee) $39.00

[ ] **Book #606   How To Buy Dirt Cheap From The Government.** Property seized in drug raids is being auctioned off in all parts of the United States. Also IRS sales, tax sales. All kinds of property is being sold---cars, house, computers, boats, trucks, office equipment. (Money-Back Guarantee) $39.95

[ ] **Book #607   The Book of Money Sources.** How to get free cash grants, loans scholarships and other financial aid from the government and little-known private sources. (Money-Back Guarantee) $29.50

[ ] **Book #608 Today's Hottest Money Making Plans.**Six complete money making plans that show you how to make money in spare time. (Money-Back Guarantee) $24.95

[ ] **Book #412 Clip Newspaper Items and make money.**Complete manual shows how you can make money by clipping newspaper items and selling to make huge profits (Money-Back Guarantee) $23.95

MAIL TO : American Publishing, P.O. Box 15196, Montclair, CA 91763-9945
NAME OF REPORT OR NUMBER _____ _____
_____ _____ _____
_____ _____ _____

Your Name_____
Address _____
City _____State_____Zip_____